The Complete Idiot's Reference Card

Windows 95 Desktop

W9-ARK-087

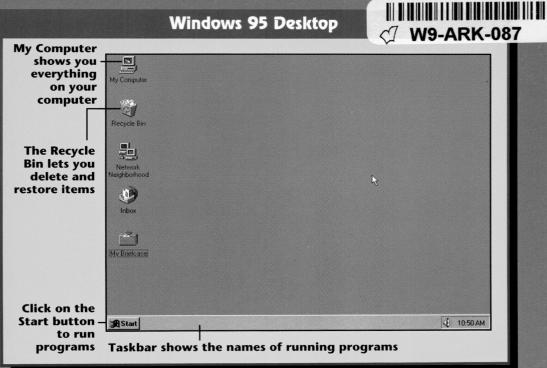

My Computer shows you everything on your computer

My Computer

Recycle Bin

The Recycle Bin lets you delete and restore items

Network Neighborhood

Inbox

My Briefcase

Click on the Start button to run programs

Start

10:50 AM

Taskbar shows the names of running programs

Windows 95 Shortcut Keys

Press	To
F1	Get Help
Ctrl+Esc	Display the taskbar and open the Start menu
Alt+F4	Exit the current program
Shift+F10	View a shortcut menu for the selected item
Alt+Tab	Cycle through the names of running programs (Hold down the Alt key while pressing Tab repeatedly.)
F2	Rename the selected folder or file
Del	Delete the selected object or file
Ctrl+Z	Undo the previous action
Ctrl+C	Copy the selected text or item
Ctrl+X	Cut the selected text or item
Ctrl+V	Paste the copied or cut text or item
Ctrl+S	Save a file
Ctrl+P	Print a file

que®

Windows 3.1 Desktop

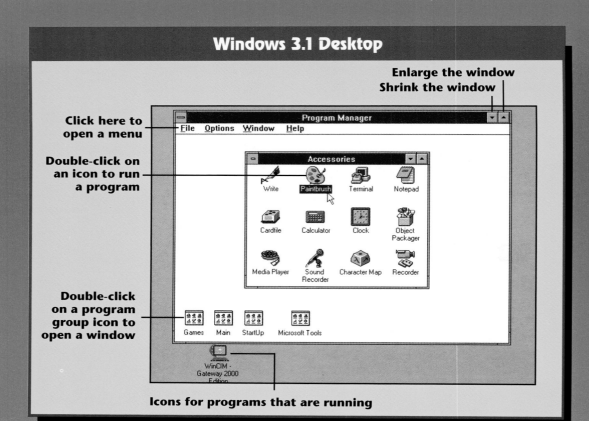

Enlarge the window
Shrink the window

Click here to open a menu

Double-click on an icon to run a program

Double-click on a program group icon to open a window

Icons for programs that are running

Windows 3.1 Shortcut Keys

Press	To
F1	Get Help
Ctrl+Esc	Display a list of running applications
Alt+Esc	Switch to the next running application
Alt+Tab	Cycle through the names of running applications (Hold down the Alt key while pressing Tab repeatedly.)
Alt+Spacebar	Open the Control menu for an application window
Alt+hyphen	Open the Control menu for a document window
Alt+F4	Quit an application or Windows
Ctrl+F4	Close a program group window
Ctrl+F6	Cycle through group windows or icons
Enter	Start the selected application
Ctrl+Z	Undo the previous action
Ctrl+C	Copy the selected text or item
Ctrl+X	Cut the selected text or item
Ctrl+V	Paste the copied or cut text or item
Ctrl+S	Save a file
Ctrl+P	Print a file

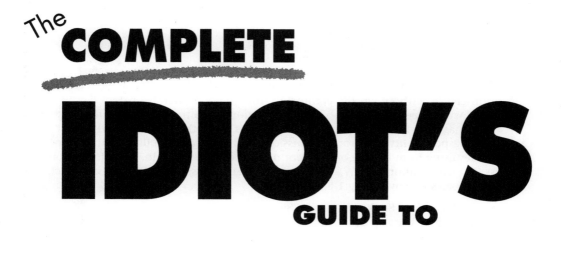

The COMPLETE IDIOT'S GUIDE TO PCs

by Joe Kraynak

A Division of Macmillan Computer Publishing
201 W. 103rd Street, Indianapolis, IN 46290

To Bob Dylan, for keeping me sane

©1996 Que Corporation

International Standard Book Number: 0-7897-0787-x
Library of Congress Catalog Card Number: 96-67562

98 97 96   8 7 6 5 4 3

Interpretation of the printing code: the rightmost double-digit number is the year of the book's first printing; the rightmost single-digit number is the number of the book's printing. For example, a printing code of 96-1 shows that this copy of the book was printed during the first printing of the book in 1996.

Screen reproductions in this book were created by means of the program Collage Plus from Inner Media, Inc., Hollis, NH.

Printed in the United States of America

Publisher
Roland Elgey

Vice President and Publisher
Marie Butler-Knight

Publishing Manager
Lynn E. Zingraf

Editorial Services Director
Elizabeth Keaffaber

Managing Editor
Michael Cunningham

Acquisitions Coordinator
Martha O'Sullivan

Product Development Specialist
Melanie Palaisa

Technical Editor
Herb Feltner

Production Editor
Kathryn Purdum

Copy Editor
San Dee Phillips

Cartoonist
Judd Winick

Cover Designer
Dan Armstrong

Book Designer
Kim Scott

Technical Specialist
Nadeem Muhammed

Production Team
*Stephen Adams, Jenny Earhart, Joan Evan, Jason Hand, Daryl Kessler,
Damon Jordan, Clint Lahnen, Michelle Lee, Ryan Oldfather, Casey Price,
Kaylene Riemen, Laura Robbins, Bobbi Satterfield, Jeff Yesh*

Indexer
John Hulse

Contents at a Glance

Contents

16 Managing Your Money (and Uncle Sam's) — 195

17 Give Me the Works: Integrated Software and Suites — 205

Introduction: What Have You Gotten Yourself into This Time?

You fell for it, too. They said the computer would make your job easier, take over some of the busy work, give you more time to play golf and bounce little Egbert on your knee. You believed them. We all did.

Now that it's time for you to start using the computer, things don't seem all that easy. The computer is about as friendly and helpful as a dead fish, and the books that came with the computer are just as bad. Sure, they have all the information you need, assuming you can find the information and translate the instructions into something that resembles English. But who has the time? You need a book that will teach you the basics: a book that tells you, in plain, simple terms, just what you need to know—no more, no less.

Welcome to The Complete Idiot's Guide to PCs

The Complete Idiot's Guide to PCs works on the premise that you don't need to be an auto mechanic in order to drive a car. In this book, I won't pack your head with high-tech fluff. I'm not going to explain how a computer chip works, how a monitor displays pretty pictures, or how a printer prints. I won't give you one hundred DOS commands, ninety of which you won't use. I promise.

Instead, you'll learn practical, hands-on stuff such as:

➤ How to kick-start your computer (and restart it when all else fails).

➤ How to get around in Microsoft Windows 3.1, 3.11, and Windows 95.

➤ How to use DOS to run other programs (and avoid DOS when possible).

➤ How to find, copy, delete, and undelete files.

➤ How to print your creations, and what to do when your printer goes on strike.

➤ How to buy a computer that's not overly obsolete.

➤ How to make your computer feel like the inferior being it is.

➤ How to get out of trouble.

You'll be surprised at how little you *need* to know in order to use a computer, and at how much you *can* know to use it more effectively.

How Do You Use This Book?

You don't have to read this book from cover to cover (although you may miss something funny if you skip around). If you're going computer shopping, skip to the "Buying and Setting Up a Computer" chapter. If you want a quick lesson in using Windows 95, skip to Chapter 4, "Windows 95: Bare Bone Basics." Each chapter is a self-contained unit that includes the information you need to survive one aspect of the computer world. However, to provide some structure to this book, I divided it into the following six parts:

➤ **Part 1** deals with the bare minimum: the parts of a computer, how to turn your computer on, and how to work with floppy disks, CD-ROM programs, and hard disks.

➤ **Part 2** provides instructions for working with the big three operating systems: Windows 95, Windows 3.1 (or 3.11), and DOS. You'll learn the basic survival skills, along with additional skills that will make you a master.

➤ **Part 3** focuses on applications (the programs you use to perform tasks such as writing letters and creating graphs). I introduce the various application types, explain how to install and run applications, and tell you how to enter commands and get help.

➤ **Part 4** teaches you everything you need to know about disks, directories (or folders), and files. Here, you'll learn how to prepare disks for storing data, copy and delete files, organize files with directories, and find misplaced files.

➤ **Part 5** launches you into the world of telecommunications. In this part, you'll learn how to select and install a modem, connect to an online service, surf the Internet, and send and receive faxes.

➤ **Part 6** provides the tools you need to prevent and recover from disasters. In addition, you'll learn how to clean up your hard disk drive, back up your files, and keep your computer running at peak performance.

How We Do Things in This Part of the Country

I used several conventions in this book to make the book easier to use. For example, when you need to type something, here's how it will appear:

type this

Just type what it says. It's as simple as that.

If you want to understand more about the command you're typing, you'll find some background information in boxes. You can quickly skip over the information I put in the boxes if you want to avoid the gory details.

There are two kinds of boxes that you'll see in this book. They're distinguished by special icons that help you learn just what you need:

Techno Talk

Skip this background fodder (technical twaddle) unless you're truly interested.

Check This Out

In these boxes, you'll find a hodgepodge of information including easy-to-understand definitions, time-saving tips, hints for staying out of trouble, and amusing anecdotes from yours truly.

Acknowledgments

Unlike most new editions, this book has undergone a major overhaul. We sent the previous edition of this book to beginning computer users, such as yourself, to review. Our reviewers said that they don't care how all the computer parts work or what they're called. They didn't want long explanations of DOS commands or exhaustive overviews of what a computer can do. They wanted instructions on how to perform specific tasks in Windows 95, Windows 3.1, and DOS. They wanted more troubleshooting information. They wanted more tips. They wanted more pictures.

So, what did we do? We did the logical thing; we cut the overviews and explanations, and added specific instructions on how to perform essential tasks. We now have *two* Windows 3.1 chapters, *two* Windows 95 chapters, and *barrels* of tips on how to get the most out of your computer. I would like to thank our reviewers for providing us with such valuable feedback.

Several other people had to don hard hats and get their hands dirty to build a better book. I owe special thanks to Melanie Palaisa (development editor) for guiding the content of this book and keeping it focused on new users. Thanks to San Dee Phillips (copy editor) for tightening my language and making me define the scary terms. And thanks to Herb C. Feltner (technical editor) for making sure the information in this book is accurate and timely. Katie Purdum (production editor) deserves a free trip to the Bahamas for shepherding the manuscript (and art) through production. And our production team merits a round of applause for transforming a collection of electronic files into such an attractive, bound book.

Special thanks to Michelle Re of Microsoft Corporation, Michael Bellefeuille of Corel Corporation, and Sheryl Ross of Intuit for supplying most of the software for this book.

Trademarks

All terms mentioned in this book that are known to be, or are suspected of being, trademarks or service marks are appropriately capitalized. Que Books cannot attest to the accuracy of this information. Use of a term in this book should not be regarded as affecting the validity of any trademark or service mark.

We'd Like to Hear from You!

As part of our continuing effort to produce books of the highest possible quality, Que would like to hear your comments. To stay competitive, we *really* want you, as a computer book reader and user, to let us know what you like or dislike most about this book or other Que products.

You can mail comments, ideas, or suggestions for improving future editions to the address below, or send us a fax at (317) 581-4663. For the online inclined, Macmillan Computer Publishing has a forum on CompuServe (type **GO QUEBOOKS** at any prompt) through which our staff and authors are available for questions and comments. The address of our Internet site is **http://www.mcp.com** (World Wide Web).

In addition to exploring our forum, please feel free to contact me personally to discuss your opinions of this book: on CompuServe, I'm at 73353,2061, and on the Internet, I'm **mpalaisa@que.mcp.com**.

Thanks in advance—your comments will help us to continue publishing the best books available on computer topics in today's market.

Melanie Palaisa
Product Development Specialist
Que Corporation
201 W. 103rd Street
Indianapolis, Indiana 46290
USA

Part 1
Basic Training

This is war! From the time you flip the power switch on your computer to the time you beat it into submission, your computer is trying to defeat you. Its tactics are irrational and overwhelming. You enter a command, and your computer displays "Bad command or filename." You click a button, and the manuscript you've been working on for hours disappears in a flash of light. You try to open a file you created and saved, and you find that it has apparently gone AWOL. With this constant barrage of illogical assaults, the computer hopes to wear you down, to force you into unconditional surrender.

To win the war (or at least put up a good fight), you need to learn about the enemy: what it's made up of, how it thinks, and how you can tell it what to do. In this part, you'll get the basic training you need to survive your first encounter with the enemy.

Chapter 1

The Top Ten Things You Need To Know

Most people like to play around with a machine until they're absolutely sure they don't know what they're doing. As a last resort, they pull out the manual and start reading. There's nothing wrong with that approach. In fact, I encourage it—the more you play, the more you learn. However, if you run into trouble when you're poking around, scan the questions in this chapter. Chances are, you'll find the answer you need.

1. How Do I Turn On My Computer?

Once all the parts of a computer are connected, turning it on is as easy as turning on your TV. Just flip the power switch on the monitor *first* (looks like a TV screen), the system unit (the box that everything else plugs into), the printer, and any other devices that look like they might be connected to your computer. Wait till all the grinding and beeping stop, and then you should be ready to go. For more information about firing up your computer, see Chapter 2, "Getting Your Computer Up and Running." If your computer is still in pieces in various boxes, see Chapter 25, "Buying and Setting Up a Computer."

2. What Will I See When the Computer Starts?

As the computer starts, it runs a series of commands, which you may see on the screen. What happens after that depends on how your computer is set up. Here are the five most common things you may see:

➤ **Microsoft Windows 95**   Many newer computers are set up to run Microsoft Windows 95. Chapter 4, "Windows 95: Bare Bone Basics," covers Windows 95.

➤ **Windows 3.1**   Lots of folks have decided to stick with the older version of Windows. If you see a screen with lots of tiny pictures on it (called *icons*), skip to Chapter 6, "Windows 3.1 Survival Guide."

➤ **The DOS prompt**   In the old days, all computers were set up to display the infamous DOS prompt. If you see something like this

      C:\>

or this

      A:\>

or this

      A>

on your screen, skip to Chapter 8, "DOS, If You Must." There, you'll learn how to deal with the DOS prompt (and how to get rid of it).

➤ **Navigator screen**   Many computer manufacturers set up the computer to display a screen that's designed to make your computer easier to use. For example, some computers come with TabWorks, a program that places your programs on tabs that you can flip through with the mouse.

➤ **A menu**   Some computers come with a menu of all the applications that are on the computer. If you see such a menu, don't panic. Just read everything on the screen (especially the stuff at the bottom). The screen will often include messages that tell you what to do next or how to get help.

3. How Do I Stick a Disk in the Computer?

That depends. If you have a compact disc (spelled with a "c" instead of "k"), you usually have to press the **Eject/Load** button on the drive to open the disc caddy. Then, you lay the disc in the caddy, pretty side up, just as if it were a music CD. With some CD-ROM players, you have to shove the caddy into the computer. With others, press the **Eject/Load** button again.

If you have a floppy disk (spelled with a "k"), grab the disk by its labeled edge, so your thumb is on the top of the label. Pull it out of its paper or plastic sleeve, and insert it into the drive. If the drive has a lever on it, flip the lever down so it crosses the slot. When you remove a disk, first make sure the drive light near the disk drive slot is NOT lit. Press the **Eject** button or flip the drive lever up so it no longer crosses the drive slot. Pull the disk gently out of the drive, and insert it back into its sleeve. In Chapter 3, you learn all about inserting and removing disks from your computer and how you take care of them.

4. What Do You Mean, Drive A, Drive B, Drive C?

Most computers have three disk drives: A, C, and D (if you're wondering what happened to B, that letter is reserved for an additional floppy disk drive). Whenever you want to work with a file that is on the disk in one of the drives, you have to "change to" or *access* that drive. You usually change drives by selecting the drive from a list of letters, or by typing the drive letter followed by a colon (for example, **a:**) and pressing **Enter**. Chapter 3 will tell you more about each of the disk drives mentioned here.

5. What Is Memory?

Lots of people confuse memory and disk storage. Your computer actually has two types of storage: permanent (magnetic disk storage) and memory (electronic storage on memory chips). A disk stores information permanently, just as a cassette tape stores sounds. When you turn the computer off, the information remains on the disk.

With memory, on the other hand, RAM (random-access memory) chips store the information electronically, allowing the computer to quickly use the information, so the computer doesn't have to keep reading from the relatively slow disk. However, when you turn off the computer, any information in RAM disappears (along with the electricity that was used to store it). This is why it is important to save your work (to disk) before turning off your computer.

By the way, computers typically have much more disk space than memory.

6. I Have a Mouse, But How Do I Use It?

If you have a mouse attached to your computer, you can use it to enter commands in most programs. First, however, you have to master the following five basic mouse moves:

➤ **Point**   Roll the mouse around on your desk until the tip of the mouse pointer is over the desired item. Nothing really happens, however, until you click, as explained next.

➤ **Click**   Press and release the mouse button without moving the mouse. Use the left mouse button unless told specifically to use the right button.

➤ **Double-click**   Hold the mouse steady, and press and release the mouse button twice pretty fast.

➤ **Drag**   Hold down the mouse button (usually the left button) while sliding the mouse over the desk or mouse pad. You drag to move things, select text or objects, or draw.

➤ **Right-click**   In Windows 95 and some new programs, you can point to an object on your screen and click the right mouse button to display a shortcut or pop-up menu. You can then click on a menu option to select it.

7. How Do I Run Programs in Windows 95?

Windows 95 has a Start button (typically in the lower-left corner of the screen, unless one of your office buddies moved it). Click the **Start** button, and a menu pops up. Now, rest the tip of the mouse pointer on **Programs**. A submenu pops up to the right of the Start menu, and lists programs and other submenus that have programs on them. Rest the mouse pointer on the name of the program you want to run, and click. Check out Chapters 4 and 5 for more information about Windows 95.

8. How Do I Run Programs from Windows 3.1?

If you have an older version of Windows (version 3.1 or 3.11), you can run programs by double-clicking on little pictures (*icons*) that represent your programs. When you start Windows (usually by typing **win** at the C:\> prompt), it displays a bunch of tiny squares called program icons, that represent groups of programs. You double-click on one of these squares, and it blossoms into a window containing more tiny pictures (called *program-item icons*). You double-click on a program-item icon, and, voilà, Windows runs the program and displays a window where you can start working (or playing). Chapters 6 and 7 will tell you more about using Windows 3.1.

9. What's the Difference Between a Program and an Application?

Nothing...other than the fact that they're spelled differently. Actually, *program* is a general term for any set of instructions that control how the computer operates. *Application* is a more specific term used to describe a program that allows you to perform a specific task with the computer. So, for example, a word-processing program (which allows you to create documents) is an application.

10. When I'm Done, Can I Just Turn It Off?

No, not until you close down the applications you've been working with. Otherwise, you may lose the work you created, and you may scramble your computer's brains. Most applications have an Exit or Quit command (usually on the File menu) that you should use to leave the application. This command does two things: 1) if you haven't saved your work, it warns you and 2) it removes the application, in an orderly fashion, from your computer's memory. If you just turn off the computer, you bypass this important safety net.

If you're working in Windows 95, you can select the **Shut Down** command from the **Start** menu. Windows 95 closes down any applications in an orderly fashion, warns you if you've done any work you haven't saved, and then displays a message telling you when it is safe to turn off your computer.

Chapter 2

Getting Your Computer Up and Running

By the End of This Chapter, You'll Be Able To:

➤ Name the parts that make up a computer

➤ Turn on your computer the right way, and then turn it off

➤ Restart your computer safely when it refuses to budge

Computers have come a long way. About six years ago, you had to perform a little ceremony to start your computer: insert a startup disk, search for hidden power switches, and even swap floppy disks in and out of your computer as you ran it. Nowadays, turning on a computer is about as simple as turning on a television set. You just press a couple buttons, and watch your computer leap into action.

In this chapter, you'll learn how to turn on all the computer parts in the proper order. As an added bonus, I'll tell you the proper names of all the parts, just in case you encounter one in your next crossword puzzle.

Naming the Parts of Your Computer

When you're sitting at the computer, you really don't need to know the names of all the parts to explain your frustration when something doesn't work the way *you* think it should. You can simply point and say, "That thing there started grinding, so I pressed this button, and now I can't find anything." Or, "I stuck one of these flat things in this here hole, and now I can't get it out." However, when people start talking computers at a cocktail party, you better know your part names. Carry this picture with you, if you have trouble.

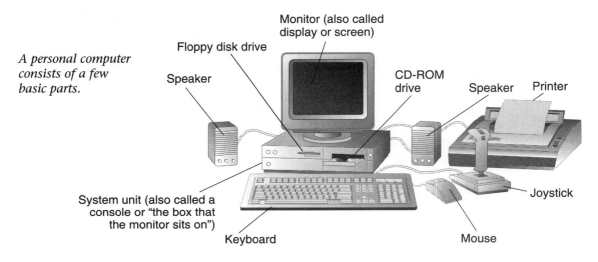

A personal computer consists of a few basic parts.

Monitor (also called display or screen)

Floppy disk drive

Speaker

CD-ROM drive

Speaker   Printer

System unit (also called a console or "the box that the monitor sits on")

Keyboard

Mouse

Joystick

PC Stands For...

Before it was hip to be politically correct, PC stood for *personal computer* and was used specifically for IBM personal computers, as opposed to Apples, Macintoshes, and Commodores (excluding Lionel Ritchie). Although many people use the term "personal computer" to describe any computer that can stand on its own two feet, I use the term specifically for IBM and compatible computers (Compaqs, Packard Bells, Gateways, and so on).

The System Unit: Brains in a Box

Although the system unit doesn't look any more impressive than a big shoe box, it contains the following elements that enable your computer to carry out the most complex operations:

➤ **Memory chips**   Also called RAM (random-access memory), these chips electronically store program instructions and data, so your computer can grab the information in a hurry. When you turn off your computer, information stored in RAM is lost.

➤ **Central processing unit** CPU, pronounced "sea-pea-you," is your computer's brain. If it's real smart, it's called a *Pentium*. Otherwise, it might be called a 486, 386, or 286.

➤ **Input and output ports** Located at the back of the system unit are several outlets into which you can plug your keyboard, mouse, monitor, printer, modem, and other devices. I'll tell you more about ports in Chapter 25.

➤ **Floppy disk drives** Appearing as slots on the front of the system unit, these devices read from and write to disks (those square plastic things you stick in the slots).

➤ **Hard disk drives** A hard disk drive is usually inside the system unit, so you can't see it or stick anything in it. The hard disk itself acts as a giant floppy disk, storing hundreds of times more information than any floppy disk can store.

➤ **CD-ROM drive** Most new computers come with a CD-ROM drive that acts a lot like a CD player. This CD player, however, can play programs, games, video clips, sound, and music.

➤ **Other goodies** The system unit might also contain a modem (for connecting to other computers using the phone), a sound card (for playing audio), and other electronic gadgets.

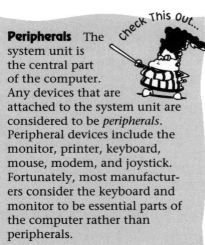

Peripherals The system unit is the central part of the computer. Any devices that are attached to the system unit are considered to be *peripherals*. Peripheral devices include the monitor, printer, keyboard, mouse, modem, and joystick. Fortunately, most manufacturers consider the keyboard and monitor to be essential parts of the computer rather than peripherals.

The Monitor: That TV Thing

The monitor is your computer's windshield. As you drive your computer, the monitor lets you see where you're going. It even collects about as much dirt as your car's windshield—everything from tiny bits of dust to globs of unidentifiable gunk.

The Keyboard (Yes, You Have To Type)

The keyboard has more keys than a high school custodian (another product of the human penchant to overcomplicate). Although the locations of keys on your keyboard may vary, all PC keyboards contain these loyal standards:

➤ **Alphanumeric keys** The keys you use to type.

➤ **Function keys** The 10 or 12 F keys ("eff" keys) at the top or left side of the keyboard: F1, F2, F3, and so on. You use these keys to enter commands quickly.

➤ **Arrow keys**   Also known as cursor-movement keys, these keys move the cursor (the blinking line or box) around on-screen.

➤ **Numeric keypad**   A group of number keys positioned like the keys on an adding machine. You use these keys to type numbers or to move around on-screen.

➤ **Ctrl and Alt keys**   The Ctrl (Control) and Alt (Alternative) keys make the other keys on the keyboard act differently from the way they normally act. For example, in Windows, you can press Alt+F4 (hold down the Alt key while pressing F4) to exit a program.

➤ **Esc key**   You can use the Esc (Escape) key in most programs to back out of or quit whatever you are currently doing.

A typical keyboard.

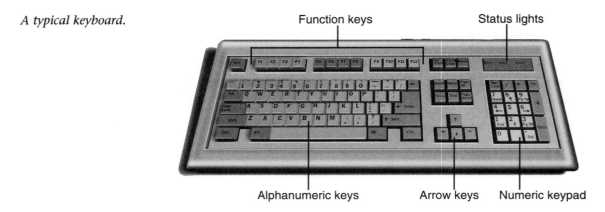

Function keys

Status lights

Alphanumeric keys   Arrow keys   Numeric keypad

The Mouse: A Rodent You Must Live With

The mouse, also called a "Mexican hairless," is a critter that sits next to the keyboard. You slide the mouse over your desktop or mouse pad to move a pointer around on the monitor. The buttons on the mouse let you select commands and other objects that appear on the monitor. You usually use the mouse to *click* or *double-click*. *Click* means you point to something (usually a menu command), and then press and release either the right or left mouse button. In this book, always click the left button, unless I specifically say otherwise. With a *double-click*, you press and release the mouse button twice real fast.

In search of the perfect pointing device, computer manufacturers have toyed with other ideas: trackballs, joysticks, touchpads, and IBM's little red button. The trackball is basically an upside-down mouse; you roll a ball to move the pointer across the screen. A joystick looks like the flight-sticks you see on arcade games; it's the best pointing device for most computer games. A touchpad is a pressure-sensitive square that you slide your finger across to move the pointer (very popular in the touchy-feely '90s).

A couple years ago, IBM came up with the ultimate pointing device (at least IBM thought so). It's sort of like a tiny red joystick/button that sits in the middle of the keyboard (typically on laptop computers). You move the button around in little circles to move the pointer. Trouble is, most businessmen couldn't find the button.

Your Modem: Calling Other Computers

If you plan on being hip, your computer should have a modem, so you can connect to the Internet and go to places such as http://www.toystory.com. The modem sits inside or outside the computer, and connects to your phone jack. It can dial numbers for you and connect to computers all over the world. I would go into more detail about the wonders of modems and telecommunications, but I've saved that for Part 5, "Reaching Out with a Modem."

Sound Cards and CD-ROM Drives

Most new computers come with a sound card and a CD-ROM drive, so the dealers can boast that they sell *multimedia* computers (computers that can play sound, pictures, and video). If your computer has a sound card, it's installed inside the system unit. If you spin your computer around and look at the back, you'll see a couple jacks where you can plug in a set of speakers or headphones.

The CD-ROM drive is next to the floppy disk drive on the front of the system unit. This drive plays compact discs (CDs), which look just like the CDs you see in your local music store. In fact, most CD-ROM players can play music CDs as well as computer CDs, so you can listen to your favorite tunes while playing Solitaire. What makes CDs so important is that a single CD can store as much information as can be stored on a mid-size hard disk, so software companies can put huge programs, killer computer games, or an entire set of encyclopedias on a single disk.

The Printer: Getting It on Paper

The printer's job is to transform the electric burps and beeps in your computer into something that normal human-type people can read. Printers range from inexpensive dot-matrix types, which print each character as a series of dots, to expensive laser print-ers, which operate like copy machines. In between are inkjet printers, which spray ink on the page (sounds messy, but it's not). For more information about the various types of printers, see Chapter 25, "Buying and Setting Up a Computer."

Software: Instructions on a Disk

Before your computer can do anything useful, it needs an education—some instructions that tell it what to do. In the computer world, these instructions are called *software*. I could bore you with a complete explanation of software, but all you need to know are the following facts:

➤ Computers need a special type of software called *the operating system software* in order to start. Common operating systems are DOS, Windows 3.1, and Windows 95.

➤ Once the computer starts, you can run other software, called *applications*. Applications include word processors, spreadsheets, games, and any other program that lets you do something specific.

➤ If you just purchased a computer, it has the operating system software on its hard disk. When you turn on your computer, the operating system runs automatically.

➤ New computers typically come with applications, as well. You can purchase additional applications at your local computer store.

➤ Software normally comes on floppy disks or CDs. You must install the software (place it on your hard disk), before you can use it.

See Chapter 9, "Selecting, Installing, and Running Programs," for more details about software.

Okay, Start 'er Up

You've probably started your computer a hundred times already. You don't need a book to tell you how to do it, right? Well, maybe you're not turning it on *properly*. Run through the following procedure to make sure you're turning on all the parts in the right order:

1. All your equipment should be plugged into a surge-protector power strip (see Chapter 25, "Buying and Setting Up a Computer"). Make sure the power strip is on.

2. Press the button on the monitor or flip its switch to turn it on. Computer manufacturers recommend that you turn on the monitor *first*. This allows you to see the startup messages, and it prevents the monitor's power surge from passing through the system unit's components. The monitor will remain blank till you turn on the system unit.

3. If you plan on printing, turn on the printer. Otherwise, leave it off. The printer consumes a lot of power; you can turn it on later, just before you decide to print.

4. If you turned on the printer, make sure its On Line light is lit (not blinking). If the light is blinking, make sure the printer has paper, and then press the **On Line** button.

5. If you have speakers or other devices connected to your computer, turn them on.

6. Make sure your floppy disk drive is empty. If it has a floppy disk in it, press the eject button on the drive and then gently remove the disk. (Don't worry about removing any CDs from the CD-ROM drive.)

7. Press the power button or flip the switch on the system unit.

8. Ahhh, this is where the fun starts. Stuff appears on-screen. Lights flash; disk drives grind. You'll hear beeps, burps, gurgles, and grunts. Eventually, your system settles down, and you see something useful on your screen.

If you hear some rude grinding and you see a message on-screen telling you to insert a system disk in drive A, don't worry. You (or someone else) may have left a disk in drive A when you turned off the computer. The computer can't find the system information it needs to wake up. No biggy; remove the disk from drive A and press **Enter**.

> **Check This Out...**
>
> **The Story of O (and I)** Most power switches or buttons are marked with the symbols I and 0. These are Egyptian hieroglyphics that stand for On (I) and Off (0). They were first observed on an ancient Egyptian computer dug up in the early 1990s. There was a book sitting next to the computer entitled *DOS for Mummies*, but experts agree that the book is of little or no significance.

Do You Have Windows 3.1, Windows 95, or DOS?

Before I can tell you what to do next, you have to figure out which operating system you have (if you don't know already). Most new computers are set up to run Windows 95 automatically, in which case, you'll see a **Start** button in the lower left corner of your screen. If you have an older system, you'll see Windows 3.1 (which displays a bunch of tiny icons) or the DOS prompt, which looks like C:\> (or something similar). The figure at the end of this section will help you identify your operating system.

If you don't see any of these common displays, scan the following list to find out what's going on:

➤ If your screen is still blank, make sure the monitor is on. If it's on, the brightness knob may be turned way down. Try turning the brightness up. The brightness controls are usually on the front, back, or side of the monitor.

➤ If you see a list of choices, the dealer probably set up something else on your computer to confuse you. Read the screen; it usually tells you what to do.

➤ If you see your kid's Christmas list, she knows a lot more about computers than she's letting on.

15

Which operating system do you have?

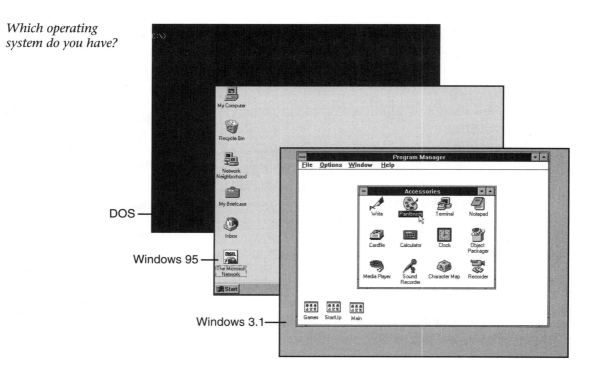

DOS

Windows 95

Windows 3.1

Restarting Your Computer When It Freezes Up

At any given moment in time, your computer may lock up, refusing to do any more work. You press **Esc**, click the mouse everywhere, press the **F1** key, and press all the other keys, and it gives you the same blank stare.

Avoid Rebooting
Reboot (warm or cold boot) your computer only as a last resort. If you are working on a project and you have to reboot, you will lose everything you did since the last time you saved your work.

When this happens, you will be tempted to turn the computer off and then on. Resist the temptation. Try to *warm boot* the computer first. Warm booting forces the computer to reread its startup instructions without turning the power off and on. To warm boot the computer, hold down the **Ctrl** key and the **Alt** key while pressing the **Del** key. This key combination, **Ctrl+Alt+Del**, is commonly referred to as the "three-key salute." Warm booting is preferred to cold booting, because it doesn't jolt your computer with another startup surge.

If you try to warm boot from Windows, you get a warning screen that explains the potential risks and your options. Read the entire screen before proceeding. In most cases, your computer is busy performing some task, or one of the applications you're running is conflicting with Windows. You can probably regain control without rebooting, simply by exiting the program that caused your computer to lock up.

If Ctrl+Alt+Del Doesn't Work...

Sometimes, the **Ctrl+Alt+Del** key combination doesn't work. You press the combination, and nothing happens. What next? If your computer has a Reset button, try pressing the **Reset** button to reboot your computer. Like **Ctrl+Alt+Del**, the Reset button reboots your computer without turning the power off and on.

The Cold Boot Restart: The Last Resort

If a **Ctrl+Alt+Del** doesn't work and your computer doesn't have a Reset button, you will have to cold boot your computer. To cold boot your computer, start by flipping the system unit power switch to the Off position. (Don't turn off the monitor or any other devices, just the system unit.)

Wait 30 to 60 seconds for the system to come to a complete rest and to allow the system to clear everything from memory. Listen to your computer carefully, and you'll be able to hear it "power down" for a few seconds. You may also hear the hard disk drive spin to a stop. This is important, because if you flip the power back on before the hard disk drive stops spinning, the "needle" (read/write head) in the drive might crash down on the "record" (disk) and destroy your data. After the sound of powering down ends, flip the system unit power switch to the On position.

Turning Everything Off

Although your computer may look like nothing more than a fancy TV, you can't just turn it off when you're finished working. Doing so could destroy data and foul up you programs. Here's the right way to turn off your computer:

1. Save any files you have open on a disk. When you have a file open, your work is stored in RAM, which is like brain cells that require electricity to work. If you turn off the electricity without saving your work on a disk, your computer forgets your work—and you probably won't remember it either.

2. Quit any programs you are currently using. When you close a program, it makes sure you've saved all your work to disk, and then it shuts itself down properly. To exit most programs, you open the program's **File** menu and select **Exit**.

3. Put your floppy disks away. Floppy disks can become damaged if you leave them in the disk drives. First, make sure that the floppy drive light goes off. Then, remove the floppy disk from the disk drive and put it away.

17

4. Make sure the hard disk drive light is off, and then turn off the system unit.

5. Turn off the monitor and any other devices that are connected to the system unit.

6. Pour libations to the computer gods. Without divine intervention, no computer task is possible.

The Least You Need To Know

In this chapter, you learned about the basic parts that make up a computer and how to turn on your computer. If you don't want to pack your memory full of details, at least remember the following:

➤ Your computer consists of hardware, such as the monitor and system unit, and software (instructions that come on disks).

➤ Every computer needs two types of software: operating system software and application software.

➤ Before you turn anything on, make sure everything is plugged in and the power strip (if you have one) is turned on.

➤ Turn on the monitor first; then turn on the system unit.

➤ If you turn on your computer and it displays the message **Non-system disk** or **disk error**, you probably left a disk in the floppy disk drive by mistake. Remove the disk and press **Enter** on the keyboard.

➤ If your computer locks up, try to warm boot it by pressing **Ctrl+Alt+Del**.

➤ Before you turn off your computer, save any work you've done and quit any programs you were using.

Chapter 3

Feeding Your Computer: Disks, Files, and Other Munchies

By the End of This Chapter, You'll Be Able To:

➤ Stick your finger in a floppy disk drive

➤ Point to drives A, C, and D

➤ Touch a floppy disk without violating its integrity

➤ Insert a disk into a disk drive (and coax one out)

Computers eat bite-sized, cracker-shaped things called *disks*. Well, they don't actually eat the disks. They just read information off the disks and write information on the disks. Your job is to stick the disks in the computer's mouth—the disk drive—without getting bit.

So, if it's that simple, why have an entire chapter devoted to it? Because it's not that simple. Computers complicate everything.

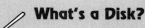

What's a Disk?

A disk is a circular piece of plastic that's covered with microscopic magnetic particles. (A floppy disk is circular on the inside, but is covered with a square plastic case.) A disk drive inside the computer can "read" the charges of the magnetic particles and convert them to electrical charges that are stored in the computer's memory. The drive can also write information from memory (RAM) to the disk the same way a cassette recorder can record sounds on a tape.

Disk Drives: Easy As A-B-C

Most computers have three disk drives, as shown here. DOS refers to the drives as A, C, and D. If you're wondering what happened to B, it's used only if the computer has a second floppy disk drive.

Your computer uses letters from the alphabet to name its disk drives.

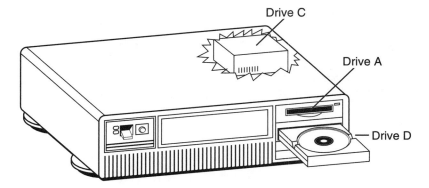

The Floppy Disk Drives: A (and Sometimes B)

Your computer's system unit has one or more slots or openings on the front, into which you can shove a floppy disk, a CD, or a tape, depending on the type of drive it is. For now, look for a narrow slot that might be horizontal or vertical. This is your computer's floppy disk drive. The drive's not floppy, the disk is; and even the disk isn't very floppy, as you will soon learn.

When feeding your computer, make sure you feed it only *floppy disks*. Use the disk identification guide that is shown here.

Disk identification guide.

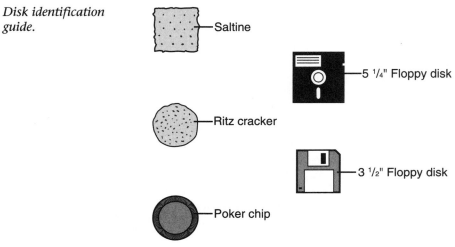

The Hard Disk Drive: C

The drive shown inside the computer is the *internal hard disk drive*, usually called drive C. Some computers have an *external* hard drive, which sits outside of the computer and is connected to the system unit by a cable (it's still drive C). With hard drives, you don't handle the disk; it's hermetically sealed inside the drive.

Two, Two, Two Disks in One

A hard disk drive can be partitioned (or divided) into one or more drives, which your computer refers to as drive C, drive D, drive E, and so on. (Don't be fooled; it's still one disk drive.) The actual hard disk drive is called the *physical* drive; each partition is called a *logical* drive.

The CD-ROM Drive: D

If you're lucky, your computer has a CD-ROM drive. If it's an internal CD-ROM drive, it will be near the floppy drives, although the CD-ROM drive is larger and is *never* vertical. If it's an external drive, it will stand alone, connected with a cable to your system unit. Either way, the CD-ROM drive is usually drive D. These drives are very similar to audio CD players; most can even play audio CDs.

You may have seen people place the system unit on its side. Hey, it saves space and looks cool. However, if your system unit has a CD-ROM drive, don't *ever* set the system unit on its side. In addition to making it nearly impossible to insert a disc in the drive, setting the system unit on its side would damage the CD-ROM drive.

Serving Information to the Computer on Floppy Disks

Think of a floppy disk as a serving tray. Whenever you want to get information into the computer, you must deliver the information on a floppy disk. Likewise, if there is something in your computer that you want to store for safekeeping or share with another user, you can copy the information from the computer to a floppy disk.

Two characteristics describe floppy disks: *size* and *capacity*. Size you can measure with a ruler. The size tells you which floppy drive the disk will fit in. You can get 3 1/2" disks or 5 1/4" disks, as shown here.

Techno Talk

Can My Drive Read This Disk? In general, a disk drive can read disks that are equal to or less than its own capacity. A high-capacity disk drive can read low-capacity disks, but the reverse will not work; a low-capacity disk drive cannot read high-capacity disks. Fortunately, manufacturers have stopped making and using low-capacity drives.

Capacity refers to the amount of information the disk can hold; it's sort of like pints, quarts, and gallons. Capacity is measured in *kilobytes* (*K*) and *megabytes* (*MB*). Each *byte* consists of eight *bits* and is used to store a single character—A, B, C, 1, 2, 3, and so on. (For example, 01000001 is a byte that represents an uppercase A; each 1 or 0 is a *bit*.) A kilobyte is 1,024 bytes—1,024 characters. A megabyte is a little over a million bytes. A gigabyte is a little over 1,000 megabytes. Grababyte means to go get lunch.

A disk's capacity depends on whether it stores information on one side of the disk (single-sided) or both sides (double-sided) and on how much information it lets you cram into a given amount of space (the disk's *density*).

To understand density, think of a disk covered with magnetic dust. Each particle of dust stores one piece of data. No matter how large or small the particle, it still stores only one piece of data. With low-density disks, the particles are large, so the disk can hold fewer particles (less data). With high-density disks, the particles are small, so more particles can be packed into less space and the disk can store more data.

The following table shows the four basic types of floppy disks and how much information each type can hold.

Four Basic Types of Floppy Disks

Disk Size	Disk Type	Disk Capacity
5 ¹/₄"	Double-sided Double-density (DS/DD)	360K
5 ¹/₄"	Double-sided High-density (DS/HD)	1.2MB
3 ¹/₂"	Double-sided Double-density (DS/DD)	720K
3 ¹/₂"	Double-sided High-density (DS/HD)	1.44MB

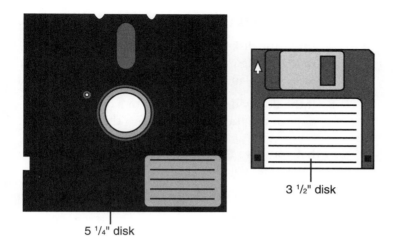

Floppy disks come in two sizes.

3 ½" disk

5 ¼" disk

Floppy Disk Handling DOs and DON'Ts

Every beginning computer book contains a list of precautions telling you what *not* to do to a disk. Don't touch it here, don't touch it there, don't get it near any magnets, blah blah blah.... Although these are good warnings, by the time you get done reading them, you're too afraid to even pick up a disk.

My recommendation is to chill out when it comes to disks. They're pretty sturdy, especially the 3 ½" variety. Throw a disk across the room; it'll survive. Touch the exposed part (God forbid), and your data will probably remain intact. The best advice I can give you is to treat a disk as if it is your favorite CD or cassette tape. However, if you really want to ruin a disk, perform the following acts of destruction:

➤ Chew on it like a pen cap.

➤ Use a disk as a coaster to keep those ugly rings off your desk.

➤ Take a refrigerator magnet and rub it all over the disk in tiny circles. (Usually, if you just rest the magnet on the disk it won't do anything.)

➤ Walk on the disk with spike heels.

Sticking It in, Pulling It Out

A disk will fit into a floppy drive in any number of ways: upside-down, sideways, even backward. But a disk drive is like one of those dollar changer machines; if you don't insert the disk the right way, the drive won't be able to read it. To insert the disk properly,

Check This Out...

Wait Till the Drive Light's Off Pulling a disk out of its drive when the drive light is on is like pulling a piece of bacon out of Rover's mouth while he's chewing on it. If the drive light is on, the drive is reading or writing to the disk. If you pull the disk out, the read/write head is going to scrape over the surface of the disk, scrambling the data and possibly damaging the read-write mechanism in the disk drive.

1. Hold the disk by its label, with the label facing up.

2. Insert the disk into the drive, as shown in the following figure. (If the disk slot is vertical, hold the disk so the label faces away from the eject button.)

3. If the floppy drive has a lever or a door, close the door or flip the lever so it covers the slot.

Now that you have the disk in the drive, how do you get it out? Here's what you do:

1. Make sure the drive light is off.

2. If the drive has an eject button, press the button, and the disk will pop out like a piece of toast. If the drive has a lever or door, flip the lever or open the door, and the disk will partially pop out.

3. Gently pull the disk from the drive. Insert the disk into its pouch so the label faces out.

A disk drive cannot read a disk unless the disk is inserted properly.

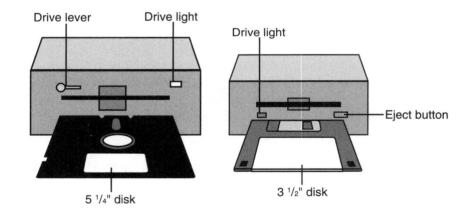

Making a Floppy Disk Useful

You get a brand new box of disks. Can you use them to store information? Maybe. If the disks came preformatted, you can use them right out of the box. If they are not *formatted*, you'll have to format them yourself, with the help of DOS or Windows (see Chapter 19, "Formatting and Copying Floppy Disks").

Formatting divides a disk into small storage areas and creates a *file allocation table* (FAT) on the disk. Whenever you save a file to disk, the parts of the file are saved in one or more of these storage areas. The FAT functions as an inventory chart, telling your computer the location of information in all of its storage areas.

Format New Disks Only

You normally format a disk only once: when it is brand new. If you format a disk that contains data, that data is erased during the formatting process. Before you format a disk, make sure the disk is blank or that it contains data you will never again need.

Loading and Unloading CDs

You can't just slide a CD into your computer like a nickel in a slot machine. You have to serve it to your computer on a tray, just as if you were placing an audio CD in your CD player. And you have to be just as careful handling these CD-ROMs. Hold the CD only by its edges, so you don't get any gooey fingerprints on the surface that the CD-ROM player has to read.

Some CD-ROM drives come with a removable carriage. You remove the CD from its jewel case, place the CD into the carriage, and then insert the carriage into the drive. Other drives have a built-in carriage that's sort of like a dresser drawer. You press a button to open the carriage, and then you place the CD in the carriage and push it closed (or press the **Load/Eject** button, which automatically closes the carriage).

If you ever have trouble "playing" a CD in your CD-ROM drive, it might be because the CD is dirty. To clean the CD, wipe it off with a soft, lint-free cloth from the center of the CD out to its edges. Don't wipe in little circles, no matter what your mother says. If something sticky gets on it, spray a little window cleaner on it, and then wipe. Let the CD dry thoroughly before inserting it in the drive.

Inside the Belly of Your Computer: The Hard Disk

Like I said earlier, floppy disks are bite-sized morsels—mere finger-food for a computer. Any computer worth its salt can gobble up a handful of floppy disks in a matter of seconds and still be grumbling for more. To prevent the computer from always asking for more disks, computer engineers have given modern computers the equivalent of stomachs. The stomachs are called *hard disk drives*, and these hard disks can store lots of information.

The hard disk drive is like a big floppy disk drive complete with disk (you don't take the disk out, it stays in the drive forever). A medium-sized hard disk drive can store over 500 megabytes, the equivalent of about 350 3 ½-inch, high-density floppy disks. Many new computers come with a hard drive that can store over one gigabyte—1,000 megabytes! Sound excessive? When you consider that Microsoft Windows 95 consumes about 80 megabytes, a gigabyte doesn't look all that big.

To get information to the hard disk, you copy information to it from floppy disks or CDs, or you save the files you create directly to the hard disk. The information stays on the hard disk until you choose to erase the information. When the computer needs information, it goes directly to the hard disk, reads the information into memory, and continues working.

Don't Feed the Animals: Diskless Workstations

If your computer is part of a network, it may not have any floppy disk drives or a hard disk drive. If that's the case, forget all this babble about floppy disks and hard disks. Your network probably has a *server* with a disk drive as big as an elephant that stores all the information and programs everyone in the company needs. A person called the *network administrator* acts as the zookeeper, feeding the server, making sure all the information you need is on hand, and keeping the server happy.

You may have heard the buzz about IBM's new computers that come without a hard disk drive. Supposedly, before the year 2000, we'll all be using remote storage facilities on the Internet, so we won't need hard disk space (IBM is betting on it, anyway). IBM and a couple other companies are creating inexpensive computers that basically connect to the Internet and use its resources instead of the resources of the computer itself. These computers are supposed to sell for about 500 bucks.

The Food on the Disks: Files

Information doesn't just slosh around on a disk like slop in a bucket. Each packet of information is stored as a separate file that has its own name.

Your computer uses two types of files: *data files* and *program files*. Data files are the files you create and save—your business letters, reports, the pictures you draw, the results of any games you save. Program files are the files you get when you purchase a program. These files contain the instructions that tell your computer how to perform a task. A program may consist of a hundred or more interrelated files.

Getting Your Act Together with Directories

Because hard disks can store thousands of files, you need to create *directories* and *subdirectories* (called *folders* in Windows 95) to help organize your files. To understand directories, think of your disk as a city. All your files are like little houses inside the city. Directories are like postal zones, grouping the files to make them easier to locate. In this analogy, a directory name is like a ZIP code. Whenever you are looking for a file, you can use the directory name to help you determine the file's general location.

Directories on Floppy Disks? Some users like to create directories on their floppy disks. Although it can be done, floppy disks usually store less than 25 files, so you don't really need to organize them in directories.

Whenever you install a program, the installation utility (which places the program on your hard disk) automatically creates a directory for the program. For your own files, the easiest way to create directories is to use File Manager (in Windows 3.1) or Windows Explorer (in Windows 95). You can also use DOS to create directories. See Chapter 20, "Making and Deleting Directories (or Folders)," for more information.

Directories and subdirectories form a structure, shown in the picture, that looks like a family tree. The directory at the top of the tree is called the *root directory* (every disk has one). Why the root is at the top of the tree is beyond me, but that's the way it is. This tree structure is standard to many file management programs, including DOS, so you will soon get tired of seeing it.

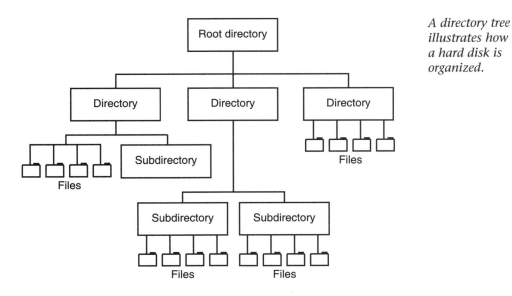

A directory tree illustrates how a hard disk is organized.

To understand how your computer locates files, it's helpful to look at the directory tree in terms of a *path*. Whenever you tell your computer where a file is located, you're essentially telling it to follow a specific path through the directory tree. For example, you may need to tell your computer to get the CUB file that's in subdirectory LION, which is in the directory ZOO, on drive C. The path would be C:\ZOO\LION\CUB.

Once you get accustomed to using directories, they're pretty straightforward; just weave through your directory tree to your destination. We'll talk more about directories in Chapter 20.

The Least You Need To Know

In this chapter, I've given you a lot to chew on. Make sure the following stuff sticks to your ribs:

➤ Most computers have three disk drives: A (the floppy drive), C (the hard disk), and D (the CD-ROM drive).

➤ There are four types of floppy disks: 5 $1/4$" double-density (360K), 5 1/4" high-density (1.2MB), 3 $1/2$" double-density (720K), and 3 1/2" high-density (1.44MB).

➤ A high-density floppy disk drive can read high-density and low-density disks, but a low-density disk drive can read only low-density disks.

➤ Do not pull a floppy disk out of a drive when the drive light is lit.

➤ Never turn off the computer when the hard disk drive is lit. (Okay, this wasn't covered in this chapter, but it's an important reminder.)

➤ Whenever you create something on the computer, you should save it in a file on disk.

Part 2
Doing Windows 95, Windows 3.1, and DOS

You've turned on your computer only to find yourself facing a new challenge: how to deal with that stuff on your screen. Maybe you're facing the ugly DOS prompt, maybe you've managed to move up to Windows 3.1, or perhaps you're staring at the new kid on the block—Windows 95. Whatever the case, you have to know how to work with this beast if you're going to have any fun.

In this part, you'll learn how to use the three most popular operating systems around: Windows 95, Windows 3.1, and DOS. By the end of this section, you'll know the basics for performing just about any computer task on just about any computer you're likely to face. Plus, you'll learn some tricks to get the most out of your operating system.

Chapter 4

Windows 95: Bare Bone Basics

By the End of This Chapter, You'll Be Able To:

➤ Start Windows without even saying "hello" to DOS

➤ Run a program simply by picking it from a menu

➤ Rearrange the program windows on the Windows 95 desktop

➤ Pick a running program from the taskbar

If you took Mick Jagger's advice to "Start it up!" (or if the manufacturer of your new computer installed Windows 95 on your hard disk), you're now facing the opening Windows 95 screen, a Spartan screen with a lowly Start button that lets you run all your programs. But how do you start? And how do you navigate this brave, new operating system? In this chapter, you'll find the answers you need and specific instructions on how to perform the most basic Windows 95 tasks.

We Now Have Control of Your TV

There's no starting Windows 95; there's no stopping it, either. Once it's installed, it comes up whenever you turn on your computer. You won't even see a DOS prompt. What you will see is the simplified Windows *desktop*, shown in the following figure.

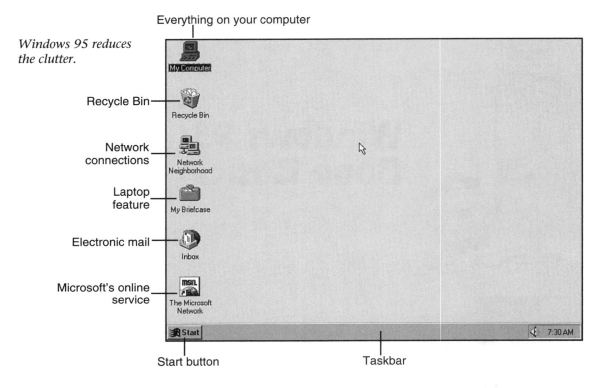

Everything on your computer

Windows 95 reduces the clutter.

Recycle Bin

Network connections

Laptop feature

Electronic mail

Microsoft's online service

Start button

Taskbar

For more information about My Computer and using Windows to manage disks, files, and folders, see Part 4, "Managing Disks, Directories, and Files." For more about the Recycle Bin, see "Trashing Files in the Recycle Bin," in Chapter 5.

Taking Off with the Start Button

Granted, the Windows 95 screen looks about as barren as the Bonneville Salt Flats. It does, however, contain the one item you need to start working: a Start button. You click the big **Start** button, and a menu with seven options appears. Slide the mouse pointer up to the word Programs (you don't have to click on it), and another menu appears listing all the programs you can run. Move the mouse pointer so that it rests on the program you want to run, and then click the icon to run the desired program.

Although the Start menu is designed to make your computer easier to use, it can be a bit difficult to navigate at first. Here are a few tips to help you through your first encounter:

➤ If you rest the mouse pointer on an option that's followed by a right arrow, a submenu appears, listing additional options. You might have to go through several layers of submenus before you see the name of a program you want to run.

➤ Options that are followed by three dots (...) open a dialog box, which allows you to carry out an operation. For example, the Shut Down... option displays a dialog box that lets you shut down Windows.

➤ If you select an option that has no dots or arrow after it, you run a program. For example, if you open the **Start** menu and click **Help**, Windows opens the Help window, offering a list of help topics.

Program groups   Programs you can run

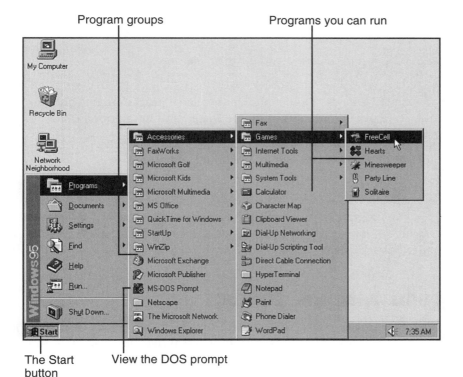

The Start button is your ignition key to Windows 95.

The Start button   View the DOS prompt

Use the Programs That Come with Windows 95

Chances are that your computer came loaded with all sorts of software. If you purchased a family PC, it probably came with Microsoft Works, maybe Fine Artist, and a couple other top-of-the-line programs. But even if your computer wasn't garnished with additional programs, Windows 95 has several programs you can use to write letters, draw pictures, and perform other tasks.

To run any of these programs, click the **Start** button, point to **Programs**, point to **Accessories**, and then click the program you want to run:

33

Calculator displays an on-screen calculator that you can use to perform addition, subtraction, division, and multiplication.

 HyperTerminal is a telecommunications program you can use (with a modem) to connect to other computers.

 Notepad is a text editing program which is useful for typing notes and other brief documents.

 WordPad is a more advanced word processing program that allows you to create fancier, longer documents.

 Paint is a graphics program for creating and printing pictures.

 Phone Dialer works with a modem and a phone to create a programmable phone. You can enter and store phone numbers in Phone Dialer, and have Phone Dialer place calls for you.

Games is a group of simple computer games, including Solitaire.

System Tools is a collection of programs that help you maintain your system. These tools include a backup program, a program for fixing your hard disk, and a hard disk defragmenter, which can increase the speed of your disk. See Chapter 27, "Optimizing Your Computer," for details.

Juggling Programs with the Taskbar

Program Juggling There are other ways to switch from one program to another. Try this: Hold down the **Alt** key and press the **Tab** key once, twice, three times. Each time you press Tab, the name of another running program appears. When you release the Alt key, Windows switches to that program. You can also press **Ctrl+Esc** to open the Start menu.

Multitasking (working with several programs at once) in previous versions of Windows was like taking a Zen lesson in resignation: If you clicked on the wrong spot, the window you were working in disappeared under an avalanche of other windows. If you were lucky, you might see an edge of the window that you could click to get it to jump in front of the other windows.

Windows 95 makes it much easier to switch from one program to another. Windows 95 displays a *taskbar* at the bottom of the screen, giving you a button for each program that's running. If you happen to lose a window at the bottom of a stack, just click on its name in the taskbar to get it back.

Keep in mind that each program you have open (the program button appears on the taskbar) uses part of your computer's memory. As you use more memory, the program you're using runs slower. If you're not using a program, exit it.

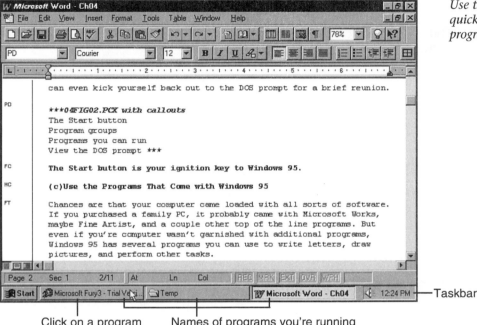

Use the taskbar to quickly switch to a program.

Click on a program to go to it.

Names of programs you're running

Taskbar

Stupid Taskbar Tricks

Normally, the taskbar just lurks at the bottom of the screen until you need it. If you're bored, however, the taskbar offers some mild entertainment. Try the following:

➤ Drag the taskbar to the top of the screen or to the left or right side of the screen to move it.

➤ Move the mouse pointer over one edge of the taskbar until the pointer turns into a double-headed arrow. Then, drag the edge up or down to resize the taskbar.

➤ Double-click the time in the taskbar. This displays a dialog box that lets you set the time and date.

➤ Right-click on a blank area of the taskbar, and click **Properties**. A dialog box appears, allowing you to change the way the taskbar behaves.

Taskbar Woes

If your taskbar "disappears," you may have turned on the **Auto Hide** option in the Taskbar Properties dialog box. If Auto Hide is on, you can bring the taskbar into view by resting the mouse pointer at the edge of the screen where the bar typically appears (the bottom of the screen, unless you moved the taskbar) and the taskbar pops into view. To turn off Auto Hide, right-click on a blank area of the taskbar, select **Properties**, click **Auto Hide**, and click OK.

The taskbar might also disappear if you shrink it. In this case, rest the mouse pointer at the edge of the screen where the taskbar usually appears; the mouse pointer should turn into a double-headed arrow. Hold down the mouse button, and drag away from the edge of the screen. This makes the taskbar bigger, so you can see it.

Dealing with Windows

Working in Windows is like being the dealer in a card game. Whenever you start a program or maximize an icon, a new window appears on-screen in front of the other windows. Open enough windows, and pretty soon, your screen looks like you've just dealt a hand of 52-card pickup. To switch to a window or reorganize the windows on the desktop, use any of the following tricks:

➤ If you can see any part of the window, click on it to move it to the front of the stack.

➤ To quickly arrange the windows, right-click on a blank area of the taskbar, and, from the shortcut menu that appears, choose one of the following options: **Tile Horizontally**, **Tile Vertically**, or **Cascade**. With Cascade, you can see the title bar (at the top) of each window. Click inside a title bar to move the window to the front.

➤ To close a window (and exit the program), click the **Close** button (the one with the X on it), located in the upper right corner of the window (see the next figure).

➤ To make a window take up the whole screen, click the **Maximize** button (just to the left of the Close button). The Maximize button then turns into a Restore button, which allows you to return the window to its previous size.

➤ To shrink a window, click the **Minimize** button (two buttons to the left of the Close button). The minimized window appears as a button on the taskbar. Click the button on the taskbar to reopen the window.

➤ To resize or reshape a window, place your mouse pointer in the lower right corner of the window, and when the pointer turns to a double-headed arrow, drag the corner of the window.

➤ To move a window, drag its title bar. (You can't move a maximized window, because it takes up the whole screen.)

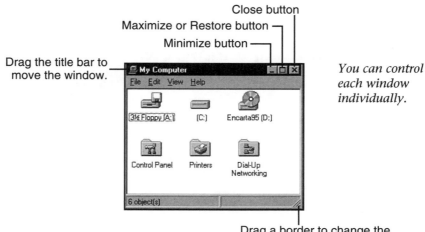

Close button

Maximize or Restore button

Minimize button

Drag the title bar to
move the window.

*You can control
each window
individually.*

Drag a border to change the
window size and shape.

Seeing More with Scroll Bars

Think of a window as...well, a window. When you look through a window, you don't see
everything that's on the other side of the window. You see only a portion of it.

A Windows window is the same. If a window cannot display everything it contains, a
scroll bar appears along the right side or bottom of the window. You can use the scroll
bar to bring the hidden contents of the window into view, as follows:

Scroll box   Move the mouse pointer over the scroll box, hold down the mouse
button, and then drag the box to the area of the window you want to view. For
example, to move to the middle of the window's contents, drag the scroll box to the
middle of the bar.

Scroll bar   Click once inside the scroll bar, on either side of the scroll box, to move
the view one screenful at a time. For example, if you click once below the scroll box,
you will see the next windowful of information.

Scroll arrows   Click once on an arrow to scroll incrementally (typically one line at
a time) in the direction of the arrow. Hold down the mouse button to scroll continuously in that direction.

Barking Out Orders in Windows 95

Until the programming wizards work out the bugs in voice-activated computing, we have to settle for selecting menu commands and clicking on little on-screen pictures. The following sections will help you survive this transitional period.

Take Your Pick: Using a Pull-Down Menu

Pull-down menus are lists of commands and options that hide inside a bar just below a program's title bar. You click on the menu's name to open it, and then you click on the command you want to use. When you open a pull-down menu, you get a list of commands that may vary in appearance:

Do It Quick with Keystrokes
Notice that some commands are followed by a keyboard short-cut. For example, the Print command may be followed by Ctrl+P. You can use these keyboard shortcuts to bypass the menus. Simply hold down the first key while pressing the second key. In this example, hold down **Ctrl** while pressing **P**.

➤ **Dimmed commands** are not accessible. For example, if you try to select the Copy command but have nothing selected, the Copy command appears dim.

➤ **A command followed by an arrow** opens a submenu that contains additional commands.

➤ **A command followed by an ellipsis (...)** opens a dialog box that requests additional information. Skip ahead to the next section to figure out what to do.

➤ **A command preceded by a check mark** is an option that you can turn on or off. The check mark indicates that the option is on. Selecting the option removes the check mark and turns it off.

Conversing with Windows Through Dialog Boxes

If you pick a command that's followed by an ellipsis (...), Windows shoves a dialog box at you, asking for more information. You have to fill out the form and then give your ok before Windows will proceed.

Each dialog box contains one or more of the following elements:

Tabs allow you to flip through the "pages" of options. Click a tab to view a set of related options.

List boxes provide available choices. To select an item in the list, click it.

Drop-down lists are similar to list boxes, but only one item in the list is shown. To see the rest of the items, click the down arrow to the right of the list box.

Text boxes (not shown in following figure) allow you to type an entry. To activate a text box, click inside it. To edit text that's already in the box, use the arrow keys to move the insertion point, and then use the **Del** or **Backspace** keys to delete existing characters. Then type your entry.

Check boxes allow you to select one or more items in a group of options. For example, if you are styling text, you may select Bold and Italic to have the text appear in both bold and italic type. To select an item, click on it.

Option buttons are like check boxes, but you can select only one option button in a group. Clicking on one button deselects any option that is already selected.

Spin boxes usually have a numerical entry with an up and down arrow button to the right of it. You increase the number by clicking the up arrow, or decrease it by clicking the down arrow.

Command buttons allow you to enter or cancel your selections. Once you have responded to the dialog box by entering your choices, you click a command button to finalize the entry. Most dialog boxes have at least three command buttons: one to give your final ok, another to cancel your selections, and one to get help.

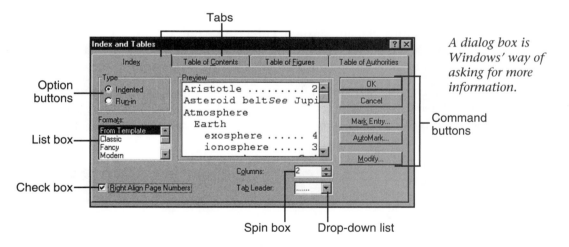

A dialog box is Windows' way of asking for more information.

Many Windows 95 dialog boxes offer an additional feature that lets you get help. If you see a dialog box that has a question mark button in the upper right corner, you can click the button for help. A question mark then appears next to the mouse pointer. You can click an option in the dialog box, and Windows will display a box describing the option. Click outside the Help box to turn it off.

Right-Clicking for Quick Commands

Frantically searching for a use for the right mouse button, programmers have recently developed *context-sensitive menus*. Here's how they work. Move the mouse pointer over an object (say a window's title bar, an icon, a file, or some text you selected), and then click the *right* mouse button. Up pops a small shortcut menu that lists all the options available for that object.

Right-Clicking in Dialog Boxes If you come across a dialog box in Windows 95, try right-clicking on an option name inside the box. A box should pop up, displaying **What's This?** Click **What's This?** to find out more about the option.

For example, say you right-click the **My Computer** icon. The menu you get offers options for opening the window, exploring its contents (with Windows Explorer), finding an item, creating a shortcut (sort of a copy of the icon), or changing the icon's properties. In short, you don't really have to know what you're doing; just right-click and pick an option. Try right-clicking on a blank area of the Windows desktop or on the time of day (right side of the taskbar) to see more examples of shortcut menus.

Taking Shortcuts with Toolbars

Most Windows 95 programs display one or more *toolbars* just below the menu bar. Each toolbar contains buttons that allow you to enter commands quickly by bypassing the menus. For example, instead of opening the **File** menu, selecting **Print**, and then entering options in the Print dialog box, you can simply click the **Print** button to start printing.

Each tiny button usually has an even tinier picture that supposedly represents what the button does. However, deciphering the meaning of these pictures can be slightly difficult. To help, many programs offer *tool tips*. You rest the mouse pointer on the button, and a little box appears, displaying the name of the button.

Toolbar —
Tool tip —

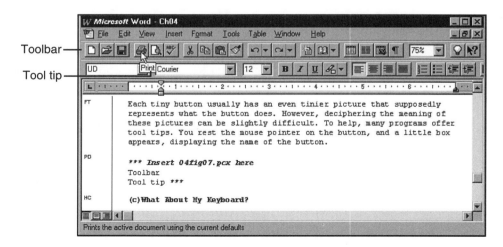

What About My Keyboard?

In Windows 95, the mouse definitely rules. However, Windows 95 does offer some keystrokes you can use to bypass the normal Windows mouse moves. Here's a list of common keystroke shortcuts:

Press	To
F1	Get help in a program or dialog box
Alt+F4	Exit the current program
Shift+F10	View a shortcut menu for a selected item
Ctrl+Esc	Open the Start menu
Alt+Tab	Switch to the previous window
Ctrl+C	Copy the selected object
Ctrl+X	Cut the selected object
Ctrl+V	Paste the copied or cut object
Ctrl+Z	Undo the previous action
Del	Delete the selected item

Help Is on Its Way

If you get stuck in Windows 95, you don't have to flip through a book looking for help. Instead, open the **Start** menu and click **Help**. The Help window appears, offering a table of contents and an index. Click the **Contents** tab if you're searching for general information about how to perform a task or use Windows. Double-click **Tour: Ten minutes to using Windows** for an animated, interactive lesson on the basics of using Windows 95. For help with specific tasks, such as running programs or working with files, double-click **How To**.

For specific help, click the **Index** tab. This tab provides an alphabetical listing of help topics that would make the most ambitious librarian cringe. The easiest way to find a topic in this list is to click inside the text box at the top, and then start typing the name of the topic. As you type, the list scrolls to show the name of the topic that matches your entry.

The **Find** tab offers a more extensive search tool. Instead of searching only through the index of topics, Find searches the contents of the Help system. If you're having trouble tracking down the information you need, click the **Find** tab and start searching.

The Windows 95 help system teaches you the basics.

To learn how to perform a specific task, double-click How To.

View an animated tutorial

Had Enough? Shut It Down

As with any operating system or application, you can't just flip the power switch on your computer when you're done. If you try that, the computer gets revenge by deleting your work and possibly refusing to start the next time. To shut down Windows 95, first exit any applications you were running (remember, they're in the taskbar). Then, open the **Start** menu and select **Shut Down**.

A dialog box appears asking if you want to shut down the computer or reboot it. Click the desired option, and then click the **Yes** button. Wait until Windows tells you that it is now safe to shut down your computer. Okay, now flip the power switch (or press the button); turn off the system unit first, and then the monitor.

The Least You Need To Know

All hype aside, you want Windows 95. When you get it, keep the following in mind:

➤ Windows 95 starts automatically when you turn on your computer.

➤ To run a program, click the **Start** button and follow the menu system to your program.

➤ To get help, click the **Start** button and then click **Help**.

➤ The taskbar displays buttons for all the programs you're running.

➤ To exit Windows 95, click the **Start** button and select **Shut Down**.

Chapter 5

Windows 95 Tips, Tricks, and Traps

By the End of This Chapter, You'll Be Able To:

➤ Make Windows search for files on your hard disk

➤ Nuke files with the Recycle Bin (and get them back)

➤ Place icons for running your favorite programs right on the Windows desktop

➤ Customize Windows 95 to suit your tastes

You've mastered the basics. You can run a program, rearrange program windows on the screen, and even jump around with the taskbar. But there's more to Windows 95 than just running programs. You have to be able to find programs and files on your system, use the Recycle Bin to trash and recover files, change the look and sound of Windows, and much, much more. In this chapter, you'll learn additional techniques for working in Windows 95 and for customizing it to look and behave the way you want it to.

Finding Files and Programs on Your Computer

A gigabyte hard drive is standard on most new computers. That's great, but it ends up turning your computer into a huge junkyard filled with thousands of files. If you misplace a file or your favorite program wasn't added to the Start menu, finding it can be difficult. However, Windows 95 does offer some tools for tracking down lost files and folders.

Before you go snooping around on your hard disk, you should meet Windows 95's two new disk management tools: My Computer and Windows Explorer. My Computer appears as an icon in the upper-left corner of your screen whenever you start Windows. It's intended to give you easy access to your disks and files, the Windows Control Panel, and to your printer settings. Windows Explorer (on the Start/Programs menu) is more of a full-featured file-management tool for helping you keep your disks and files tidy. Both tools allow you to display the contents of your disks and folders (aka directories).

Check This Out...

Quickly Open Saved Documents

If you recently created or worked on a document, its name is added to the Start/Documents sub-menu. To open the document, click **Start**, point to **Documents**, and click on the name of the desired document.

For general information about disks, folders, and files, see Chapter 3. For specifics on how to use Windows Explorer and My Computer to work with disks, directories, and files, see Part 4, "Managing Disks, Directories, and Files."

Windows 95 has two disk and file management tools.

My Computer quickly shows what's on your computer.

Windows Explorer helps you manage disks, folders, and files.

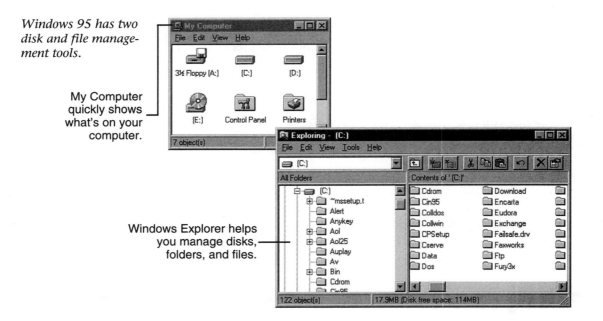

Searching for Files and Folders on Your Hard Disk

If you have no idea where to look for a file or folder, have Windows 95 search for you. Open the **Start** menu, point to **Find**, and click **Files or Folders**. This displays a dialog box, asking you to specify what you're looking for.

In the **Named** text box, type the name of the file or folder you're looking for. If you can't remember the entire name, type the first few letters of the name. Open the **Look in** drop-down list, and select the drive on which you think the file or folder is stored. Click the **Find Now** button. Windows searches the specified disk, and displays the names and locations of all the files and folders that matched your entry.

Windows will search for files and folders on your hard disk.

Select the drive you want to search.

This tab lets you search the contents of files.

Type the name of the file or a portion of it.

If you can't remember the name of a file, but you do remember some unique text inside the file, you can use the **Advanced** tab in the Find: All Files dialog box. Click the tab, click inside the **Containing text** box, and type the unique text (for example, a person's name or address, or a topic title). Windows will search the contents of the files on your disk and display a list of files that contain the text.

Listing Files and Folders in My Computer

Windows 95 gives you two ways to poke around on your computer. You can double-click the **My Computer** icon (located on the desktop), or you can use Windows Explorer. If you double-click the **My Computer** icon, Windows displays icons for all the disk drives on your computer, plus two folder icons: Control Panel (which allows you to change system settings) and Printers (for setting up a printer). You might also have a Dial-Up Networking icon, if you chose to install this feature. To find out what's on a disk or in a folder, double-click its icon.

Use My Computer to browse the contents of a disk or folder.

Double-click on a disk icon or folder to open it.

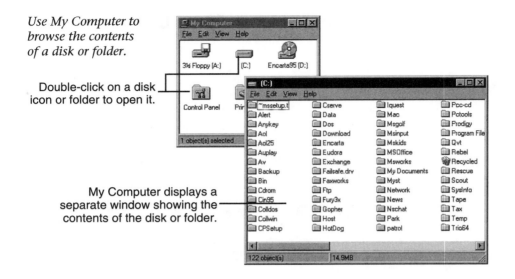

My Computer displays a separate window showing the contents of the disk or folder.

Poking Around with Windows Explorer

Windows Explorer is My Computer's superior twin. It allows you to perform the same basic tasks as you can perform in My Computer, but provides better tools for managing disks, folders, and files. To run Explorer, open the **Start** menu, point to **Programs**, and select **Windows Explorer**. You see a two-pane window, with a directory tree on the left and a file list on the right. You can use the Explorer to copy, move, and delete files and folders (directories), just as you could in the Windows 3.1 File Manager. For details, see Part 4, "Managing Disks, Directories, and Files."

Customizing My Computer and Windows Explorer

My Computer and Windows Explorer can seem a little unwieldy at times. The files may not be listed in the best order, the icons may seem too big or small, and there must be a faster way to enter commands. To take control of My Computer or Windows Explorer, try the following:

They Really Work the Same Way Once you're inside My Computer or Windows Explorer, you use the same commands and options to change the settings.

➤ To change the look of the icons in My Computer or Windows Explorer, open the **View** menu, and select **Large Icons**, **Small Icons** (small icons with folders on the left), **List** (small icons with folders at the top), or **Details** (to display additional information such as the date and time files were created).

➤ To rearrange the icons, open the **View** menu, point to **Arrange Icons**, and select **by Name** (list alphabetically by file name), **by Type** (list alphabetically by file extension), **by Size**, or **by Date**. You can also choose **Auto Arrange** to have the icons rearranged automatically whenever you drag an icon. (Extensions consist of three or fewer characters tacked on at the end of a file name. They indicate the file type—for example, .DOC for document.)

➤ You can have My Computer use a single window (instead of opening a new window for each folder you select). Open the **View** menu and select **Options**. In the dialog box that appears, click **Browse folders by using a single window**, and then click **OK**.

➤ To display a toolbar that allows you to quickly enter commands, in either My Computer or Windows Explorer open the **View** menu and select **Toolbar**. The following figure shows how to use the toolbar to perform basic tasks.

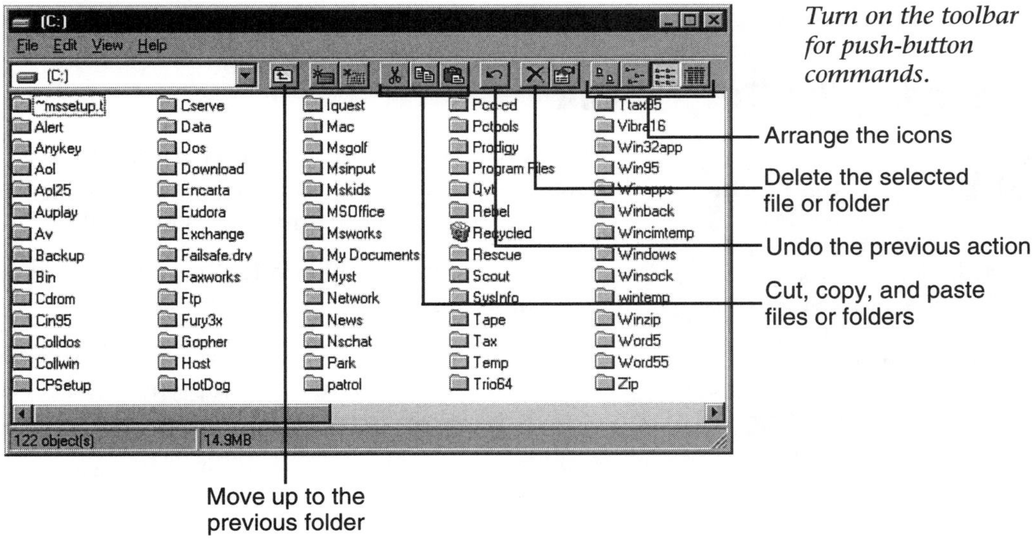

Turn on the toolbar for push-button commands.

— Arrange the icons

— Delete the selected file or folder

— Undo the previous action

— Cut, copy, and paste files or folders

Move up to the previous folder

Trashing Files in the Recycle Bin

Windows 95 has an on-screen trash can in which you can dump the files and icons you no longer need. Simply drag an icon from the Windows desktop or from My Computer or Windows Explorer over the Recycle Bin icon, and release the mouse button. The file is moved to the Recycle Bin. The file is not really deleted though, until you *empty* the Recycle Bin. Until you empty the Recycle Bin, you can still recover a file that you deleted by mistake. There are other ways to send files to the Recycle Bin:

➤ Right-click on a file or folder, and select **Delete** from the shortcut menu.

➤ Select the file or folder, and then click the **Delete** button in the toolbar (the button with the **X** on it).

➤ Select the file or folder, and then press the **Del** key on your keyboard.

Recovering Deleted Files

Pulling things out of the Recycle Bin is as easy as dragging them into it. Double-click the **Recycle Bin** icon, to display its contents. Click on the item you want to restore (**Ctrl+click** to select additional items). Then, perform one of the following steps:

➤ To restore the selected items to their original locations, open the **File** menu, and select **Restore**.

➤ Drag the selected item onto the Windows desktop or into a folder using My Computer or Windows Explorer.

Emptying the Recycle Bin

Out of Disk Space? If you get an error message saying you are out of disk space, before you begin deleting programs and files that you still may need, check the Recycle Bin to make sure you're keeping it empty.

The recycle bin can consume ten percent or more of your hard disk space with the files you pitch in there. To reclaim this disk space, you can empty the Recycle Bin:

1. Double-click the **Recycle Bin** icon, located on the desktop.

2. Make sure you will never ever need any of the files in the Recycle Bin. After emptying the Recycle Bin, retrieving files is nearly impossible.

3. Open the **File** menu, and select **Empty Recycle Bin**.

Changing the Recycle Bin's Properties

As I mentioned, the Recycle Bin is set up to use ten percent of your hard disk space to store deleted files. When the ten percent is used up, the Recycle Bin automatically deletes the oldest deleted files, so you can't restore them. You can increase the amount of disk space Recycle Bin uses, to play it safe, or, if you're running low on hard disk space, you can reduce the percentage. You can adjust other settings as well:

➤ To change the Recycle Bin's properties, right-click the **Recycle Bin** icon, and click **Properties**.

➤ If you have more than one hard drive, you can click **Configure drives independently**, and then use the drive tabs to set Recycle Bin options for each drive.

➤ To change the amount of disk space that the Recycle Bin uses, drag the **Maximum size of Recycle Bin** slider to the left or right to change the percentage of disk space it uses.

➤ If you don't want the safety of the Recycle Bin, you can disable it by selecting **Do not move files to the Recycle Bin**. However, if you select this option, you won't be able to recover accidentally deleted files later.

Playing CDs with AutoPlay

Windows 95 has a feature called AutoPlay that tries to run a CD as soon as you load it into the CD-ROM drive. If you have the Windows 95 CD, insert it now to see AutoPlay in action. If your CD player can handle audio (music) CDs, and you have one handy, take out the Windows 95 CD and insert the audio CD. Windows starts playing it automatically, and you see a CD control panel like the one shown here.

Stop

Play

Eject

Pause

AutoPlay automatically plays an audio CD when you load it.

Not all programs that come on CD support AutoPlay. You may have to install the program, as explained in Chapter 9, "Selecting, Installing, and Running Programs."

Check This Out...

Bypassing AutoPlay

If you don't want the audio CD or program CD to play automatically when you insert it, hold down the **Shift** key while loading the CD.

Customizing Windows 95

Your colleague down the hall has a neat screen saver playing on *his* computer. And your pal across the street has icons for all her favorite programs right on the Windows desktop! You want to do all this; you want to be cool, too. But where do you start? In the following sections, you'll find tips and tricks for taking control of Windows 95 and making your life easier.

Making Shortcuts to Your Favorite Programs

Meandering through the Start menu and its many submenus is time-consuming. You probably use only five or six programs a day, so why can't Windows display the five or six icons you need? It can. Windows 95 lets you clone program icons and place them right on the desktop, where you can get at them in a hurry. Windows 95 refers to these clones as *shortcuts*.

You can create shortcuts for any of your Windows or DOS programs simply by holding down the **Ctrl+Shift** keys while dragging the icon that represents the program's executable file from Windows Explorer or My Computer onto the Windows desktop. For Windows programs, these icons usually appear as pretty pictures that represent the programs. For DOS programs, the icons usually resemble tiny windows.

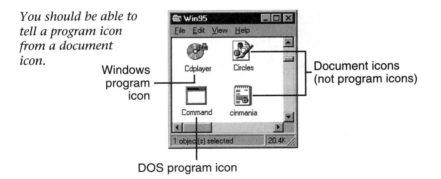

You should be able to tell a program icon from a document icon.

Windows program icon

Document icons (not program icons)

DOS program icon

If the picture on the icon doesn't help you, look at the icon's name. If it ends in .COM, .BAT, or .EXE, the icon could be the one that runs the program. The only trouble is that Windows 95 doesn't display the end of file names (file name extensions) as the default. To have Windows display file name extensions, open the View menu in My Computer or Windows Explorer, click **Options**, click the **View** tab in the dialog box that appears, click **Hide MS-DOS File Extensions** (to remove the check mark), and click **OK**.

Now that you know how to tell the difference between program icons and data icons, take the following steps to create a shortcut for running a program:

1. Find the icon you want to clone. Open either My Computer or Windows Explorer and locate the folder that contains the program to which you want a shortcut.

   Tip: Open the **View** menu, point to **Arrange** icons, and click **by Type**. This groups all the icons that have the same extension together, so it is easier to find program files (that have the EXE, BAT, or COM extensions).

2. Hold down the right mouse button, and drag the icon from My Computer or Windows Explorer onto a blank area of the Windows desktop. (If Windows Explorer takes up the whole screen, and you can't see the desktop, click the **Restore** button in the upper-right corner of the Windows Explorer window.)

3. Release the mouse button, and click **Create Shortcut(s) Here**.

> **You Can't Clone an Icon from the Start Menu** The logical place to find program icons is on the Start menu. Wouldn't it be great if you could create a shortcut simply by dragging the program from the Start menu to the Windows desktop? Well, you can't, so stop dreaming.

You can arrange the icons on the Windows desktop. Right-click on a blank area of the desktop, point to **Arrange** Icons, and click on the desired arrangement. (**Auto Arrange** is a good choice.) You can rename the icon by clicking on its name (below the icon) and typing the new name.

Create a shortcut by dragging an icon onto the Windows desktop.

Drag the icon to the desktop.

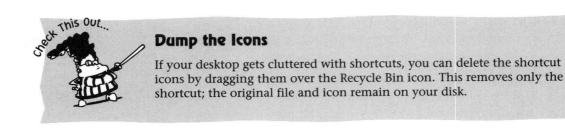

Dump the Icons

If your desktop gets cluttered with shortcuts, you can delete the shortcut icons by dragging them over the Recycle Bin icon. This removes only the shortcut; the original file and icon remain on your disk.

Rearranging Items on the Start Menu

As you know, the Start menu contains Windows programs and other programs that are installed on your computer. However, your favorite programs may not appear on the menu, or the menu may have too many submenus for your liking. Does that mean you have to live with it? Heck no, change it.

First, click the **Start** menu, point to **Settings**, and click **Taskbar**. This displays the Taskbar Properties dialog box. Click the **Start Menu Programs** tab. Now, do any of the following to customize your Start menu:

➤ To add a program to the Start menu or one of its submenus, click the **Add** button. This starts a wizard (a series of dialog boxes that leads you through the process). Follow the on-screen instructions to complete the operation.

➤ To remove a program from the Start menu, click the **Remove** button. This displays a list of all the Start menu items. To view the items on a submenu, click the plus sign next to the menu's name. Select the item you want to remove, and click the **Remove** button.

➤ To rearrange items on the Start menu, click the **Advanced** button. Again, you can click the plus sign next to a submenu name to view its contents. You can drag items up or down on the menu, drag programs to different submenus, and even delete items.

➤ To have a program start when you start Windows, drag its icon into the StartUp folder.

Top o' the Start Menu

To quickly add a program to the top of the Start menu, display the program's icon in My Computer or Windows Explorer. Drag the icon onto the Start button, and release the mouse button.

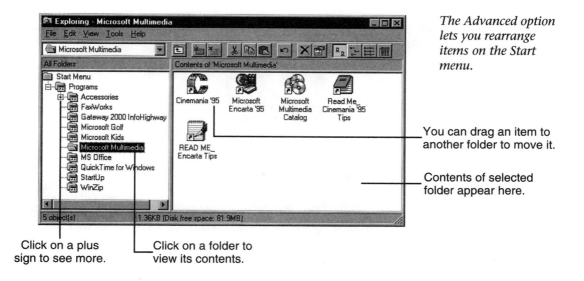

The Advanced option lets you rearrange items on the Start menu.

You can drag an item to another folder to move it.

Contents of selected folder appear here.

Click on a plus sign to see more.

Click on a folder to view its contents.

Turning on a Screen Saver

You've probably seen the winged toasters flying across somebody's screen at work, or the flying Windows, or maybe crawling cockroaches. These *screen savers* were originally developed to prevent stagnant images from being permanently *burned in* to the screen. Newer monitors don't really benefit from screen savers anymore, but they're still fun. Windows comes with a couple screen savers you can turn on or off.

To turn a screen saver on, right-click on a blank area of the Windows desktop, and select **Properties**. In the Display Properties dialog box, click the **Screen Saver** tab. Open the **Screen Saver** drop-down list, and click on the desired screen saver (you can click **Preview** to see what it will look like). Click on the arrows to the right of the **Wait ___ minutes** spin box to specify how long your system must remain inactive (no typing, no mouse movement) before the screen saver kicks in.

If you have a monitor with energy-saving features built in, you can configure those options here as well. Monitors use a lot of energy, so make use of these features.

Now, when the screen saver turns on, all you have to do to start working again is move your mouse pointer or press a key.

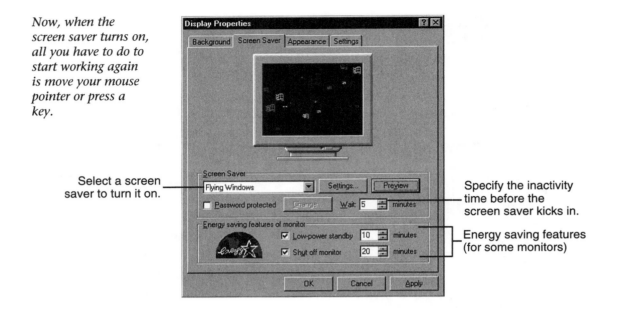

Select a screen saver to turn it on.

Specify the inactivity time before the screen saver kicks in.

Energy saving features (for some monitors)

Changing the Look of Windows 95

Computers are personal, and people seem to enjoy customizing their displays by turning on background graphics, changing the screen colors, and changing other display properties to give their screens a unique look.

To change the appearance of your Windows desktop, right-click on a blank area of the desktop, and click **Properties** to display the Display Properties dialog box. Then, experiment with the following:

➤ Click the **Background** tab; select an item from the **Pattern** or **Wallpaper** list to change the look of the Windows desktop.

➤ Click the **Appearance** tab and try selecting different color schemes from the **Scheme** drop-down list.

➤ If you don't like any of the color schemes, assign colors to various items on the desktop. Open the **Item** list, and pick the item whose appearance you want to change. Use the Size, Color, and Font options to change the look of the selected item.

➤ Click the **Settings** tab. Make sure the **Color Palette** option is set to 256 or greater. You can drag the Desktop Area slider to the left to make items appear bigger on-screen, or to the right to make them smaller (and fit more objects on the screen).

If you like the way your desktop looks in the preview area of the dialog box, click **OK**. If you really messed up the desktop, click **Cancel**.

Making Windows Sound Off

All computers have some way of making sounds. New computers, equipped with a sound card and speakers, can play any sound that has been recorded and saved as a file—everything from the patented Homer Simpson belch to a snippet from Beethoven's Fifth. Older computers are equipped with a built-in speaker designed to emit only an occasional beep. However, a special program called a PC speaker driver can make even these built-in speakers emit interesting (although low-quality) sounds.

If your computer is capable of emitting sounds when you start Windows, run a program, close a window, or perform other actions, you can take advantage of all the sounds that come with Windows. You can turn on jungle sounds to make Windows sound like an old Tarzan movie, or turn on Robotz for a futuristic effect. When you select a sound scheme, Windows assigns a specific sound to each window action, such as opening a menu or closing a dialog box.

To pick a sound scheme for Windows, click the **Start** button, point to **Settings**, and click **Control Panel**. Double-click the **Sounds** icon. Open the **Schemes** drop-down list, and select the sound scheme you want to use.

> **Customized Sound Schemes** You can assign any sound to any windows activity. In the Events list, click on the activity to which you want to assign a sound, such as Menu Command. Then, click the **Browse** button, and select the sound you want to assign to this activity. Click **OK**.

Using the Windows Control Panel

You can write a whole book on how to use the Windows Control Panel to customize Windows. But I'm not going to do that to you. I will, however, give you a quick way to open the Control Panel: Double-click **My Computer**, and double-click **Control Panel**. And I will give you a list and brief descriptions of what you'll find in the Control Panel:

Accessibility Options

Accessibility Options   If you have some hearing loss, vision impairment, or have difficulty moving the mouse or using the keyboard, double-click on this icon. Windows offers some helpful customization options.

Add New Hardware

Add New Hardware   If you connected a new device to your system, run the **Add New Hardware Wizard**. The Wizard leads you step-by-step through the process of setting up the new device. See the next section, "Plug-and-Play with Windows 95," for details.

55

Add/Remove
Programs

Add/Remove Programs   Double-click on this icon to install a new program. See Chapter 9, "Selecting, Installing, and Running Programs," for details.

Date/Time

Date/Time   Double-click on this icon to change the system date and time. (It's quicker to just double-click on the time in the taskbar.)

Display

Display   These are the same options you get when you right-click on the Windows desktop and select Properties.

Fonts

Fonts   This icon opens a dialog box that allows you to add or remove fonts (type styles and sizes) from your computer.

Joystick

Joystick   If you have a joystick connected to your computer, this icon lets you set up, configure, calibrate, and test the joystick.

Keyboard

Keyboard   Double-click on this icon to set the speed at which characters (or spaces) repeat when you hold down a key, and to set the amount of time you have to hold down a key before it starts repeating.

Modems

Modems   If you have a modem, you can double-click on this icon to set it up and change any modem settings that might be giving you problems.

Mouse

Mouse   Change how fast or slow your mouse pointer travels across the screen, and control how fast you have to click twice for a double-click. You can also set your mouse up to swap the functions of the left and right mouse buttons.

Multimedia

Multimedia   This icon displays a dialog box that lets you enter settings for the audio, visual, MIDI, and CD devices installed on your system. (Great way to crank up your speaker volume.)

Passwords

Passwords   To prevent unauthorized use of your computer, double-click on this icon and enter a password. (Just be sure you remember your password.)

Printers

Printers   This icon displays a dialog box that lets you select the printer you want to use and enter settings to specify how you want the printer to operate. See Chapter 10, "Program Rites and Rituals," for details.

Sounds

Sounds   You already encountered this one.

System

System   This icon gives you a peek at what's on your system, and allows you to change system settings.

When you double-click on most of these icons, you get a dialog box that lets you enter your preferences. Remember, if you don't understand an option in a dialog box, right-click on the option, and then select **What's This?**

Plug-and-Play with Windows 95

I had my first plug-and-play encounter with Windows 95 when I installed the program. Before installation, my external CD-ROM drive and my mouse were working fine. After installation, I had no mouse pointer. I "plugged" all right, and then I played the rest of the day—and part of the next day—trying to get all my equipment to live in harmony once again.

To be honest, I wasn't actually using plug-and-play technology. For this technology to work, your computer (and any equipment you install) must be designed for plug-and-play. The equipment I was using was designed more for "bet-you-can't-make-this-work."

When computer manufacturers get this plug-and-play thing in gear, with Windows 95 you'll be able to add peripheral devices (modems, CD-ROM drives, and so on) by plugging in the expansion card (the circuit board) and turning on your computer. Windows 95 will then identify the card for you, work out any conflicts with other cards, and configure the card for optimum performance.

Even without plug-and-play expansion cards, however, Windows 95 can help you install new hardware. After following the instructions that came with the device you purchased, double-click **My Computer**, double-click the **Control Panel** icon, and then double-click the **Add New Hardware** icon. The Add New Hardware Wizard appears. This wizard consists of a series of dialog boxes that lead you through the process of setting up the new device to work in Windows. Follow the on-screen instructions to complete the operation.

Windows 95 can search for any new devices you connected to your computer.

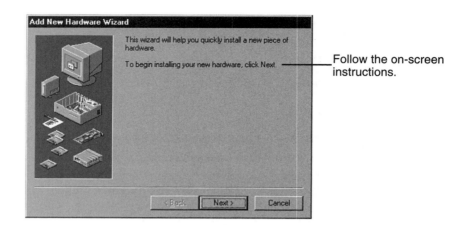

Follow the on-screen instructions.

Check This Out...

Addressing Your Card

When you install a circuit board that does not support plug-and-play technology, you might have to adjust the *interrupt* and *memory address* of the card. If two cards in your computer have the same settings, one of the cards won't work. To change the settings on the card, you must flip tiny switches on the cards or move tiny jumper sleeves. In either case, the process can cause hair loss and hives. With plug-and-play, you don't have to mess with any switches.

The Least You Need To Know

Okay, I admit I packed a lot into this chapter, but wasn't it worth it? In case you missed the important information, here are the top seven tips from this chapter (in my opinion anyway):

➤ Click **Start**, point to **Find**, and click **Files or Folders** to search for files or folders on your disks.

➤ To quickly open a document you worked on and saved, click **Start**, point to **Documents**, and click the document's name.

➤ To create a shortcut on the Windows desktop, hold down the **Ctrl+Shift** keys while dragging the icon from My Computer or Windows Explorer onto a blank area of the desktop.

➤ To change the amount of disk space the Recycle Bin consumes, right-click the **Recycle Bin** icon, and click **Properties**.

➤ To change the display properties, right-click on a blank area of the Windows desktop, and click **Properties**.

➤ To place a program at the top of the Start menu, drag its icon onto the **Start** button.

➤ To change the system date or time, double-click on the time in the taskbar.

Chapter 6

Windows 3.1 Survival Guide

By the End of This Chapter, You'll Be Able To:

➤ Use the old version of Windows, if you haven't yet switched to Windows 95

➤ Get help in Microsoft Windows

➤ Run Windows' animated tutorial

➤ Use the applications that come with Windows, including a couple of neat games

Windows has given DOS a new meaning: Disabled Operating System. With Windows running, you won't even know DOS is there. In place of the DOS prompt, you get menus, pictures, and, best of all, a pointer that lets you poke at all the other things. In other words, you get something called a *graphical user interface* (GUI), which is designed to make your computer easier to use.

Gooey Stuff

Some people, not me of course, joke that GUI (pronounced "GOO-ey") actually stands for "graphical unfriendly interface." As with most jokes, this one has some truth; before Windows can make your computer easier to use, you have to know how to get around in Windows.

Bye-Bye DOS! Starting Windows

Before you can take advantage of Windows' bells and whistles, you have to do something mundane like start it from the DOS prompt (unless your computer is set up to run Windows automatically). Here's what you do:

1. Change to the drive that contains your Windows files. For example, type **c:** at the DOS prompt and press **Enter**.

2. Change to the directory that contains your Windows files. For example, if the name of the directory is WINDOWS, type

   cd \windows

   at the prompt, and then press **Enter**.

3. Type **win** and press **Enter**. DOS starts Windows. The Windows title screen appears for a few moments, and then you see the Windows Program Manager, as shown in the following figure.

Start Windows Automatically

You can set up your computer to start Windows whenever you turn on the computer. See Chapter 9, "Selecting, Installing, and Running Programs," for details.

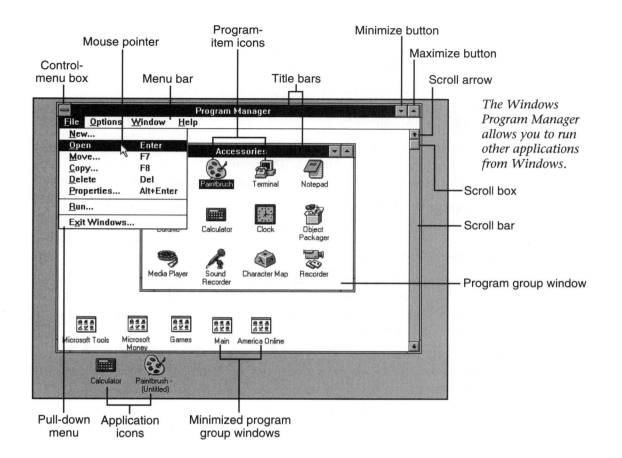

Control-menu box · Mouse pointer · Menu bar · Program-item icons · Title bars · Minimize button · Maximize button · Scroll arrow

The Windows Program Manager allows you to run other applications from Windows.

Scroll box · Scroll bar · Program group window

Pull-down menu · Application icons · Minimized program group windows

Windows Anatomy 101

So, now that you know the names of all those doohickeys on the screen, you're probably wondering what each one does. Here's a quick rundown (don't be afraid to poke around on your own):

➤ The **mouse pointer**, which looks like an arrow, should appear somewhere on the screen (assuming you are using a mouse). If you don't see it right away, roll the mouse around on your desk to bring the pointer into view.

➤ The **title bar** shows the name of the window or application (as if I needed to tell you that).

➤ A **program group window** contains a group of related program-item icons. What are program-item icons? Read on.

➤ **Program-item icons** are small pictures that represent applications that are not running. Double-click on one of the icons now. A window should open. Double-click on the box in the upper left corner of the window to close it.

➤ The **Minimize button** shrinks a window down to a mere icon. To restore the window to its original condition, click the program's icon and then click **Restore**. Go ahead, click any Minimize button now.

➤ The **Maximize button** makes a window take up the whole screen. If you see a Maximize button on-screen now, click it. The button then changes to a double-headed **Restore** button, which allows you to return the window to its previous size.

➤ The **Control-menu** box displays a menu that allows you to close the window or change its size and location. Click any Control-menu box now to see a list of commands. Click the button again to close the menu. (You can double-click the **Control-menu** box to close a window.)

➤ The **menu bar** contains a list of the available pull-down menus. Each menu contains a list of related commands. In the menu bar, click **Window** to open the Window menu. Click it again to close the menu. You'll come across pull-down menu bars in all Windows applications.

➤ **Scroll bars** appear on a window if the window contains more information than it can display. Use the scroll bars to view the contents of the window that are not currently shown.

➤ An **application icon** is a small picture that represents an application that is currently running but that has been minimized. The application is still running, but it is running in the background. You can restore the application to window status by double-clicking its application icon.

Take Windows Lessons from Windows 3.1

Windows 95 comes with its own Help system that can teach you the basics of moving around in Windows, running applications, entering commands, managing disks and files, and so on. Simply click the **Start** button and select **Help.** Then click the **Contents** tab. A list of help topics appears; click the desired topic. To move around in the Help system, use the following controls:

➤ Click on a green, underlined term or topic to display more information.

➤ Click the **Back** button (just below the menu bar) to display the previous screenful of information.

➤ Click on a green term with a dotted underline to display a box that explains the term in greater detail. Click outside the box to close it.

➤ Click the **Search** button (below the menu bar) to search for information about a specific term or topic.

Most computer books keep it a secret that Windows 3.1 comes with its own animated tutorial. Why would you need a book if you can learn from the program itself? My point exactly. Here's how you run the tutorial:

1. Click **Help** on the Program Manager menu bar. The Help menu opens. (If the Windows Tutorial option is not there, either you don't have Windows 3.1, or whoever installed Windows did not install the Help files.)

2. Click **Windows Tutorial**. The tutorial starts.

3. Read and follow the on-screen instructions. The tutorial takes about ten to fifteen minutes. (To exit the tutorial at any time, press the **Esc** key.)

Climbing Out of Windows

The first thing you should know about any program, including Windows, is how to get out of the program. To exit Windows, do any one of the following:

➤ Click the **Control-menu** box in the upper left corner of the Program Manager window, and then click **Close**. Press **Enter**.

➤ Double-click the **Control-menu** box. Press **Enter**.

➤ Press **Alt+F4** and then press **Enter**.

Save Your Work

If you try to exit Windows without saving your work, Windows will display a message asking if you want to save your work before leaving. To save your work, click **Yes**. If asked to name your file, type a name, eight characters or fewer, and don't use any spaces or funky characters such as * / or :. Stick with letters and numbers for now.

Using the Windows Applications

In addition to making your computer easier to use, Windows comes with several useful applications, as shown here. To run an application, double-click its icon.

Paint program

Copies files, formats disks, and performs other file management tasks

Word processing program | Telecommunications (modem) program

Windows comes with games and several basic applications.

Displays any data that you cut or copy in a Windows program

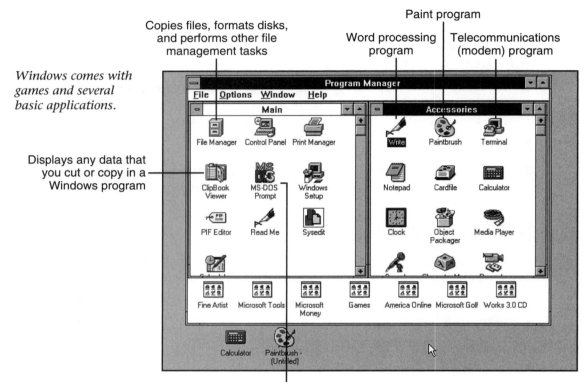

Lets you go to the DOS prompt

Play Solitaire
The Solitaire game that comes with Windows is good practice for learning how to use the mouse. That's what I tell my boss, anyway.

You are not limited to the applications that come with Windows. Many software companies (more than you can count on your fingers and toes) create applications that run under Windows and have the same look and feel as all Windows applications.

Launching Applications from Windows

Whenever you install a Windows application (see Chapter 9), you get one or more new program-item icons (usually inside a new program group window). To run the application, you double-click its icon. If you can't see the program-item icon, it's probably in a shrunken program group window. Double-click the group icon to display the window, and then double-click the program-item icon.

If the thought of running several applications at the same time excites you, then minimize the application's window and double-click another program-item icon. For you channel surfers, here's a quick list of ways to switch from one running application to another:

➤ If part of the application's window is visible, click on any exposed part. The selected window moves to the front of the pile and becomes the *active* window.

➤ Press **Ctrl+Esc**, and then double-click the desired application in the Task List.

➤ Click the **Control-menu** box in the upper left corner of any application window, select **Switch To**, and then double-click the desired application.

➤ Hold down the **Alt** key while pressing the **Tab** key one or more times until the name of the desired application appears. Then release the **Alt** key.

Entering Commands and Options

In the old days, you entered commands by typing them or by pressing function keys. You pretty much had to know what you were doing to get anything done. Now, things are easier. Windows has ushered in the era of pull-down menus and buttons. You simply point-and-click to enter commands.

Picking Commands from Pull-Down Menus

All Windows applications offer some sort of menu system, the most popular of which is the *pull-down menu*. These menus hide inside a menu bar located just below the application's title bar. To open a menu, you click its name. To enter a command or select an option from the menu, you click it. What happens next depends on the appearance of the command:

➤ **Dimmed commands** are inaccessible. For example, if you try to select the Paste command before you copied anything, the Paste command appears dim.

➤ **A command followed by an arrow** opens a submenu that contains additional commands.

➤ **A command followed by an ellipsis (...)** opens a dialog box that requests additional information. Skip ahead to the next section to figure out what to do.

➤ **A command preceded by a check mark** is an option that you can turn on or off. The check mark indicates that the option is on. Selecting the option removes the check mark and turns it off.

Bypass the Menus

Notice that some menu commands are followed by a keyboard shortcut. For example, the Save command may be followed by Ctrl+S. You can use these keyboard shortcuts to bypass the menus. Simply hold down the first key while pressing the second key. In this example, hold down **Ctrl** while pressing **S**.

Providing More Information with Dialog Boxes

If you pick a command that's followed by anellipsis (...), Windows displays a dialog box, asking for more information. It's sort of a fill-in-the-blanks form. You must enter the requested information, or select the desired options and settings, and then click the **OK** button to confirm.

A dialog box is Window's way of asking for more information.

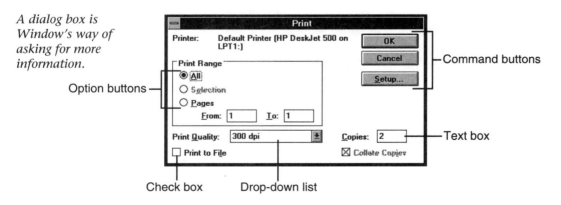

Each dialog box contains one or more of the following elements:

Tabs (not shown in picture) allow you to flip through the "pages" of options. Click a tab to view a set of related options.

List boxes (not shown in picture) provide available choices. To select an item in the list, click it.

Drop-down lists are similar to list boxes, but only one item in the list is shown. To see the rest of the items, click the down arrow to the right of the list box.

Text boxes allow you to type an entry. To activate a text box, click inside it. To edit text that's already in the box, use the arrow keys to move the insertion point, and then use the **Del** or **Backspace** keys to delete existing characters. Then type your entry.

Check boxes allow you to select one or more items in a group of options. For example, if you are styling text, you may select Bold and Italic to have the text appear in both bold and italic type. To select an item, click on it.

Option buttons are like check boxes, but you can select only one option button in a group. Clicking one button deselects any option that is already selected.

Command buttons allow you to enter or cancel your selections. Once you have responded to the dialog box by entering your choices, you click a command button to finalize the entry. Most dialog boxes have at least three command buttons: one to give your final okay, another to cancel your selections, and one to get help.

Seeing More with Scroll Bars

If you open a window, and it contains more information than it can display on a single screen, you'll see *scroll bars* at the right and/or bottom of the screen. You can use the scroll bar to bring the hidden contents of the window into view, as follows:

Scroll box Move the mouse pointer over the scroll box, hold down the mouse button, and then drag the box to the area of the window you want to view. For example, to move to the middle of the window's contents, drag the scroll box to the middle of the bar.

Scroll bar Click once inside the scroll bar, on either side of the scroll box, to move the view one screenful at a time. For example, if you click once below the scroll box, you will see the next windowful of information.

Scroll arrows Click once on an arrow to scroll incrementally (typically one line at a time) in the direction of the arrow. Hold down the mouse button to scroll continuously in that direction.

Juggling Windows on Your Screen

As you run programs, open documents, and play games, your screen starts to look like some sort of manic collage. You need some way to take control of all the windows, resize them, and arrange them on the Windows desktop. The following sections tell you just what to do.

Moving a Window to the Top

Before you can work (or play) inside a window, it has to be on top and active. If you can see any part of a window, the easiest way to move the window to the top is to click on the exposed portion of the window. The window automatically jumps to the front and covers anything else on-screen.

Finding Lost Windows

If you cannot see the desired window, click on **Window** on the menu bar, and then select the name of the window you want to go to. The selected window is then moved to the front and is activated. If that doesn't work, press **Ctrl+Esc** and then choose the window from the Task List.

Arranging Windows On-Screen

When you're holding a handful of cards and you want to see what you have, you fan the cards. In Windows, you can view a portion of each window on-screen by using a similar technique. You can tell Windows to display the windows side-by-side (*tiled*) or overlapping (*cascade*). Here's how: Click **Window** on the menu bar and click **Cascade** or **Tile**. Although cascaded windows overlap, you can still see the title bar of each window, so you can quickly switch to a window by clicking on its title bar.

Resizing and Moving Windows

As you rearrange windows on-screen, you may want to shrink windows that are less important or that contain fewer icons; or you may want to enlarge more important windows. You may also want to move the windows to different locations. The picture here shows you what to do.

Drag the title bar to move the window.

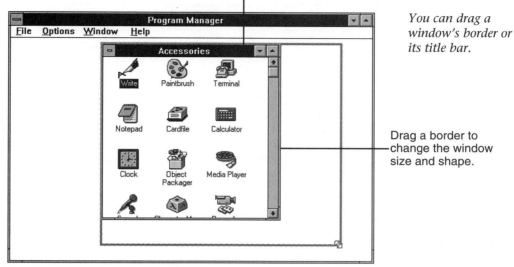

You can drag a window's border or its title bar.

Drag a border to change the window size and shape.

What About My Keyboard?

Your keyboard isn't obsolete just yet. Although Windows works best with a mouse, you can still use your keyboard to manipulate windows. The keyboard shortcuts listed in the following table explain how.

Windows Keyboard Shortcuts

Press	To
Alt+Esc	Cycle through the application windows and icons.
Ctrl+F6 (or Ctrl+Tab)	Cycle through program group icons and windows.
Alt+Spacebar	Open the Control menu for an application window or icon.
Alt+− (hyphen)	Open the Control menu for a program group window or icon, or for a document window or icon.
Arrow keys	Move from one icon to another in the active program group window.
Alt (or F10)	Activate the pull-down menu bar.
Alt+selection letter	Open a pull-down menu from the menu bar or select an option in a dialog box.

continues

Windows Keyboard Shortcuts   Continued

Press	To
Enter	Run the application whose icon is highlighted, or restore a window that has been reduced to an icon.
Esc	Close a menu or dialog box.
Ctrl+Esc	View the task list, which allows you to switch to a different application.
F1	Get help.
Ctrl+F4	Minimize the selected program group window.
Alt+F4	Exit the active application or exit Windows.

The Least You Need To Know

Microsoft Windows comes with a book that's over 600 pages long, so there's a lot more that you can know about Windows. However, the following details will help you survive your first day on the job:

➤ To start Windows, change to the Windows directory (usually C:\WINDOWS), type **win**, and press **Enter**.

➤ To quit Windows, double-click the **Program Manager's Control-menu box**.

➤ To run an application in Windows, change to the program group window that contains the program item icon for the application you want to use, and then double-click the application's icon.

➤ To open a pull-down menu, click the name of the menu in the menu bar.

➤ To select a command from a menu, click the command.

➤ The buttons in the upper right corner of a window allow you to maximize, minimize, or restore the window to its previous size.

➤ You can bring a window to the top of the stack by clicking on any portion of the window.

➤ You can resize a window by dragging one of the window's borders.

Chapter 7

Windows 3.1: Beyond the Basics

By the End of This Chapter, You'll Be Able To:

➤ Make Windows start when you turn on your computer

➤ Make your own program groups

➤ Make an icon for running a DOS program

➤ Change the look of Windows

➤ Use more of your hard disk space as memory

In the previous chapter, you got your feet wet with Windows 3.1. You can now run programs, enter commands, and even talk back to dialog boxes. Now, you want to do more. You want to master Windows, turn on a screen saver, and make your very own program group window with icons for all your favorite applications. Maybe, you even want to change the system settings to give Windows more memory. Well, you've come to the right place.

Forcing Windows to Start Automatically

Windows 3.1 or 3.11? Windows 3.1 and Windows 3.11 (often referred to as *Windows for Workgroups*) are essentially the same, at least on the surface. The one big difference you might notice if you used both versions is that the File Manager looks different.

The computer manufacturer may have already set up your computer to run Windows automatically when you turn on your computer. Or maybe, you had one of your weekend hacker friends do it for you. However, if your computer still starts with the DOS prompt, you can set it up to start Windows instead. Here's what you do:

1. Run Windows from the DOS prompt as you normally would.

2. Open Program Manager's **File** menu and select **Run**. The Run dialog box appears.

3. Type **sysedit** and press **Enter**. This runs System Editor, a program that lets you edit your startup files.

4. Click inside the AUTOEXEC.BAT title bar. AUTOEXEC.BAT is a file that runs a set (*batch*) of startup commands when you turn your computer on.

5. Click at the end of the last text line in the window, and press **Enter**. This creates a new command line.

6. Type **c:\windows\win** to add a command that runs Windows.

7. Open the **File** menu and select **Save**.

8. Open the **File** menu and select **Exit**.

You can add a command to AUTOEXEC.BAT to have Windows run at startup.

Type **c:\windows\win** here.

```
System Configuration Editor
File   Edit   Search   Window

C:\WINDOWS\SCHDPLUS.INI
C:\WINDOWS\MSMAIL.INI
C:\WINDOWS\SYSTEM.INI
C:\WINDOWS\WIN.INI
C:\CONFIG.SYS
C:\AUTOEXEC.BAT

LH C:\WINDOWS\SMARTDRV.EXE
LH C:\DOS\MSCDEX.EXE /D:MTMIDE01 /M:10
SET MSINPUT=C:\MSINPUT
rem C:\MSINPUT\MOUSE\MOUSE.EXE
PATH=C:\;C:\DOS;C:\WINDOWS;C:\TRIO64;c:\pctools;c:\zip;c:\nc;c:\windows\s
SET PATH=C:\IW;%PATH%
C:\TRIO64\S3REFRSH 91a0
SET TEMP=C:\TEMP
REM following line modified by InternetWorks Setup
REM SHARESHARE /L:500 /F:5100
c:\windows\win
```

You can test this by exiting Windows and then rebooting (press **Ctrl+Alt+Del**). Windows will now run whenever you turn on your computer.

Running Applications at Startup

If you always use a specific application in Windows, or if you just like to play a quick game of Solitaire before starting your day, you can have Windows run the application whenever you start Windows.

First, double-click the **StartUp** program group icon to open the StartUp program window. Open the program group window that contains the application you want to run at startup. Now, hold down the **Ctrl** key while dragging the program-item icon into the StartUp window. When you release the mouse button, Windows places the icon in the StartUp group. After you reboot your computer, any applications that you place in this group will run automatically when you start Windows.

Making Your Own Program Groups

Windows comes with a few of its own program groups, and whenever you install a Windows application, it creates its own program group. After awhile, program groups pepper your screen, making it difficult to find the applications you use most. So why not do something about it? Create your own program group, and stick the icons you use most in that group:

Restoring Windows Program Groups If you accidentally delete a Windows program group (Accessories, StartUp, Main, or Games), you can get it back. Open Program Manager's **File** menu and select **Run**. Type **c:\windows\setup /p** and press **Enter**.

1. Open Program Manager's **File** menu and select **New**. A dialog box appears, asking if you want to create a new Program Group or Program Item.

2. Click **Program Group**, and click **OK**. The Program Group Properties dialog box appears.

3. In the Description text box, type a name for the group (for example, **Jane's Group**).

4. Click **OK**. A new group window appears, but it's empty. Skip to the next section to learn how to stick icons in this window.

Copying and Moving Icons to Your Program Group

Once you create a group, you'll want to fill it with icons for the applications you use most. You do this by dragging icons from other program group windows into your new window:

➤ To copy an icon, hold down the **Ctrl** key while dragging the icon from its original program group window to your new window.

➤ To move an icon, drag it from its original program group window to your new window.

You can drag program-item icons from one window to another.

To copy an icon, hold down the Ctrl key while dragging an icon.

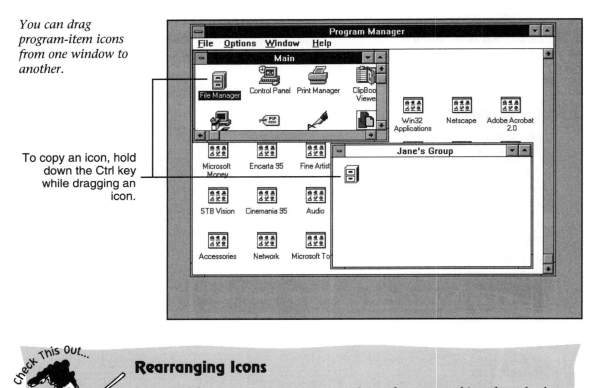

Rearranging Icons

Program Manager can rearrange your icons for you, making them look nice and neat. To arrange the icons in a program group window, open the Window; then open Program Manager's **Window** menu, and select **Arrange Icons**. To arrange the program group icons, make sure all program groups appear as icons (are minimized). Then, open the **Windows** menu and select **Arrange Icons**.

Making an Icon for a DOS Program

When you install Windows, it searches your hard disk for DOS programs and creates icons for them. If you install a DOS program after installing Windows, however, you have to tell Windows to make an icon for it. Here's how:

1. If the DOS program is not installed, follow the installation instructions to install it from the DOS prompt. See Chapter 9, "Selecting, Installing, and Running Programs," for details.

2. Double-click the **Main** group icon. The Main group window appears.

3. Double-click the **Windows Setup** icon. The Windows Setup window appears.

4. Open the **Options** menu and select **Set Up Applications**. The Setup Applications dialog box appears.

5. Click on **Ask you to specify an application**, and click **OK**. A dialog box appears, asking you to specify the name of the file that runs the program and the name of the group window in which you want the icon to appear.

6. Click the **Browse** button. The Set Up Applications dialog box appears, prompting you to select the drive, directory, and name of the file that runs the program. (Any file that ends in .BAT, .COM, .EXE, or .PIF can run a program.)

Select the program's directory.

Select the file that runs the program.

Use the Browse button to find the file that runs the program.

Select the drive where the program's files are stored.

7. Click the arrow to the right of the **Drives** option, and click the letter of the drive that contains the program's files.

8. Double-click the directory that contains the application. (To move up in the directory tree, double-click the topmost directory or drive letter.)

9. Click the name of the file that runs the program in the **File Name** list. (If you see a file that ends in .PIF, pick that one, because it has the information that Windows needs to run the program properly.)

10. Click **OK**.

11. From the **Add to Program Group** drop-down list, click the program group in which you want the icon to appear.

12. Click **OK**. If all goes as planned, Windows creates a program information file (PIF) for the application, assigns it an icon, and places the icon in the specified group.

If Windows displays a message saying that it cannot set up this program, click **OK**. Then, open the program group in which you want the icon to appear. Open the **File** menu and select **New**. Click **Program Item** and click **OK**. In the Description text box, type the program's name. Click the **Browse** button, use the dialog box that appears to select the file that runs the program (a file ending in .EXE, .BAT, or .COM), and click **OK**. This returns you to the Program Item Properties dialog box; click **OK**. You now have an icon that can run your DOS program. The only trouble with this approach is that Windows doesn't use a PIF file to run the program—this may or may not cause a problem in how the program runs.

PIFs

Windows likes to have a PIF (program information file) for every DOS program. A PIF contains all the information Windows needs to run a DOS program properly. Some DOS programs come with their own PIFs. For others, Windows Setup can create a PIF. However, if the program doesn't have one, and if Windows can't create one, you may have to run the program without a PIF, by running its BAT, EXE, or COM file. Some programs (especially games) may have trouble running without a PIF.

Customizing Windows 3.1

Customizing sounds like an advanced technique that only experienced computer technicians are qualified to do. But you've already customized Windows by making it start automatically and by playing with program groups. And it's no big deal, right? The following customization options let you have a little more fun playing with how Windows looks and behaves.

Turning On Windows Wallpaper

Windows has a dingy gray background that looks like it came out of some old Bela Lugosi movie. To jazz up your Windows background, you can turn on *wallpaper*, a graphic image that sits behind Program Manager and gives you something more interesting to look at. You can select one of the wallpaper designs that comes with Windows by performing the following steps:

1. Open the **Main** program group window.

2. Double-click the **Control Panel** icon. The Control Panel window appears.

3. Double-click the **Desktop** icon. The Desktop dialog box appears, allowing you to change the Desktop settings.

4. Open the **Wallpaper File** drop-down list. A list of graphics files, all having the extension .BMP, appears.

5. Click the graphics file you want to use as your Windows background.

6. Click **Center** or **Tile**. If the image you select is not big enough to fill the screen, Windows centers the image, or tiles several copies of the image to fill the screen.

7. Click **OK** button. The selected graphic appears on-screen, if you have your windows minimized.

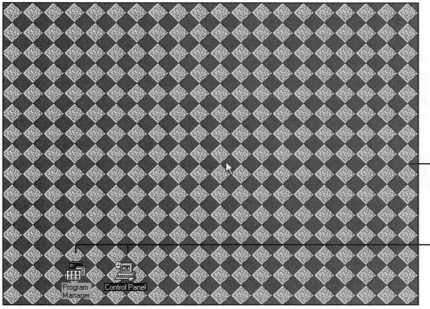

Hanging wallpaper in Windows is a snap.

This is the ARCADE.BMP wallpaper tiled.

These windows are minimized.

Turning On a Screen Saver

With older computer monitors, if you left a particular image on the screen for a long time, it could burn itself into the screen, creating a permanent ghost image on the screen. Programmers developed screen savers to prevent this from happening. If the screen didn't change for a given amount of time, the screen saver would either blank the screen or display moving pictures (fish, flying toasters, creeping cockroaches, you name it). Although newer monitors don't really benefit from screen savers, they're still fun.

Windows comes with a couple of its own screen savers. To turn on one of these screen savers, open the **Main** group window, double-click **Control Panel**, and double-click on **Desktop**. Open the **Screen Savers** drop-down list, and click the screen saver you want to use. You can also change any of the screen saver settings:

➤ Click the arrows to the right of the **Delay** spin box to set the amount of time Windows must remain inactive before the screen saver kicks in.

➤ Click the **Setup** button, and enter any other settings. For example, if you chose the Flying Windows screen saver, you can change the number of flying windows and the speed at which they fly.

➤ Click the **Test** button to view the screen saver in action.

Attaching Sounds to Windows Events

Turning Off the Sounds
When you get tired of the sounds (and you will), open the **Main** group window again, open the **Control Panel** and double-click **Sound**. In the Sound dialog box, click **Enable System Sounds** to remove the X in the check box.

Does your computer make sounds when you start Windows, exit, or enter commands? Do you want it to? If your computer is capable of emitting more than an occasional beep, if it has a sound card or a PC speaker driver, you can control the sounds your computer makes in Windows. (A PC speaker driver is a program that helps the dimestore speaker inside the system unit emit more complex sounds.)

To assign sounds to Windows events, first open the **Main** group window, double-click the **Control Panel** icon, and then double-click the **Sound** icon. A dialog box appears listing Windows events on the left and available sound files on the right. (If the lists are dim, your computer isn't capable of playing the sounds.) Simply click an event, and then click the sound that you want to assign to the event. You can use the **Test** button to play a sound. When you're done assigning sounds to events, click **OK**.

Click the event to which you
want to assign a sound.

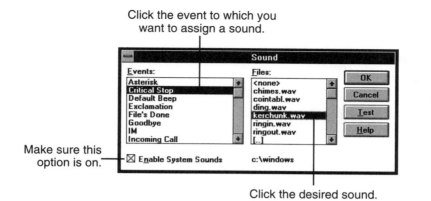

*In Windows, you
can assign sounds to
specific Windows
actions.*

Make sure this
option is on.

Click the desired sound.

Setting the System Time and Date

Computers have built-in clocks that keep track of the
time and date, even when the computer is off. Many
programs can insert the system date and time in your
documents, so you don't have to type it. Like any
clock, your computer's clock can lose or gain time. Or
if you live in an area that has daylight savings time,
you may need to adjust the time twice a year.

The process is fairly simple. Open the **Main** group
window, double-click the **Control Panel** icon, and
then double-click the **Date/Time** icon. A dialog box
appears, showing the current settings. Click the
number you want to change (for example, the month,
day, hour, or minute), and then click the arrows to
the right of the setting to increase or decrease it.
Do the same for any other settings you want to
change, and then click **OK**.

**Using the
Windows
Clock** Windows
comes with an on-
screen clock. To turn
it on, open the **Accessories**
group, and double-click the
Clock icon. To have the clock
remain in front of all the other
windows, open its **Control**
menu, and click **Always on
Top**. You can use the Settings
menu to change to a Analog
clock (one with hands) or
Digital (one with fingers…er,
numbers).

Controlling the Behavior of Your Mouse

Here's a perfect April Fool's joke for your home or office. You can switch the left and right
mouse buttons in Windows, so the left button acts as the right button and vice versa. (Or
you can do this if you're a lefty, but it's not as much fun.) You can also change the speed

that the mouse pointer moves across the screen, and the speed at which you have to click twice for Windows to recognize it as a double-click.

To change the mouse settings, open the **Main** group window, double-click the **Control Panel** icon, and double-click on the **Mouse** icon. You can then use the Mouse dialog box to change the settings:

➤ Drag the **Mouse Tracking Speed** slider to the left to slow down the speed at which the mouse pointer moves across the screen. Or drag to the right to speed it up.

➤ Drag the **Double Click Speed** slider to the left to slow down the speed at which you have to click twice for a double-click. Or drag it to the right to speed it up.

➤ To reverse the functions of the left and right mouse buttons, click **Swap Left/Right Buttons**. If you do this, you have to right-click to open menus, run applications, and select options.

➤ To make the mouse pointer do a stutter step across the screen when you move it, click **Mouse Trails** to turn it on. Click **OK** when you're done.

Preventing Changes to the Windows Desktop

If you have kids or meddlesome colleagues, they can mess up the Windows desktop in a lot less time than it took you to carefully construct it. They might leave a program group open, minimize Program Manager, or just trash your icon arrangements. And Windows is set up to save any changes they've made when you exit. If you want to lock your changes in place, open the Program Manager's **Options** menu, and select **Save Settings on Exit** to turn the option off.

Now, if someone rearranges the items on your desktop, all you have to do is quit Windows and restart it to recover your desktop. If *you* make changes to your Windows desktop, those changes will be lost the next time you start Windows. To save the changes, hold down the **Shift** key while double-clicking the **Control menu** box in the upper-left corner of the Program Manager window.

Giving Windows More (Virtual) Memory

Windows requires about 4 megabytes of RAM (random-access memory) in order to function properly. If your programs require more, Windows can use disk space as memory (called *virtual memory*). It's slow, but slow memory is better than no memory.

To check (or change) the amount of disk space Windows is using as memory, open the **Main** group window, double-click the **Control Panel** icon, and double-click the

Enhanced icon. Click the **Virtual Memory** button and click **Change**. Now, make your changes:

➤ Windows is set up to use disk space on drive C as virtual memory. If you have another hard drive with more free space, open the **Drive** drop-down list and select that drive.

➤ Windows creates a *temporary* swap file that it uses as memory. To increase the speed of the swap file, open the **Type** drop-down list, and select **Permanent**. A temporary swap file uses free space from anywhere on the disk. A permanent swap file uses the largest block of free space on your disk, making it work faster. However, if you don't have a big block of free space, Windows won't let you create a permanent swap file. Give it a try, anyway.

➤ In the **New Size** text box, type the amount of disk space you want to use as virtual memory. The number must be less than or equal to the Maximum size listed. If you have the disk space, try cranking this up to 5000 or more kilobytes (5 megabytes).

You can check your PC's virtual memory.

Select Temporary or Permanent.

Type a new size that is less than or equal to the recommended maximum size.

83

The Least You Need To Know

Managing Disk Space

If you want to create a permanent swap file, but your hard disk does not have a large block of free space, you can clean up your disk to create more free space. See Chapter 27, "Optimizing Your Computer," for details.

In this chapter, you learned that Windows 3.1 isn't a stone tablet. You can configure it to suit your tastes and make your job easier. Here's a quick review of some of the cool things you can do:

➤ You can have Windows start automatically by adding the WIN command to the AUTOEXEC.BAT file.

➤ You can run Windows applications automatically by dragging their icons to the StartUp program group window.

➤ To create a program group window, open Program Manager's **File** menu and select **New**. Click **Program Group** and click **OK**.

➤ You can copy program-item icons by dragging them from one program group window to another.

➤ The Windows Control Panel has all the icons you need for customizing Windows.

➤ Virtual memory is disk space that Windows uses as memory. Because it's on a disk, it's much slower than real memory.

Chapter 8

DOS, If You Must

By the End of This Chapter, You'll Be Able To:

➤ Pronounce DOS correctly (hint: rhymes with "sauce")

➤ Enter five harmless DOS commands

➤ Run a DOS program

➤ Figure out what's on a disk

It's time for DOS to wander off onto an ice floe somewhere and die a peaceful death. DOS (pronounced "dawss") has simply outlived its usefulness. Its commands are cryptic, its prompt is clueless, and its error messages are downright rude. We want menus. We want tiny pictures of things. We want Microsoft Windows.

However…as long as there are DOS programs, and as long computer stores sell old games that run only under DOS, you're going to need to know a little bit about DOS. In this chapter, you'll learn the least you need to know to survive the DOS prompt.

What Exactly Does DOS Do, Anyway?

DOS is the boss, the supervisor, of your computer. As boss, DOS performs the following duties:

➤ **Traffic cop** DOS tells your computer how to interpret input (from the keyboard and mouse), how to process data, and how to produce output (on the monitor or printer).

➤ **Program launcher** You can run your other programs from the DOS prompt. DOS retreats to the background (where it belongs), silently managing any communications between the other program and your computer.

➤ **Jack-of-all-trades** DOS gives you the tools to manage your disks and files: to prepare disks to store information, to copy files to a disk, to move or rename files, and to delete files.

Facing the DOS Prompt

When you boot your computer, you may see the DOS prompt (as shown in the following figure), displaying the letter of the active drive and hinting that you can enter a command. It doesn't tell you much else. To enter a command, you type the command and press the **Enter** key. But what do you type and how do you type it? You'll learn all that later in this chapter.

The nefarious DOS prompt.

```
c:\>
```

If you don't get the ugly DOS prompt when you start your computer, your computer may be set up to automatically run Windows or some other program. In such a case, you can probably avoid DOS, and skip the rest of this chapter. However, if you want to do all the fun stuff in this chapter, you can exit the program you're in, or skip ahead to the next section, "Doing DOS from Windows."

Doing DOS from Windows

Windows hasn't completely abandoned DOS (although Windows 95 tries real hard). Both Windows 3.1 and Windows 95 provide a way to go out to the DOS prompt. In Windows 95, click the **Start** button, point to **Programs**, and then click **MS-DOS Prompt**. In Windows 3.1, open the **Main** program group window, and double-click the **MS-DOS Prompt** icon. Regardless of which version of Windows or DOS you're using, the DOS commands explained in this chapter all work the same way.

Sometimes, Windows displays the DOS prompt inside a window, sort of pretending that DOS is a Windows program. Other times, Windows runs DOS in full-screen mode, giving you a black screen with the diminutive, off-white DOS prompt. To switch from window-size DOS to full-screen DOS (or vice versa), press **Alt+Enter**. Because Windows uses memory to create a window, DOS will use *less* memory when run in full-screen mode.

DOS Games Are Temperamental

If you're going to DOS to run a computer game in Windows 3.1, you may need to completely exit Windows. Most DOS games require a lot of memory, and if Windows is consuming part of that memory, there may not be enough left for the game. However, Windows 95 does a fairly good job of managing memory so there is enough for the game.

Harmless DOS Commands, Just for Practice

Before you get into the heavy, important DOS commands where mistakes do count, try a few light commands that can't hurt anything. (Oh yeah, if any of the DOS commands in this section don't work, try typing **cd\dos** and pressing **Enter**. Then enter the command again.)

Internal and External Commands

A *DOS command* is an order that you tell DOS to carry out. There are two types of DOS commands: *internal* and *external*. Internal commands, such as DIR, are stored in memory for quick access. External commands, such as FORMAT, are small programs that are stored on disk. When you enter an external command, DOS runs the program required to perform the task.

What's Today's Date?

Unless you picked up your computer at a garage sale or an auction (circa 1984), it has an internal, battery-powered clock that keeps track of the date and time. To tell DOS to display the date on-screen, do this:

1. Type **date** and press **Enter**. DOS displays something like the following:

   Current date is Tue 06-01-96
   Enter new date:

2. If the date is correct, press **Enter**. If the date is incorrect, type the correct date in the form mm-dd-yy (for example, 07-04-96) and press **Enter**.

Capitalization Doesn't Matter

Don't worry about capitalization: date, DATE, and dAte are all the same to DOS. However, if you leave out a space, add too many spaces, or use punctuation marks that I don't tell you to use, DOS won't recognize the command. For example, if you typed **date.** and pressed **Enter**, DOS would display the message **Invalid date**.

What Version of DOS Do You Have?

Every time Microsoft Corporation releases an updated version of DOS, the version number increases, and the program can do more new things or can do old things better. Hence, DOS 6.2 is better than DOS 4.01. To find out which version of DOS you have, type **ver** and press **Enter** (VER stands for "version"). DOS displays the version number on-screen.

Sweeping Up the Screen

Now that you have the date and DOS version number displayed on-screen, your screen looks like an alphabetical junkyard. To clear the screen, type **cls** and press **Enter**. (CLS stands for CLear Screen.)

Giving DOS a Makeover

The DOS prompt shows only the letter of the active disk drive (for example, **A:\>**, **B:\>**, or **C:\>**). You can change the look of the DOS prompt by using the PROMPT command. Type one of these funky prompt commands:

➤ Type **prompt nq** and press **Enter**. $n tells DOS to display the current drive, and $q tells it to display the equal sign (=). The prompt now looks like **C=**.

➤ Type **prompt $v nb** and press **Enter**. $v tells DOS to display the DOS version number, and $b tells it to display a vertical line called the pipe symbol (|). The prompt now looks like **MS-DOS Version 5.0 C|** (why you would want a prompt like this is beyond me).

When you are done fooling around, type **prompt pg** and press **Enter**. $p tells DOS to display the names of all the directories leading up to the current directory (along with the current directory's name), and $g tells DOS to display the right angle bracket (>). The remaining commands in this chapter assume that you can see the drive and directory names at the DOS prompt.

Dissecting a DOS Command

A typical DOS command, **copy c:\data\johnson.ltr b: /v** consists of the following elements:

Command   This is the name of the DOS command (in this case, COPY). It tells DOS which action you want DOS to carry out.

Delimiters   Spaces and special characters (such as /, \, and :) that break down the command line for DOS. Think of delimiters as the spaces between words in a sentence.

Parameters   Specify the objects on which you want DOS to perform the action. In the preceding example, c:\data\johnson.ltr is the parameter.

Switches   Allow you to control how the command performs its action. In this case, the /V switch tells DOS to verify the copy operation to make sure the copy matches the original.

What Kind of Computer Do You Have?

If you have DOS version 6.0 or later, you have a program called Microsoft Diagnostics that can display more information about your computer than you probably want to know. To run the diagnostic program, do this:

1. Type **msd** and press **Enter**. The Microsoft Diagnostics screen appears, as shown in the following figure.

2. To exit the diagnostic program, press **F3**, or press **Alt+F** and then **X**.

Check This Out...

> ### Use MSD to Shop
>
> Next time you're at your local neighborhood computer store, try running Microsoft Diagnostics from some of the computers on display. You'll probably end up knowing more than the salespeople about the computers they're selling.

Processing chip type   Amount of memory   Available disk drives

If you have DOS 6.0, you can view information about your computer.

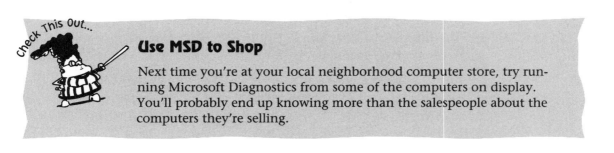

DOS version

Gimme Help

DOS versions 5.0 and later include a help system (clever idea, eh?) that you can access by typing **help** and pressing **Enter**. A list of all the available DOS commands appears, as shown here. Press the **Page Down** key to see more of the list. Press the **Tab** key to move from one command to another. Press **Enter** to view help for the currently selected command.

```
  File  Search                                                    Help
                    MS-DOS Help: Command Reference
 Use the scroll bars to see more commands. Or, press the PAGE DOWN key. For
 more information about using MS-DOS Help, choose How to Use MS-DOS Help
 from the Help menu, or press F1. To exit MS-DOS Help, press ALT, F, X.

 <What's New in MS-DOS 6.22?>

 <ANSI.SYS>              <EMM386.EXE>            <Multi-config>
 <Append>               <Erase>                 <Nlsfunc>
 <Attrib>               <Exit>                  <Numlock>
 <Batch commands>       <Expand>                <Path>
 <Break>                <Fasthelp>              <Pause>
 <Buffers>              <Fastopen>              <Power>
 <Call>                 <Fc>                    <POWER.EXE>
 <Cd>                   <Fcbs>                  <Print>
 <Chcp>                 <Fdisk>                 <Prompt>
 <Chdir>                <Files>                 <Qbasic>
 <Chkdsk>               <Find>                  <RAMDRIVE.SYS>
 <CHKSTATE.SYS>         <For>                   <Rd>
 <Choice>               <Format>                <Rem>
 <Cls>                  <Goto>                  <Ren>
 <Command>              <Graphics>              <Rename>
 <Alt+C=Contents> <Alt+N=Next> <Alt+B=Back>              00006:002
```

Tab to a command and press Enter
for help about that command.

DOS versions 5.0 and later provide on-line help for every DOS command.

Where Have All the Files Gone?

If you're going to make it in DOS, you have to master its filing system. This system can be summed up in three words: *disks*, *directories*, and *files*. Each disk is capable of storing gobs of files, too many to keep track of in any single location. So, DOS uses *directories* to group the files. To figure out where DOS is hiding all your files, you have to know how to change from one drive to another, switch to a directory, and display file lists. You'll learn all this in the following sections.

Changing to a Disk Drive: The Old Shell Game

To change to a disk drive, type the letter of the drive followed by a colon (:) and press **Enter**. For example, if you have a disk in drive A, type **a:** and press **Enter**. The DOS prompt then changes to A:\>. To change back to drive C, type **c:** and press **Enter**.

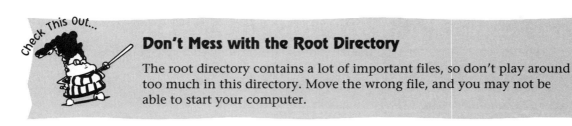

Unformatted Disk Need Not Apply

Before you change to a disk drive, make sure the drive contains a formatted disk (your hard disk, CDs, and the program disks you purchase are already formatted). If you change to a drive that does not contain a formatted disk, the following error message will appear:

Not ready reading drive A
Abort, Retry, Fail?

Insert a formatted disk in the drive, close the drive door, and press **R** for Retry.

Changing to a Directory

When DOS activates a disk drive, DOS automatically looks for files in the first directory on the disk: the *root directory*. If the files are in a different directory, you must change to that directory by entering the CHDIR or CD (Change Directory) command. You'll practice changing directories in the next few sections. For details on how to create and delete directories, see Chapter 20, "Making and Deleting Directories (or Folders)."

Going to the House of DOS: The DOS Directory

Depending on how your computer is set up, you may have to change to the DOS directory to enter a DOS command. Here's how you do it:

1. Type **c:** and press **Enter** to change to drive C. C:\> appears on-screen.

2. Type **cd \dos** and press **Enter** (CD stands for Change Directory). **C:\DOS>** appears on-screen. You are now in the house of DOS.

Going Back to the Root Cellar

To change back to the root directory, type **cd ** and press **Enter**. The DOS prompt changes back to C:\>.

Don't Mess with the Root Directory

The root directory contains a lot of important files, so don't play around too much in this directory. Move the wrong file, and you may not be able to start your computer.

Changing to a Subdirectory

Let's say you want to work with the files in a subdirectory (a directory that's under another directory). For example, suppose you want to work with the files in C:\DATA\BOOKS (assuming you have this directory on your hard disk). You can change to the subdirectory in either of two ways. The first way is to enter two CD commands:

1. Type **c:** and press **Enter** to change to drive C.

2. Type **cd \data** and press **Enter** to change to C:\DATA. (The backslash \ tells DOS to start at the root directory.)

3. Type **cd books** and press **Enter** to change to C:\DATA\BOOKS. (Note that the backslash is omitted here, because you don't want to start back at the root directory.)

The other way to change to a subdirectory is to use a single CD command followed by a complete list of directories that lead to the subdirectory. This list of directories is also known as a *path*. Here's what you do:

1. Type **c:** and press **Enter** to change to drive C.

2. Type **cd \data\books** and press **Enter**.

In addition to moving down the directory tree, you can move up the tree. Type **cd ..** and press **Enter** to move up one directory in the tree.

So What's in This Directory?

Once you have changed to the drive and directory that contains the files you want to work with, you can view a list of the files on that drive and directory. To view a list of files, type **dir** and press **Enter**. A file list appears.

Whoa! Slowing Down the File List

If the file list contains too many files to fit on one screen, the list scrolls off the top of the screen, making you feel as though you are falling very fast. To prevent the list from scrolling off the screen, you have three options:

➤ Type **dir /w** and press **Enter**. The /W (wide) switch tells DOS to display only the names of the files and to display the file names in several columns across the screen.

➤ Type **dir /p** and press **Enter**. (The /P stands for Pause.) DOS displays only one screenful of file names at a time. You can press any key to see the next screenful of names.

➤ Type **dir /a:d** and press **Enter**. (The /A:D stands for Attribute:Directories.) DOS displays the names of the directories under the current directory. No file names are displayed.

Narrowing the File List

You may not want to view all the files in a directory. You may, for example, want to view only those files that end in .EXE, .BAT, or .COM (these are files that run programs). To view a group of files, you can use *wild-card characters*.

Dealing with Wild Cards

A wild-card character is any character that takes the place of another character or a group of characters. Think of a wild-card character as a wild card in a game of poker. If the Joker is wild, you can use it in place of any card in the entire deck of cards. In DOS, you can use two wild characters: a question mark (?) and an asterisk (*). The question mark stands in for any single character. The asterisk stands in for any group of characters.

Here are some ways you can use wild-card entries with the DIR command:

Type **dir *.com** and press **Enter** to view a list of all files with the .COM file name extension (for example, HELP.COM, EDIT.COM, and TREE.COM).

Type **dir ???.*** and press **Enter** to view a list of all files that have a file name of three letters or fewer (for example, EGA.CPI, SYS.COM, and FC.EXE).

Type **dir s???.*** and press **Enter** to view a list of all files whose file name starts with S and has four letters or fewer (for example, SORT.EXE and SYS.COM).

Wild Cards and Switches

You can use a wild-card entry with a switch. For example, if you type **dir *.com /w**, DOS will display only those files with the .COM extension and will display them in several columns across the screen.

To learn more about managing disks, files, and directories in DOS or Windows, see Part 4, "Managing Disks, Directories, and Files."

Ditching DOS: Running Another Program

The easiest way to deal with DOS is to avoid it; run one of your programs and have DOS retreat backstage where it belongs. To run a DOS program, you change to the directory where the program's files are stored and then enter the command for running the program. For example, you may enter **wp** to run WordPerfect. For more details about running programs, see Chapter 9, "Selecting, Installing, and Running Programs."

The Least You Need To Know

Until Bill Gates descends from the mountain and announces that "DOS is dead," you'll need to know the basics of working at the DOS prompt:

➤ The DOS prompt shows the letter of the current drive and the name of the directory.

➤ To change to drive A, shove a formatted disk into drive A; type **a:** and press **Enter**.

➤ To change to a directory, type **cd** ***dirname*** (where *dirname* is the name of the directory) and press **Enter**.

➤ To view a list of files in a directory, type **dir** and press **Enter**. Type **dir /w** if the list flies past the screen.

➤ To run a program from the DOS prompt, change to the drive and directory that contains the program's files, type the command to run the program, and then press **Enter**.

Part 3
Doing Something Useful with Programs

You didn't buy a computer so you could watch the pretty pictures or drag icons across the screen. You got a computer so you could do some work…or play a few games. This section provides a tour of the various applications you can run on your computer—programs for creating letters, balancing your checkbook, drawing pictures, managing your schedule, learning something, and even having some fun.

And that's not all. You'll also learn what to do when you bring a new application home—how to install it on your hard drive (or play a CD), enter commands, and use the application without flipping through the documentation.

Chapter 9

Selecting, Installing, and Running Programs

By the End of This Chapter, You'll Be Able To:

➤ Explain what applications are and what they do

➤ Pick the right application for the right job

➤ Look at a box in your software store and figure out whether your computer can run the application

➤ Put your fancy new application on your hard disk and run it

Before you can do anything useful with your computer, you must run two types of programs: an *operating system* (such as DOS or Windows) and an *application*. The operating system is fairly boring. Unless you're a bona fide nerd, you won't deal with it very much. Applications are why you own your computer; it lets you create newsletters, calculate your finances, play games, get up-to-the-minute sports scores, and even go shopping.

In this chapter, you will learn the basics about applications, including how to install a new application on your hard disk and how to run an application.

Check This Out...

Terminology Break

Before you get too far into the chapter, you should understand the terms *software*, *program*, and *application*. *Software* consists of any instructions that tell your computer (the hardware) what to do. A *program* is a complete set of instructions. A program can be an *operating system* (such as DOS) or an *application*. An application is a program that allows you to do something useful, such as type a letter or shoot incoming aliens out of the sky. To further confuse you, the terms *program* and *application* are commonly used interchangeably.

The Right Application for the Right Job

When choosing an application, first ask yourself what you want the application to do. As the next table shows, each type of application specializes in performing a specific task. The remaining chapters of Part III go into more detail about each type of application.

Types of Applications

Use This Application	To
Database	Store and manipulate information, analyze data, generate client reports, and print mailing labels.
Desktop publishing	Create and print newsletters, flyers, brochures, business cards, and books.
Educational	Play games (both educational and otherwise), compose music, and research topics.
Finance/Accounting	Print checks, balance a checkbook, manage payroll, and update inventory records.
Graphics	Create graphs, illustrate manuals, design machinery, and make slide shows.
Integrated	Perform combined tasks of word processor, spreadsheet, database, communications, and graphics applications. Some software manufacturers bundle a full-featured program (such as a word processor, spreadsheet, and database) and market the program as a suite, which acts as an integrated package.
PIM	PIM stands for Personal Information Manager. You use this type of application to keep track of meetings and appointments.

Use This Application	To
Spreadsheet	Balance accounts, keep track of schedules, track materials, estimate job costs, determine averages, automate quality control, and do graphs.
Telecommunications	Transfer data between two computers, access online information, and cruise the Internet.
Utilities	Enhance the capabilities of your computer, maintain your computer and files, make your system easier to use.
Word processor	Write letters and reports, compose books, and write articles.

Can Your Computer Run This Application?

You can't run all applications on all computers. Before you buy any application, make sure your computer can run it. The minimum hardware and software requirements are printed on the outside of every software package.

Look for the following information:

Computer type   Typically, you can't run a Macintosh application on an IBM-compatible computer. Make sure the application is for an IBM or compatible computer.

Operating system   Try to find applications that are designed specifically for the operating system you use: Windows 95, Windows 3.1, or DOS. Windows 95 and Windows 3.1 are both capable of running DOS programs, but Windows 3.1 cannot run Windows 95 programs, and DOS cannot run any Windows programs.

CPU requirements   CPU stands for *central processing unit*. This is the brain of the computer. If the application requires at least a 486 chip, and you have a 386 chip, your computer won't be able to run the application effectively. The name or number of the chip inside your computer should appear on the front of your system unit. (Note: a Pentium is a step up from a 486.)

Type of monitor   Here are the monitor types from worst to best:

➤ CGA (Color Graphics Adapter)

➤ EGA (Enhanced Graphics Adapter)

➤ VGA (Video Graphics Array)

➤ SVGA (Super VGA)

If an application requires a VGA monitor, and you have an SVGA, no problem. If the application requires an SVGA and you have VGA, EGA, or CGA, you will have problems.

Mouse   If you use Windows (3.1 or 95), you need a mouse (or some other pointing device). A standard, Microsoft two-button mouse is sufficient. Some mice come with three buttons, but you rarely use the middle button. Instead of a mouse, you can use a trackball, which is sort of like an upside-down mouse; you roll a ball to move the mouse pointer, and then you click a button. Many laptop and notebook computers have built-in pointing devices, which serve the same function as a mouse.

Joystick   Although most computer games allow you to use your keyboard, games are usually more fun if you have a joystick. Digital joysticks are the current trend.

CD-ROM drive   If you have a CD-ROM drive, it usually pays to get the CD-ROM version of the application. This makes it easier to install, and the CD-ROM version might come with a few extras. Check for the required speed of the drive, as well.

Sound card   Most new applications require sound cards. If you plan on running any cool games, using a multimedia encyclopedia, or even exploring the Internet, you'll need a sound card. Some applications can use the old 8-bit sound card, but newer applications require a 16-bit or better sound card, which enables stereo output.

Amount of memory (RAM)   If your computer does not have the required memory, it may not be able to run the application or the application may cause the computer to crash (freeze up).

Hard disk requirements   Before using most applications, you must install (copy) the program files from the floppy disks or CD-ROM you bought to your hard disk. Make sure you have enough space on your hard disk to accommodate the new application. Later in this chapter, I'll show you how to check computer disk space.

Don't be concerned if some of the requirements described here are not shown on the application box. Here is an example of the computer requirements for the CD version of Microsoft Publisher (Microsoft's desktop publishing application):

➤ Personal computer with a 386DX or higher processor (486 recommended)

➤ Microsoft Windows 95 operating system or Microsoft Windows NT Workstation 3.51 or later; please note product does not run on Windows version 3.1 or earlier

➤ 6MB of memory for Windows 95 (8MB recommended); 12 MB memory for Windows NT Workstation

➤ Hard-disk space required: 6 MB minimum, 32 MB maximum

➤ One CD-ROM disk drive

➤ VGA or 8514/A graphics card or compatible video graphics adapter and monitor (Super VGA 256-color recommended)

➤ Microsoft mouse or compatible pointing device

How Crowded Is Your Hard Disk?

As you install more applications, your hard disk becomes more and more crowded. It may not contain enough free space to store another application. There are several ways to find out how much free space you have on your hard disk.

If you have DOS 6.0 or later, you can get all the information you need from Microsoft Diagnostics. Here's what you do:

1. Display the DOS prompt. In Windows 95, you can go to DOS by selecting **Start**, **Programs**, **MS-DOS Prompt**. In Windows 3.1, double-click the **MS-DOS Prompt** icon in the Main program group.

2. Type **msd** and press **Enter**. Microsoft Diagnostics appears on-screen.

3. To find out more about a specific system element, click the desired button or type the highlighted letter in its name. The following screen shows what I got by clicking the **Disk Drives** button.

In addition to the amount of disk space that's available, Microsoft Diagnostics shows you the type of CPU your computer has, the amount of memory, and the version of DOS you're using.

Microsoft diagnostics can tell you how your computer stacks up.

Floppy disk drive types

Free space

Total space

```
═══════════════ Disk Drives ═══════════════
Drive  Type                              Free Space  Total Size
─────  ────                              ──── ─────  ───── ────
  A:   Floppy Drive, 3.5" 1.44M
       80 Cylinders, 2 Heads
       512 Bytes/Sector, 18 Sectors/Track
  C:   Fixed Disk, CMOS Type 1             126M        695M
       707 Cylinders, 32 Heads
       512 Bytes/Sector, 63 Sectors/Track
  D:   Fixed Disk, CMOS Type 2             622M       1031M
       524 Cylinders, 64 Heads
       512 Bytes/Sector, 63 Sectors/Track
  E:   CD-ROM Drive
MSCDEX Version 2.25 Installed
LASTDRIVE=Z:

                        OK
```

If you don't have Microsoft Diagnostics (or even if you do), there are other ways to check your hard disk space:

➤ **In Windows 95:** Click the **Start** button, point to **Programs**, and click **Windows Explorer.** Change to the drive on which you want to install the application (usually drive C). The amount of free disk space appears in the status bar at the bottom of the Windows Explorer window.

➤ **In Windows 3.1:** Run File Manager (see Chapter 7). Click the drive for which you want to check the space. In the lower left corner of the window, File Manager displays the amount of free disk space.

➤ **In DOS:** At the DOS prompt, change to the disk drive you want to check. Type **chkdsk** and press **Enter**. DOS displays information about your disk drive, including total disk space and free disk space.

Check This Out...

Free Space, Not Total Space A hard disk is a lot like a house: it seems big until you move in. When looking at the amount of disk space, make sure you look at the *Free* Space not the Total Space. Half your disk space may already be occupied.

Disk space is given in *bytes*. To convert bytes to *megabytes* (1 million bytes), add commas to the number. For example, if DOS says there are 40456798 bytes, add commas to make the number look like this: 40,456,798. The disk has 40 million bytes—about 40 megabytes.

If you're running low on disk space, turn to Chapter 27, "Optimizing Your Computer." There, you will learn how to remove applications from your hard disk, and how to find and delete useless files.

104

How Much Memory Does Your Computer Have?

If you're not sure how much memory (RAM) your computer has, there are a few ways to find out:

➤ Watch your monitor when you turn on your computer. Whenever a computer starts, it checks its memory and displays the amount of memory in the upper left corner of the screen.

➤ If you have Windows 95, double-click the **My Computer** icon on the Windows desktop, double-click the **Control Panel** and the **System** icon. In the System Properties dialog box that appears (see the next figure), click the **Performance** tab. In the Performance status area, look at how much total memory is installed in your computer.

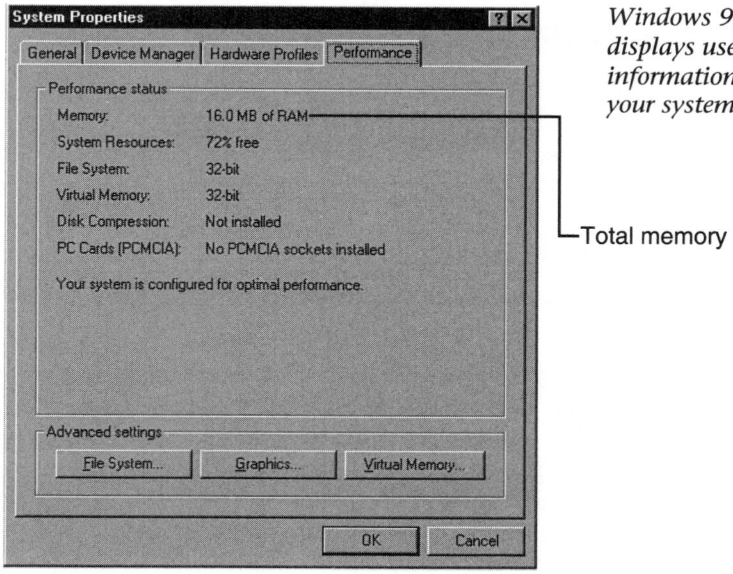

Windows 95 displays useful information about your system.

Total memory

➤ If all else fails, you can check the memory at the DOS prompt. At the DOS prompt, type **mem** and press **Enter**. DOS displays the amount of memory installed in your computer.

Memory Types

Most new computers use three types of memory: *conventional*, *extended*, and *virtual*. Conventional memory is what most applications use; it is the first 640 kilobytes of memory. Extended memory consists of additional RAM chips. Windows has a built-in memory-management system that makes this memory available to Windows applications. Virtual memory is disk space that Windows can use as memory. However, because a disk drive transfers information more slowly than RAM transfers information, virtual memory is very slow.

If you're concerned that your computer does not have the memory required to run an application, see Chapter 27, "Optimizing Your Computer."

Installing Your Brand New Application

Although "installing an application" sounds about as complicated as installing central air conditioning, it's more like installing a toaster. Most applications come with an installation program (called setup or install) that does everything for you. You just relax, eat donuts, swap disks in and out of a drive, and answer a few questions along the way.

Before You Install the Application

Back in the old days, when people still ran applications from floppy disks, the standard advice was to write-protect your new program disks, make copies of them, and use the copies to run the application. With the advent of hard disks and CD-ROM drives, this advice has pretty much outlived its usefulness. Nowadays, you either get the application on a CD (which you can't erase by mistake), or you install the application on your hard disk and never use the original floppy disks again. My advice? Don't worry about write-protecting and copying disks.

The procedure for installing an application varies, depending on whether you're installing the application in Windows 95, Windows 3.1, or DOS. The following sections lead you through the procedure for each of these operating systems. However, the procedure for installing from floppy disks and CDs doesn't differ all that much. The only difference is that with a CD, you won't have to swap discs in and out of the CD-ROM drive, so it's much faster.

Adding Programs in Windows 95

Windows 95 has an Add/Remove Programs *wizard* that can lead you step-by-step through the process of installing any Windows or DOS application (assuming that the application comes with a Setup or Install utility). To run the wizard and install a program in Windows 95, take the following steps:

1. Click the **Start** button, point to **Settings**, and click **Control Panel**. The Control Panel window appears.

2. Double-click the **Add/Remove Programs** icon. The Add/Remove Programs Properties dialog box appears.

3. Click the **Install** button. This starts the wizard. A dialog box appears, telling you to insert the first floppy disk or the CD.

4. Insert the floppy disk or CD as instructed, and then click the **Next** button. Windows searches the floppy disk or CD for a file called SETUP.EXE or INSTALL.EXE, and displays the file's name in the next dialog box.

CD-ROM Installations
When you install an application that comes on CD-ROM, the installation program usually gives you the option of installing the entire application or installing only the startup files. By installing only the startup files, you use little space on your hard disk (typically one to two megabytes), and the application runs from the CD-ROM.

5. Click the **Finish** button. Windows starts the installation program. Follow the on-screen instructions to complete the process.

Installing a Windows 3.1 Application

Unlike Windows 95, Windows 3.1 isn't going to poke around on the program disks or CD to find the Setup or Install utility. You have to find it yourself. However, the process is not a major challenge. Just take the following steps:

1. Insert the first floppy disk of the set (it's clearly marked), or insert the application's CD into the appropriate drive.

2. In Program Manager, open the **File** menu and select **Run**. The Run dialog box appears, prompting you to type the command you want to run.

3. Click the **Browse** button. The Browse dialog box appears, showing the folders on the current disk drive.

4. Open the **Drives** drop-down list, and click the letter of the drive that contains the floppy disk or CD. The Filename list displays the names of all the files you can run.

5. Click the **Setup** or **Install** file, or a file that has a similar name, and click the **OK** button. This returns you to the Run dialog box and inserts the selected file name in the Command Line text box.

6. Click **OK**. Windows starts the Setup or Install utility. Follow the on-screen instructions to complete the installation.

Setting Up Ancient DOS Applications

Windows 3.1 helps you install applications. Windows 95 provides even more help. But DOS expects you to know what you're doing. If you're holding out with DOS, then take the following steps to install a DOS application:

1. Insert program disk 1 in drive A or B.

2. Make sure the DOS prompt is displayed. It looks something like C:\>.

3. Type **a:** or **b:** and press **Enter** to change to the drive that has the disk in it.

4. Type **dir /w** and press **Enter**. DOS displays a list of files.

5. Look for a file named SETUP or INSTALL that has a three-letter extension such as .BAT, .COM, or .EXE.

6. Type the file name that looks promising (you don't have to type the period or three-letter extension).

7. Press **Enter**.

8. If nothing happens, try steps 4–7 again, but type a different file name in step 6.

9. Follow the on-screen instructions.

Registering Your Application

Once you have installed your application, you should register it. I know, you want to play with the application first, but if you do that, you'll never get around to registering the application, so do it now.

Why should you register? There are several reasons. By registering, you let the manufacturer know that you have a legal copy of the application (not a copy you pirated off of Uncle Fred). If you run into trouble later, the manufacturer will know that you paid for the application and will be more likely to help you solve the problem (assuming you can get through to their tech support department). In addition, if the manufacturer develops a newer version of the application, registered users can usually acquire the application at a reduced price.

Getting Your Application Up and Running

The chapters in Part 2 explained how to run applications from Windows 3.1, Windows 95, and the DOS prompt. But that was a long time ago. So here's a quick review of how to run your applications from various operating systems:

> **In Windows 95**, if you installed a Windows application, an icon is added to the Start, Programs menu. Click the **Start** button, move the mouse pointer over **Programs**, and click the name of the application you want to run. If you're running a CD-ROM program, you may have to insert the application's CD into the CD-ROM drive before attempting to run the program.

> If you installed a DOS application, no icon is added to the Programs menu. To run the DOS application, click the **Start** button, and then click **Run** to display the Run dialog box. Click the **Browse** button to display the Browse dialog box that shows the folders on the current drive. Change to the drive and folder where the application's files are stored. Click the name of the file that runs the application, click **Open**, and then click the **OK** button in the Run dialog box.

> **In Windows 3.1**, open the program-group window that contains the application's icon, and then double-click the application's icon.

> **From the DOS prompt**, change to the drive and directory that contains the application's files, type the command that runs the application, and press **Enter**.

Check This Out...

Register by Modem Many software companies now allow you to register your new applications via modem. Typically, after you install the application, a dialog box pops up on your screen, asking if you want to register via modem. You select **Yes**, and then follow the on-screen instructions. The application takes care of the rest (dialing the phone, sending the information, and so on).

Check This Out...

Add DOS Applications to the Start Menu You can add your DOS application to the Windows 95 Start menu. Open the **Start** menu, point to **Settings**, and click **Taskbar**. Click the **Start Menu Programs** tab, and then click the **Add** button. Follow the on-screen instructions to add the application to the Programs menu. See Chapter 5, "Windows 95 Tips, Tricks, and Traps," for details.

109

Executable Files

If you can't remember the command for running the application, look for a file whose name ends in .BAT, .COM, or .EXE. These are the files that start applications. In Windows, you can run the file by double-clicking it in File Manager or Windows Explorer. Or, start the file at the DOS prompt by typing its name (the part before the period), and pressing **Enter**.

Meeting Your Application for the First Time

After you run (start) the application, it may take a while for the computer to read the application from disk and load it into RAM. How fast the application loads depends on the speed of your computer and the complexity of the application. When the application is loaded, you'll see a main menu, a pull-down menu bar, or a blank work area. In any case, this is the screen on which you will start working.

In any application, you need to know how to save your work (in a file), close and open files, and print your creations. The procedures are fairly similar in any application; see Chapter 10, "Program Rites and Rituals," for details.

Help! Finding Your Way Out of Software Oblivion

F1, the Universal Help Key When in doubt, try pressing the **F1** key. Many applications use this key to display context-sensitive help. With a good context-sensitive Help system, you can usually get by without the documentation. But don't tell anyone I said so.

When you're using an application and you get in a jam, you can often get the help you need from the application itself. Most applications offer two forms of help: context-sensitive help and a help index. *Context-sensitive help* provides information about the screen you're currently working on. The application knows the task you're trying to perform, so when you ask for help, the application offers the information it thinks you need. A *help index*, on the other hand, lets you choose a help topic from a list of topics.

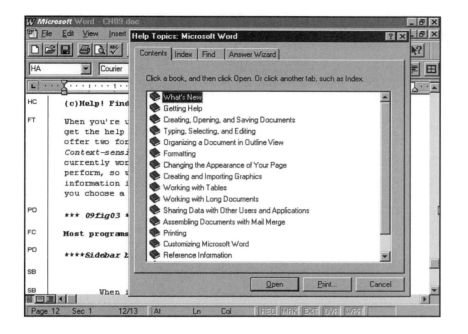

Most programs offer a list of help topics that act as documentation.

The Least You Need To Know

So much for application basic training. Try to remember these survival skills for your future forays into the application jungle.

➤ Read the box before you buy the application.

➤ Know your computer. If you have DOS 6.0 or later, type **msd** at the DOS prompt, and press **Enter** to learn about your computer.

➤ Most applications come with an installation utility that installs the application for you. This application creates the required directory on the hard disk, and copies the program files to the directory. The installation application may also decompress the files if they are in a compressed format.

➤ To run a DOS application, type the command required to start the application, and then press **Enter**.

➤ To run a Windows application, double-click the application's icon.

➤ Many applications come with a context-sensitive Help system that provides information for the task you are currently trying to perform. (When in doubt, try pressing **F1** for help.)

Chapter 10

Program Rites and Rituals

By the End of This Chapter, You'll Be Able To:

➤ Save what you've been typing

➤ Give your creations legal names

➤ Name five reasons why your computer might refuse to save a file

➤ Set up your printer in Windows or DOS

Whether you use a word processor to write love letters to your new beau or use a spreadsheet to analyze your mutual fund portfolio, you need to know a few basic tasks, such as how to save and print the files you create. Although this sounds pretty easy, saving and printing files can become the biggest obstacle for new users. In this chapter, you'll learn how to hurdle this obstacle with ease.

Saving and Naming Your Creations

As you smugly type away, your thoughts dancing across the screen, the computer stores your priceless creations in a very tentative area—RAM. If a squirrel fries himself on your power line, or someone trips the circuit breaker by running the toaster and microwave at the same time, your data is history. Why? Because RAM stores data electronically; no

What's a File? A file is a collection of information stored as a single unit on a disk. Each file has a unique name that identifies it.

electricity, no data. That's why it's important to save your work to a disk, a permanent storage area.

There's a First Time for Everything

The first time you save a file, your application asks for two things: the name you want to give the file, and the name of the drive and directory (or folder in Windows 95) where you want the file stored. For most applications, you'll use the standard operating procedure described here for saving files to your computer's hard disk:

1. Open the **File** menu, and select the **Save** command. A dialog box, usually called the **Save As** dialog box, appears asking you to name the file.

2. Click inside the **File Name** text box, and type a name for the file. In Windows 95, the name can be up to 255 characters long, and you can use spaces. In Windows 3.1 or DOS, the name can be only 8 characters long, no spaces. See "File Name Rules and Regulations," later in this chapter for details.

Omit the Extension If you don't supply an extension, most applications add a period and three letter extension to the file name automatically. For example, Word adds the extension .DOC, and Excel adds the extension .XLS.

3. (Optional) Following the name you typed, type a period followed by a three-character *file name extension*. An extension indicates the file type. For example, you might type **.doc** (word processor DOCument file), or **.xls** (for an eXceL Spreadsheet).

4. If desired, select the drive and directory where you want the file saved. If you don't specify a directory, the application picks a directory for you. To pick a drive and directory:

   Click the arrow to the right of the **Drives** list, and then click the letter of the desired drive.

   In the **Directories** list, double-click the desired directory. (To move up the directory tree, double-click the drive letter or directory name at the top of the list.)

5. Click the **OK** or **Save** button. The file is saved to the disk.

From now on, saving this file is easy; you don't have to name it or tell the application where to store it. The application saves your changes in the file you created and named. You should save your file every five to ten minutes, to avoid losing any work. In most applications, you can quickly save a file by pressing **Ctrl+S**.

Select a drive and directory.

The Save As dialog box asks you to name the file.

Type a file name.

When you save a file, most applications create a backup file (usually using the same name but adding the .BAK extension). The new version of the file (the one with your changes) replaces the old version; the old version then becomes the .BAK file. If you really mess up a file and save it, you can open the .BAK file and use it to restore your file to its original condition (before you messed it up).

When There Is No Fancy Directory Tree

With some DOS applications, you won't get a dialog box that lets you select a drive and directory from a list. You may simply be prompted to name the file. In such a case, if you want to save the file to a particular drive and directory, you must type a complete path. Here are some examples of how you can do this:

a:sales.rpt saves the file called SALES.RPT to the disk in drive A. (Make sure there's a disk in drive A first.)

c:\sales\1996\salefigs.xls saves a file called SALEFIGS.XLS to drive C in the \SALES\1996 subdirectory.

d:\personal\bookidea.doc saves a file called BOOKIDEA.DOC to drive D in the \PERSONAL directory.

> **Directory Must Exist** You can save a file only to a directory that already exists. You can use the DOS MD (Make Directory) command or the Windows File Manager or Explorer to make a directory. See Chapter 20 for details.

115

File Name Rules and Regulations

With the arrival of Windows 95, you can now give your files just about any name you can dream up: everything from LETTER.DOC to I love my job! Windows 95 file names can contain up to 255 characters, including spaces, but they cannot include \ / : * ? " < > or l. If you're still using DOS and Windows 3.1, the rules are much more strict:

➤ A file name consists of a *base name* (up to eight characters) and an optional *extension* (up to three characters), for example, CHAPTER9.DOC.

➤ The base name and extension must be separated by a period.

➤ You cannot use any of the following characters:

" . / \ [ ] : * < > l + ; , ? space

(You can use the period to separate the base name and extension, but nowhere else.)

➤ Although you cannot use spaces, you can be tricky and use the underline character _ to represent a space.

What D'Ya Mean, Can't Save File?

Occasionally, your application might refuse to save a file, rarely telling you what you're doing wrong. It could be something simple such as a mistyped file name, or maybe the disk is so full it can't store another file. If you get a cryptic error message, use the following list to decipher it:

Invalid file name: Retype the file name following the file name rules given earlier.

Invalid drive or directory: You probably tried to save the file to a drive or directory that does not exist. Save the file to an existing directory, or create the directory before trying to save to it. If you are trying to save the file to a floppy disk, make sure there is a formatted disk in the drive.

Disk full: The file you're trying to save is too big for the free space that's available on the disk. Save the file to a different disk, or delete some files off the disk you're using.

Error writing to device: You tried to save the file to a drive that does not exist or to a floppy drive that has no disk in it. Make sure you've typed the correct drive letter. If saving to a floppy disk, make sure there is a formatted disk in the drive and that the disk is not *write-protected*.

How does a disk become write-protected? Look at the back of a 3^1/$_2$-inch disk (the side opposite the label), and hold it so that the metal cover is at the bottom. In the upper left corner of the disk is a sliding tab. If you slide the tab to the top, you uncover a hole; the disk is now write-protected. Slide the tab down to cover the hole, and the disk is no longer write-protected. 5^1/$_4$-inch disks have a notch on one edge of the disk. You can write-protect the disk by placing a piece of tape or a write-protect sticker over the notch. Because you can't write to a CD-ROM disc, there's no need to write-protect it.

Closing Files When You're Done

When you're done with a file, you should close it. This takes it out of your computer's memory (RAM), making that space available for other files and applications. Before closing a file, save it one last time; open the **File** menu and select **Save**. To close a file in most applications, you open the **File** menu and select **Close**. Here are a couple other ways to close files:

➤ In Windows 95 only, click the **Close** button (the X button) in the upper right corner of the document's window.

➤ Double-click the **Control-Menu** box in the upper left corner of the document's window.

Don't confuse the document window's Close button with the application window's Close button. Clicking on the document window's Close button closes the file. The application window's Close button exits the application, and closes any document windows that might be open.

Most applications have a safety net that prevents you from losing any changes you've made to a file. If you've made changes to a file and haven't saved your changes, and you choose to exit the application, it displays a prompt, asking if you want to save the changes before exiting. Once you've given your ok (or choose not to save your changes), the application closes itself down. The worst thing you can do to your data is to flip the power off before exiting your applications; doing this is a sure way to lose data.

These buttons control the application
window, not the document window.

*You can quickly close
a file by closing its
window.*

Double-click
the Control-Menu
box to close the
document window.

Click here to close the
document window.

```
W Microsoft Word - Part03                                    _ 6 X
File  Edit  View  Insert  Format  Tools  Table  Window  Help    _ 6 X

PD        Courier          12    B  I  U        79%

***Insert drawing P-III here and wrap text.***

(a)Part Three

(b)Doing Something Useful with Applications

You didn't buy a computer so you could watch the pretty pictures or
drag icons across the screen. You got a computer so you could do some
work...or play a few games. This section provides a tour of the
various applications you can run on your computer[md]programs for
creating letters, balancing your checkbook, drawing pictures, managing
your schedule, learning something, and even having some fun.

And that's not all. You'll also learn what to do when you bring a new
application home[md]how to install it on your hard drive (or play a
CD), enter commands, and use the application without flipping through
the documentation. By the end of this section, you'll know how to take
any application out of its box and put it to work.

Page 1    Sec 1    1/1    At 1"    Ln 1    Col 1    REC  MRK  EXT  OVR  WPH
```

Opening Saved Files

Saved files are essentially stapled to your disk drive. They stay there, waiting to be called into action. To open a file, you typically open the **File** menu, select **Open**, and then use the dialog box that appears to select the drive, directory, and name of the file. The specific procedure may differ depending on the application. However, the following steps provide a general guide for opening files in a Windows application:

1. Run the application you used to create the file.

2. If the file you want to open is on a floppy disk, insert the disk into the drive.

3. Open the **File** menu and select **Open**. (If you are using a DOS application, the command may be different.) A dialog box appears, asking you to specify the name and location of the file you want to open.

4. Select the letter of the drive where the file is stored. In Windows 3.1, you can select the drive from the **Drives** list. In Windows 95, open the **Look in** drop-down list, and select the drive letter.

5. In the list of directories (or folders), double-click the desired directory.

6. To view the names of only those files that end with a specific extension, click the arrow to the right of the **Files of Type** list, and click the desired file type. The application displays a list of files.

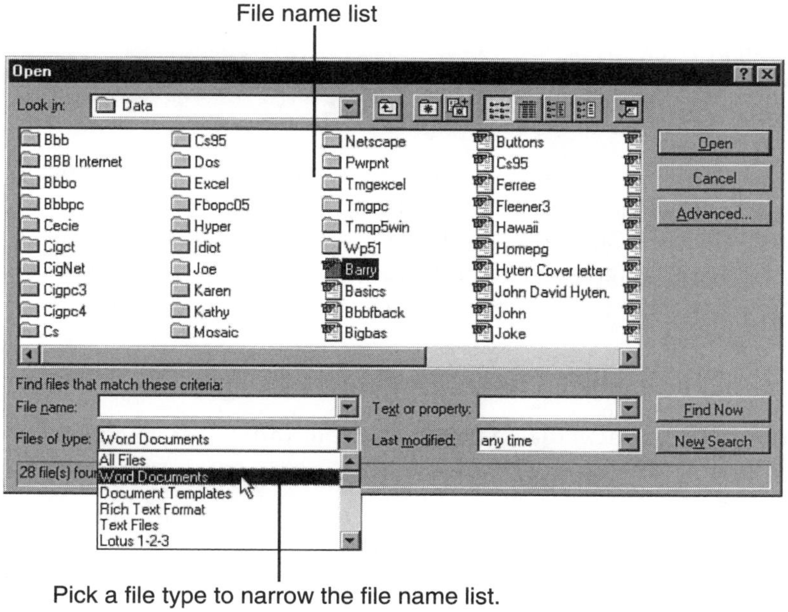

File name list

Select the drive, directory, and name of the file you want to open.

Pick a file type to narrow the file name list.

7. Click the desired file in the **File Name** list.

8. Click the **Open** or **OK** button. The application opens the file and displays its contents on-screen.

Windows applications commonly add the names of the most recently opened files to the bottom of the File menu. To open one of these files, open the **File** menu and click the file's name. Windows 95 keeps track of recently opened files, as well. Click the **Start** button and point to **Documents** to see the list.

Opening Files from Other Applications

Techno Talk

Most applications allow you to open files that were created using other applications. The application can convert the foreign file into a useable format. The Files of Type drop-down list typically displays the types of files that the current application can convert and use.

Setting Up To Print a File

You can't just plug your printer into the printer port on your system unit and expect it to work. No, that would be far too easy. You also need to install a *printer driver*—instructions that tell your applications how to use your printer.

119

If you have Windows, you install one printer driver that tells Windows how to communicate with the printer. All the Windows applications you use communicate with the printer through Windows. If you don't have Windows, you have to set up a separate printer driver for each application. The following sections explain how to make sure Windows or your application is using the correct printer driver, and, if not, how you can install the correct printer driver.

Installing a Printer Driver in Windows 95

When you installed Windows 95, the installation program asked you to select your printer from a list. If you did that, Windows 95 is already set up to use your printer. If you're not sure, double-click **My Computer**, and then double-click the **Printers** icon. If there's an icon for your printer, right-click it, and make sure there's a check mark next to **Set As Default**. If there is no icon for your printer, take the following steps to install a printer driver for your printer:

1. Double-click the **Add Printer** icon. The Add Printer Wizard appears.

2. Click the **Next** button. The next dialog box asks if you want to set up a network or local (desktop) printer.

3. Make sure **Local printer** is selected, and click the **Next** button. A list of printer manufacturers and printer makes and models appears.

4. Take one of the following steps:

   ➤ If your printer came with a disk that has the printer driver for Windows 95, insert the disk, click on the **Have Disk** button, and follow the on-screen instructions to select the printer driver. Click on the **Next** button.

   ➤ If you don't have a disk for the printer, you must use a printer driver that comes with Windows 95. Click on the manufacturer of your printer in the **Manufacturers** list, and then click on the specific printer model in the **Printers** list. Click on the **Next** button.

5. Select the port into which you plugged your printer. This is usually LPT1. Click the **Next** button. You are now asked to type a name for the printer.

6. (Optional) Type a name for the printer. If you want to use this printer as the default printer, click **Yes**. Then, click the **Next** button.

7. Windows asks if you want to print a test page. Click **Yes**, and then click the **Finish** button. If you don't have a disk for the printer, a dialog box appears telling you to insert the Windows 95 CD or one of the Windows 95 floppy disks.

8. Insert the Windows 95 CD or the specified floppy disk into the appropriate drive, and click **OK**. Windows copies the specified printer driver and prints a test page to make sure it's working properly.

If your printer did not appear on the list of printers, and the printer did not come with its own Windows 95 driver, you have several options:

➤ Select a printer that is like the one you have. For example, if an older model of your printer is listed, try selecting the older model.

➤ Select **Generic/Text Only** to print plain text. You won't be able to print fancy fonts or enhancements.

➤ Call the printer manufacturer or Microsoft Corporation, and ask them to send you an updated Windows 95 driver for your printer.

Installing a Printer Driver in Windows 3.1

Like Windows 95, Windows 3.1 uses a single printer driver that services all the Windows applications you use. Before printing, you should check to make sure that the correct printer driver is selected. Open the **Main** group window, double-click the **Control Panel** icon, and double-click **Printers**. If your printer is not selected as the default printer, click the printer's name, and click the **Set As Default Printer** button. Click the **Close** button when you're done.

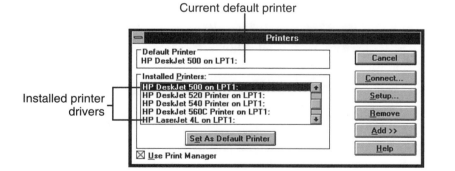

Current default printer

Installed printer drivers

The Windows 3.1 Printers dialog box.

If you get a new printer (or if none of the listed printer drivers matches your printer), you'll need to install a new printer driver. Here's what you do:

1. Open the **Main** group window, and double-click the **Control Panel** icon.

2. Double-click the **Printers** icon. A list of installed printers appears in the Printers dialog box, as shown in the previous figure.

121

3. Click the **Add** button. A list of Windows supported printers appears.

4. Take one of the following steps:

   ➤ If your printer appears in the **List of Printers** at the bottom of the Printers dialog box, click its name.

   ➤ If the name of your printer is not listed (and your printer came with a printer driver on a disk), double-click **Install Unlisted or Updated Printer**. Insert the disk, type the drive letter, and click the **OK** button, select the printer driver, and click **OK**.

5. Click the **Install** button. If Windows cannot find the required printer driver on your hard disk, it prompts you to insert the Windows printer disk.

6. Insert the appropriate disk, and click **OK**. Windows copies the printer driver to your hard disk, and then displays the name of the printer in the **Installed Printers** list.

7. Click the name of the new printer driver, and then click the **Set As Default Printer** button. This tells Windows to use this printer for all print jobs.

8. Click the **Close** button.

Using a DOS Application's Printer Driver

If you create documents or spreadsheets using a DOS application, you have to install a printer driver for that application before you can print your creations. Usually, you install the printer driver when you install the application. However, if you have trouble printing from the application, you may have to try a different driver.

Because the procedure varies for each DOS application, refer to the application's documentation or Help system for instructions on how to install a printer driver. In most cases, you must run the application's Setup utility, and then enter the following information:

➤ **Printer make and model**   This tells the application which printer driver to use.

➤ **Printer port**   This tells the application which port (on the back of the system unit) you connected your printer to. If in doubt, choose the parallel printer port, also known as LPT1.

Check This Out...

Parallel and Serial Printers

All printers are commonly categorized as either *parallel* or *serial*. Parallel printers connect to one of the system unit's parallel printer ports: LPT1 or LPT2. A serial printer connects to the system unit's serial port: COM1, COM2, or COM3. Most people use parallel printers, because they're faster; a parallel cable can transfer several instructions at once, whereas a serial cable transfers them one at a time. However, serial communications are more reliable over long distances, so if you need to place the printer far from your system unit (over 20 feet), a serial printer may be a better choice.

Before You Print

You can avoid nine out of ten printing problems by making sure your printer is ready. Is it connected and turned on? Does it have enough paper to finish the job? Is the **On Line** light lit (not blinking)?

When the **On Line** light is on, the printer has paper, is turned on, and is ready to print. If the **On Line** light is not on, you can usually make it come on by filling the printer with paper, and then pressing the **On Line** button, the **Reset** button, or the **Load** button...what the heck, press all the buttons.

Printing Your Creations

Once your printer is installed and online, printing is a snap. Although the procedure for printing may vary depending on the application, the following steps work in most applications:

1. Open the document you want to print.

2. Open the **File** menu and select **Print**. The Print dialog box appears, prompting you to enter instructions. The next figure shows a typical Print dialog box. Its appearance may vary.

3. In the **Page range** section, select one of the following options:

   ➤ **All** prints the entire document.

   ➤ **Selection** prints only the selected portion of the document; you must drag the mouse over the text you want to print before selecting the Print command.

The Print dialog box lets you enter specific instructions.

Print	? ✕

Printer
Name: 🖨 HP DeskJet 500 ▾   Properties
Status: Idle
Type: HP DeskJet 500
Where: LPT1:   ☐ Print to file
Comment:

Page range   Copies
◉ All   Number of copies: 1 ▴▾
○ Current page   ○ Selection
○ Pages: ☑ Collate
Enter page numbers and/or page ranges
separated by commas. For example, 1,3,5–12

Print what: Document ▾   Print: All Pages in Range ▾

    OK   Cancel   Options...

➤ **Pages** prints only the specified pages. If you select this option, type entries in the From and To boxes to specify which pages you want to print.

4. Click the arrow to the right of the **Print Quality** option, and select the desired quality. (**High** prints sharp but slow. **Low** prints faint but fast.)

Check This Out...

Bypass the Print Dialog Box In most Windows applications, you can bypass the Print dialog box. Simply click the **Print** button in the application's toolbar. The application prints the document using the default settings.

5. To print more than one copy of the document, type the desired number of copies in the **Number of Copies** text box.

6. Click **OK**. The application starts printing the document. This could take awhile depending on the document's length and complexity; documents that have lots of pictures take a long time.

7. Go make yourself a pastrami and cheese sandwich.

🖨 If you have any printing problems, even after you've carefully followed all the steps three or four times, you can find some extra troubleshooting tips in Chapter 28.

The Windows Print Queue

Windows 3.1 and Windows 95 both have a funny way of printing. Instead of printing directly to the printer, Windows sends all the information needed to print the document(s) to your disk. The printing information is stored in something called a *print queue* (a line in which documents wait to be printed). Windows then feeds (*spools*) the printing information from the print queue to the printer as needed. If you ever need to stop, cancel, or resume printing, you have to access the queue.

In Windows 95, whenever you print, a picture of a printer appears next to the time in the taskbar. Double-click the printer to view the print queue. You can then perform the following steps to stop or resume printing:

➤ To pause all printing, open the **Printer** menu and select **Pause Printing**.

➤ To pause the printing of one or more documents, **Ctrl+click** each document in the queue, open the **Document** menu, and select **Pause Printing**.

➤ To resume printing, open the **Printer** or **Document** menu, and click **Pause Printing**.

➤ To cancel all print jobs, open the **Printer** menu and select **Purge Print Jobs**.

➤ To cancel individual print jobs, **Ctrl+click** each print job you want to cancel, and then open the **Document** menu and select **Cancel Printing**.

Windows 3.1 also has a Print Manager that controls the printing of your documents. To view the print queue in Print Manager, press **Ctrl+Esc**, click **Print Manager**, and click the **Switch To** button. You can then perform the following steps:

Reorganizing the Print Queue Once the list of print jobs is displayed, you can change the order in which the documents are printed. Simply drag a document up or down in the queue.

➤ If your printer is marked [Stalled], click it, and click the **Resume** button. Printing should start.

➤ To pause printing, click the **Pause** button.

➤ To resume printing, click the **Resume** button.

➤ To cancel a print job, click on the print job, click the **Delete** button, and click **OK**. You can delete only one print job at a time.

The Least You Need To Know

Whatever you do with a computer, you need to know how to save, open, and print files. In this chapter, you learned how to perform those basics in all your applications. Whenever you encounter a new application, keep the following in mind:

➤ To save your work, open the **File** menu and select **Save**.

➤ If you have Windows 95, file names can have up to 255 characters including spaces.

➤ In Windows 3.1 or DOS, file names can have only eight characters and cannot include spaces.

➤ To add an extension to a file name, type a period, and one to three additional characters.

➤ Before you can print, you must install a printer driver in Windows 95, Windows 3.1, or in your DOS application.

➤ To print a document from most applications, open the **File** menu and select **Print**.

126

Chapter 11

Word Processing for the Typing Impaired

By the End of This Chapter, You'll Be Able To:

➤ Type a simple letter without going insane

➤ Rearrange text with electronic scissors and tape

➤ Eliminate spelling errors, even if you don't know how to spell

➤ Name the three most popular word processing programs

A word processing program essentially transforms your computer into a, overpriced typewriter that not only makes typing a lot easier, but can actually help you compose and perfect your work. It has an endless supply of electronic paper that scrolls past the screen as you type, and because it's electronic, you don't have to worry about mistakes. Just go back and type over the errors—no messy correction fluid, no erasing, no wasted paper (for the environmentally conscious), and best of all, you don't have to replace typewriter ribbons!

A Bird's-Eye View of Word Processing

Most word processing programs that are worth their salt come with a lot of features that let you do somersaults with text and pictures. Many users spend a good part of their adult lives learning how to use these features to improve their work and to save time.

However, if you just want to type and print a simple document such as a letter, you need to know how to perform only a few simple tasks:

Type   You need to type the first draft of whatever you're working on.

Edit   Once you have created a draft of your document, you can change the information on-screen until it is just the way you want it.

Format   At any time, you can begin working on the appearance of the document. This includes setting margins and line spacing, setting tabs, changing the way the text is aligned, and changing typestyles and type sizes.

Print   You can print the document when it's complete or at any time during its creation.

Typing on Electronic Paper

Most word processing programs start you out with a blank "sheet of paper," something like the one shown here. The screen is about a third as long as a real sheet of paper, and it may be black instead of white, so you'll have to use your imagination. The program also displays a *cursor* or *insertion point*; anything you type will be inserted at this point.

You start with a blank page.

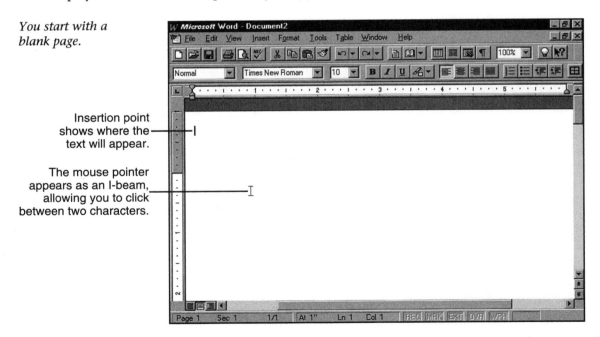

Insertion point shows where the text will appear.

The mouse pointer appears as an I-beam, allowing you to click between two characters.

Easing the Transition

Moving from a typewriter to a word processing program can be a traumatic experience. I've known several people who developed nervous tics during the transition. To prevent you from going stark raving mad during this transitional phase, I'll give you some free advice:

Press Enter only to end a paragraph. The program automatically *wraps* text from one line to the next as you type. Press **Enter** or **Return** to end a paragraph or to insert a blank line.

Don't move down until there is something to move down to. If you press the down-arrow key on a blank screen, the cursor will not move down. If you want to move the cursor down on a blank screen, you have to press **Enter** to start new paragraphs.

Text that floats off the top of the screen is NOT gone. If you type more than a screenful of text, any text that does not fit on the screen is *scrolled* off the top of the screen. You can see the text by pressing **PgUp** or using the up arrow key to move the cursor to the top of the document.

Use the arrow keys or the mouse to move the cursor. Many people try to move the cursor down by pressing the **Enter** key. This starts a new paragraph. Worse, some people try to move the cursor left by pressing the Backspace key. This moves the cursor, but it deletes any characters that get in its way. To move the cursor safely, use the arrow keys or move the mouse to the place where you want the cursor to be and click.

Delete to the right; Backspace to the left. To delete a character that the cursor is on or a character to the right of the insertion point, press the **Del** (Delete) key. To delete characters to the left of the cursor or insertion point, press the **Backspace** key.

Just do it! Once you've grasped the behavior of word processing programs, typing is easy—just do it.

To Insert or To Overstrike?

In most programs, if you move the cursor between two words or two characters and start typing, whatever you type is inserted at the cursor. Any surrounding text is bumped to the right to make room for the new kids. This is known as *Insert mode*, and it is the mode that most programs work in (unless you specify otherwise).

Check This Out...

Default Mode When a program starts in a certain mode, that mode is referred to as the *default mode*. Because nothing was specified, the program defaults to a particular setting, usually the safest or most common setting.

You can switch modes to *Overstrike mode* in order to type over what's already on-screen. If you want to replace one word with another, you simply type over the word you want to delete. In most programs, you can switch back and forth between Insert and Overstrike modes by pressing the **Ins** (**Insert**) key.

Editing: The Tools of the Trade

In a word processing program, text is like clay. You can add text anywhere, delete text, and even lop off a paragraph or two and slap them somewhere else in the document. The next few sections explain some of the word processing tools and techniques you can use to move around in a document, shuffle your text around, and make other changes.

Check This Out...

Save Early and Often

Keep in mind that until you save your work, whatever you type is stored only in your computer's electronic memory. If you turn off your computer or if the power goes out, even for a split second, your computer "forgets" your work. You have to start over. To prevent such a painful loss, open the program's **File** menu, and select **Save** (see Chapter 10 for more details on saving your file).

Zipping Around Inside a Document

When you're in a document, it's like being in a crowded city. You have all these little characters on-screen elbowing each other for a peek at the parade. You are the cursor—the little on-screen light—and you can weave your way through the crowds. To move the cursor (or insertion point), you have several options:

Mouse pointer To move the cursor with the **mouse pointer**, simply move the pointer to where you want the cursor or insertion point, and then click the left mouse button.

Arrow keys The **arrow keys** let you move the cursor up, down, left, or right one character at a time.

Ctrl+Arrow keys   To move faster (one word at a time), most programs let you use the **Ctrl** (Control) key along with the arrow keys. You hold down the **Ctrl** key while pressing the arrow key to leap from one word to the next.

Home and End keys   To move at warp speed, you can use the **Home** and **End** keys. The **Home** key usually moves the cursor to the beginning of a line. **End** moves the cursor to the end of a line. In some programs, you can use **Ctrl+Home** to move to the top of the page or document, or **Ctrl+End** to move to the bottom.

PgUp and PgDn keys   Use the **PgUp** key to move up one screen at a time, or use **PgDn** to move down one screen at a time. Remember, a screen is shorter than an actual page.

Scroll bars   Most programs also offer a scroll bar, which allows you to page up or page down with the mouse. You can click on an arrow at either end of the scroll bar to move up or down one line, drag the scroll box to scroll faster, or click inside the scroll bar (above or below the scroll box) to move up or down one screenful of text. For details on how to use scroll bars, see Chapters 4 and 6.

Rubbing Out Undesirable Characters

The simplest way to delete characters on-screen is to move the cursor to the left of the character you want to delete and press **Del**. This key works a little differently from program to program—sometimes, the cursor deletes the character it's on; other times it deletes the character to the right. You can use the **Backspace** key to delete characters, too, but it works a little differently: place the cursor to the *right* of the character you what to delete and press **Backspace**.

Selecting Chunks of Text

Automatic Rewrap   As you type corrections, add or delete words, and insert phrases into your document, you'll notice that you don't have to adjust the surrounding text to accommodate the change. The word processing program does it automatically, rewrapping the words in a paragraph to compensate for whatever change you make.

Whenever you want to do anything with the text you've typed (cut or copy the text, change the type size, or even center it), you first have to *select* the text. Although each word processing program has its own techniques for selecting text, the following are fairly standard:

➤ Drag over text to select it.

➤ Double-click on a word to select the entire word.

➤ Triple-click inside a paragraph to select the paragraph.

➤ Drag inside the selection area (the far left margin) to select lines of text.

➤ Hold down the **Shift** key while pressing the arrow keys to *stretch* the highlighting over text.

➤ Open the **Edit** menu and click **Select All** to select the entire document.

Copying, Cutting, and Pasting Text

Usually, revising a document is not a simple matter of changing a word here or there or correcting typos. You may need to delete an entire sentence or even rearrange the paragraphs to present your ideas in a more logical flow. To help you get it done, most word processing programs offer **cut**, **copy**, and **paste** commands. Using these commands is a simple four-step process:

1. Select the text.

2. Open the **Edit** menu and select **Cut** or **Copy**. The selected text is placed in a temporary holding area typically called a *Clipboard*. The **Cut** command removes the marked block from the document. **Copy** places a clone of the marked block on the Clipboard, but leaves the original alone.

3. Move the cursor to where you want the cut or copied text placed.

4. Open the **Edit** menu and select **Paste**. The text that is on the Clipboard is pasted at the cursor position. Here's a picture that illustrates what's going on.

Check This Out...

Cool Windows 95 Tip! In Windows 95, you can drag selected text (or graphics) to the Windows desktop to create *scraps*. Scraps are clippings that you can insert into other documents. An icon appears on the desktop. You can now drag this icon into the current document or another document to paste it.

What happens if you cut or delete text by mistake? If you unintentionally cut some text, you can usually get it back by pasting it. If you delete text (by pressing the **Del** key), however, the deleted text is not placed on the Clipboard, so you can't paste it back in. Is the text lost forever? Probably not. Most word processors offer an Undo command that can help you reverse the last one or more commands you entered. (If your program has pull-down menus, check the Edit menu for this command.) If you enter the **Undo** command right after you deleted the text (and before entering another command), you have a good chance of recovering the text.

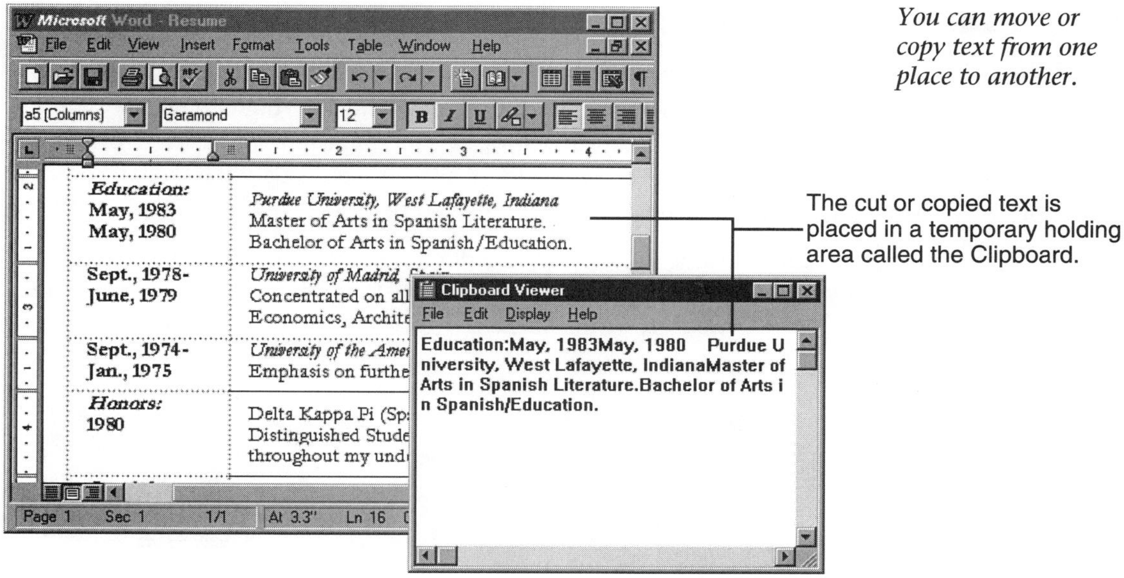

You can move or copy text from one place to another.

The cut or copied text is placed in a temporary holding area called the Clipboard.

Finding and Replacing Text

Say you write a 500-page company training manual that explains how to make a *widget*. The marketing department decides that the product will sell better if it is called a *gadget*. Now, you have to hunt down and replace all occurrences of the word "widget" with "gadget." Never fear, most word processing programs can do it for you. Simply open the **Edit** menu and choose **Replace**. You'll get a dialog box something like the one shown here that lets you specify the word you want to replace and the word you want to use as the replacement.

You can have the program search for a word or phrase and replace it with a different word or phrase.

An On-Screen Proofreader

If spelling isn't your forte, your favorite word processing feature just might be the spell checker. Many word processing programs include a spell checker that can check your document for spelling errors, typos, repeated words (such as "the the"), and incorrect capitalization (tHe). These spell checkers cannot, however, spot mistyped words; for example, it wouldn't notice if you typed "two" instead of "too" or "its" instead of "it's."

When you enter the command to spell check the document, the spell checker starts sniffing around in your document and then stops on the first questionable word it finds, as shown here. You can then skip the questionable word, replace it with a correction from the suggestion list, or type your own correction.

The spell checker stops on questionable spellings and offers suggestions.

Word being questioned

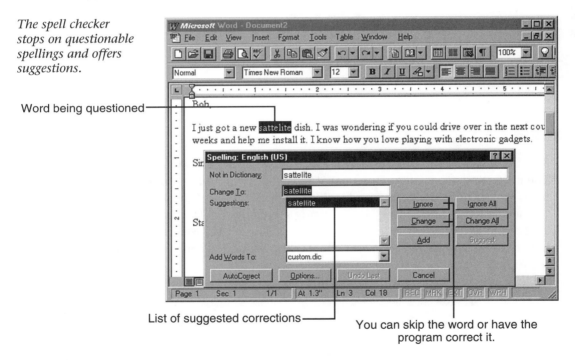

List of suggested corrections

You can skip the word or have the program correct it.

Jogging Your Memory with a Thesaurus

If you can't think of the right word, press a button to open the thesaurus. Type the best word you can come up with, and your word processing program will display a list of synonyms (words that have the same or similar meaning). You simply select a word from the list.

Formatting Your Document to Make It Look Pretty

Once you have the content of your document under control and you've fixed all your typos, misspellings, and ungrammatical grammar, you can start working on the appearance of your document—how you want it to look on paper. This is called *formatting* the document.

You can enter formatting changes before or after you type. For example, you can type an entire letter, select all the text, and then increase the type size. Or you can increase the type size before you start typing. It really doesn't matter.

You will basically format two aspects of the document: the overall page and line layout, and the look of the characters.

Changing the Page Margins

You can usually change margin settings for the entire page or for selected paragraphs. To change the page margins, look for a **Page Setup** command, usually on the **File** menu. When you enter the command, a Page Setup dialog box appears, allowing you to enter the desired margin settings in inches. Try setting the top and bottom margins to one inch, and the left and right margins to .75-inch.

Changing Paragraph Settings

In addition to changing the settings for an entire page, you can control the look of individual paragraphs. For example, you can center a title on a page, increase the space before or after a paragraph, or change the line spacing.

Where Are the Definitions?! Many spell checkers have *dictionaries* and boast the number of words included. Don't expect these dictionaries to function as Webster's Ninth. The dictionaries are used by the spell-cheking feature to determine correct spellings; most of these dictionaries do not contain definitions.

Set Margins with Print Preview If your program offers a Print preview feature, you might be able to set the page margins on the preview screen. Some programs display a set of dotted lines around the page that you can drag to set margins. In other word processors, you may have to turn on a ruler and use the ruler to change the page margins.

To format paragraphs, first select the paragraphs you want to format. Then, open the **Format** menu and select **Paragraph**. This displays a dialog box that allows you change the line spacing, alignment (left, right, or centered), and other features of the paragraph. Enter the desired settings and click **OK**.

Many word processors also display a ruler just above the document. You can drag the margin markers in the ruler to change the margins for selected paragraphs.

You can change the settings for one or more paragraphs.

Indent a paragraph.

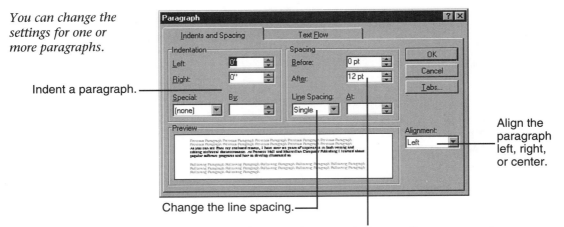

Align the paragraph left, right, or center.

Change the line spacing.

Increase the space before or after a paragraph.

Giving Your Characters More Character

To emphasize key words and phrases, many word processing programs let you select from various fonts and typestyles. In other words, you can make the letters look big and fancy like in a magazine.

What's a Font?

A *font* is any set of characters of the same *typeface* (design) and *type size* (measured in points). For example, Helvetica 12-point is a font; Helvetica is the typeface, and 12-point is the size. (Just for reference, there are 72 points in an inch.) A *typestyle* is any variation that enhances the existing font. For example, boldface, italics, and underlining are all typestyles; the character's design and size stay the same, but an aspect of the type is changed.

To change the appearance of your text, first select the text. Then, open the **Format** menu and select **Font**. The Font dialog box allows you to specify the type size and typestyle, and apply enhancements such as bold and italic. After you enter your preferences and click **OK**, the word processing program displays the text with its new look.

In Windows, you'll see some font names preceded by TT. TT stands for *TrueType*, a font designed especially for Windows. TrueType fonts are very flexible, allowing you to change the font size by *less* than one point at a time! Font names preceded by a printer icon are programmed into your printer and will usually print faster than other fonts; however, you have less control over the size of printer fonts.

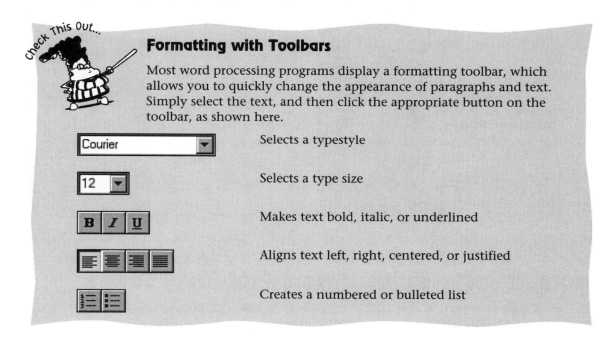

Formatting with Toolbars

Most word processing programs display a formatting toolbar, which allows you to quickly change the appearance of paragraphs and text. Simply select the text, and then click the appropriate button on the toolbar, as shown here.

Selects a typestyle

Selects a type size

Makes text bold, italic, or underlined

Aligns text left, right, centered, or justified

Creates a numbered or bulleted list

The Unveiling: Previewing Your Document

You've done all the hard work—the writing, editing, formatting, and reformatting. But how is your document going to look on paper? Before you waste paper and ink trying to find out, preview your document on-screen. The Print Preview features allows you to view entire pages of your document, so you can view its printed appearance *without* printing it. In most word processors, you simply open the **File** menu and select **Print Preview**. For details about actually printing the document, see Chapter 10, "Program Rites and Rituals."

Click this button to flip ahead or back.

Use the Print Preview feature to view pages before printing them.

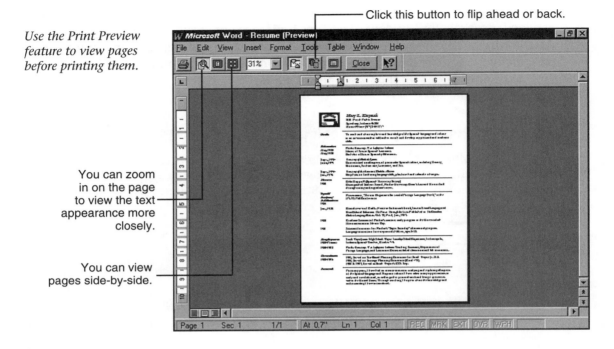

You can zoom in on the page to view the text appearance more closely.

You can view pages side-by-side.

More Power! Advanced Word Processing Tools

In documents addition to letting you type, edit, and format documents, most word processing programs come with several advanced features to help you with your work. The following list describes many of these advanced features:

OLE support Most Windows applications support a technology called OLE (pronounced "Oh-lay," short for Object Linking and Embedding). OLE allows you to drag selected objects (for instance, text or graphics) from one document to another. Make sure all your applications support OLE, so you can freely share information among your documents.

Graphics A program that supports graphics allows you to place pictures, lines, or graphs on a page. All newer word processing programs support graphics.

Multiple windows With multiple windows, you can divide your screen into two or more windows and open a different document in each window. You can then switch between windows or cut and paste text from one window to the other.

Mail merge Have you ever gotten a letter from Ed McMahon, personally addressed to you? Well, Ed personalizes those form letters by using mail merge. He combines a form letter with a list of names and addresses to create a series of letters all saying the same thing to different people.

Styles   To save time formatting, you can save several format settings as a style and apply the style to various blocks of text (usually with a single keystroke). If you change a format setting in a style, that setting is changed for all text formatted with that style.

Tables   The Tables feature can help you lay out text in columns and rows to align the text perfectly on a page. Most tables can even perform simple math, including addition, subtraction, division, and multiplication.

Which Word Processor Should I Get?

If all you want to do with your word processor is type letters, memos, and other simple documents, don't waste your money on a word processing program. Windows comes with a word processor (Write for Windows 3.1, or WordPad for Windows 95), which can get the job done. However, if you need to create tables, insert graphics, add page numbers, create indexes and tables of contents, and perform other advanced page-layout chores, pick one of the following top three word processors:

Word Pro (formerly called Ami Pro) is the best of the bunch, and currently the least expensive. Because Lotus (creator of Word Pro) is trying to gain market share, it has drastically reduced the price of its products to compete with Microsoft. Grab a copy of this program while the price is low.

Microsoft Word is the most popular word processing program in the world. Because of its ease of use, capability to handle graphics, and its powerful desktop publishing tools, you can't lose by selecting Word for Windows. (If you have Microsoft Works, you already have a slightly less powerful version of Word.)

WordPerfect used to be the most popular word processing program, but it had a difficult time figuring out how to do Windows, and its popularity took a dive. WordPerfect for Windows is still a fairly good word processing application, and if you have to use it at work, you might as well use it at home, too.

The Least You Need To Know

As you get more experienced with a word processing program, you will naturally start to use the more advanced features. When you are just starting out, however, stick to the basics:

➤ When you start a word processing program, you get a blank screen with a cursor or insertion point. Anything you type is inserted at the cursor.

➤ You can move text in most word processing programs by cutting and pasting the text.

➤ Most word processors let you undo your last action. Make sure you know how to use the Undo feature *before* you need it.

➤ To set the margins for your entire document, open the **File** menu and select **Page Setup**.

➤ To change the alignment, line spacing, or other characteristics of a paragraph, first select the paragraphs, and then open the **Format** menu and select **Paragraph**.

➤ You can format text to set off words, phrases, headings, or even entire sections of text.

➤ Before printing a document, preview it to see how it will appear in print. This saves you from wasting time, paper, and ink.

Chapter 12

Making a Spreadsheet Do Your Math Homework

By the End of This Chapter, You'll Be Able To:

➤ See the similarities between your checkbook and a spreadsheet

➤ Type text, numbers, and dates in a spreadsheet cell

➤ Add formulas to a spreadsheet to perform calculations on the values you entered

➤ Graph the values in a spreadsheet even if you don't know how to graph

There's no mystery to spreadsheets. A checkbook is a spreadsheet. A calendar is a spreadsheet. Your 1040 tax form is a spreadsheet. Any sheet that has boxes you can fill in is a type of spreadsheet.

So, what's so special about computerized spreadsheets? For one thing, they do the math for you. For example, a computerized grade book spreadsheet can add each student's grades, determine the average for each student, and even assign the correct letter grade for each average. And that's not all. The spreadsheet can also display the averages as a graph, showing how each student is doing in relation to the other students. In this chapter, you'll learn what it takes to create your own spreadsheets, and some of the things you can do with them.

A Computerized Ledger Sheet

A spreadsheet is a sheet with a spread. What's a spread? It's a grid: a series of columns and rows that intersect to form thousands of small boxes called *cells*. Most spreadsheet applications display a collection of spreadsheets in a workbook. You can flip the pages in the book by clicking on *tabs*.

A popular spreadsheet program with a sample file open.

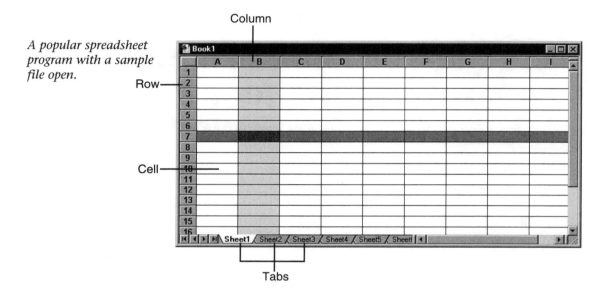

Column

Row

Cell

Tabs

Why Did the Column Cross the Row?

Look across the top of any computer spreadsheet, and you'll see the alphabet (A, B, C, and so on). Each letter stands at the top of a *column*. Down the left side of the spreadsheet, you'll see numbers representing *rows*. The place where a column and row intersect forms a box, called a *cell*. This is the basic unit of any spreadsheet. You will type text, values, and formulas in the cells to make your spreadsheet.

Check This Out...

Naming Cells and Ranges
Some spreadsheet programs let you name individual cells or groups of cells (*ranges*). You can then use the names, instead of the cell addresses, to refer to the cells.

Knowing Where a Cell Lives

If a spreadsheet loses a cell, it's in deep Voodoo. To keep track of cells, the spreadsheet uses *cell addresses*. Each cell has an address made up of a column letter and row number. For example, the cell that's formed by the intersection of column A and row 1 has the address A1 (see the previous picture).

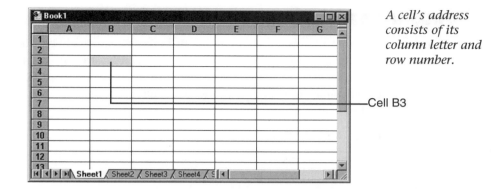

A cell's address consists of its column letter and row number.

Cell B3

Cell Hopping

Look in the upper-left corner of a new spreadsheet screen, and you'll see a cell that has a thick box around it. The thick box is the *cell selector*; it tells you which cell you're on. To jump from one cell to the next, you can use a mouse to click on the desired cell, or you can use the arrow keys or the Tab key (press **Tab** to move to the next cell to the right or **Shift+Tab** to move left). When the cell selector is on a cell, the contents of that cell are usually displayed in the *formula bar* or *input line* at the top of the screen. (Technically, the entire bar is referred to as the *formula bar*. The part in which you type is called the *input line*.)

A cell's contents appear in the input line.

Input line

When you move to a cell, its address is usually displayed at the top or bottom of the spreadsheet.

Building a Spreadsheet from the Ground Up

I bet you're just dying to know how you go about making a spreadsheet. The easiest way is to get a friend to set it up for you—to insert all the formulas and other complicated stuff. Then, all you have to do is type in your data and watch the spreadsheet do its thing. If you're a do-it-yourselfer, however, you'll need to take the following steps (don't worry, I'll go into more detail later in this chapter):

Step 1: Design the spreadsheet.

Step 2: Label the columns and rows.

Step 3: Enter your data: values and dates.

Step 4: Enter the formulas and functions that the spreadsheet will use to perform calculations.

Step 5: Perform a test run to make sure the spreadsheet works.

Step 6: Format the cells (to display dollar signs, for instance).

Step 7: Print the spreadsheet.

There's no law that says you have to perform the steps in this order. Some users like to enter their formulas before entering their data, so the formulas calculate results as they work. Regardless of how you proceed, you will probably have to go back to previous steps to fine-tune your spreadsheet.

Step 1: Designing the Spreadsheet

If you have a form that you want the spreadsheet to look like, lay the form down by your keyboard and use it as a model. For example, if you're going to use the spreadsheet to balance your checkbook, use your most recent bank statement or your checkbook register to set up the columns and rows.

If you don't have a form, draw your spreadsheet on a piece of paper or a napkin to determine the columns and rows you need. (It doesn't have to be perfect, just something to get you started.)

Step 2: Labeling Your Columns and Rows

When you have some idea of the basic structure of your spreadsheet, you're ready to enter *labels*. Labels are common-sense names for the columns and rows.

To enter a label, click in the cell where you want it to appear, type the label, and press **Enter**. If your label starts with a number (for example, 1994 Sales), you may have to type something in front of it to tell the spreadsheet to treat it as text rather than as a value. In most programs you have to type an apostrophe (') or a double quotation mark ("). Usually, whatever you type appears only in the input line until you press **Enter**. Then the label is inserted into the current cell.

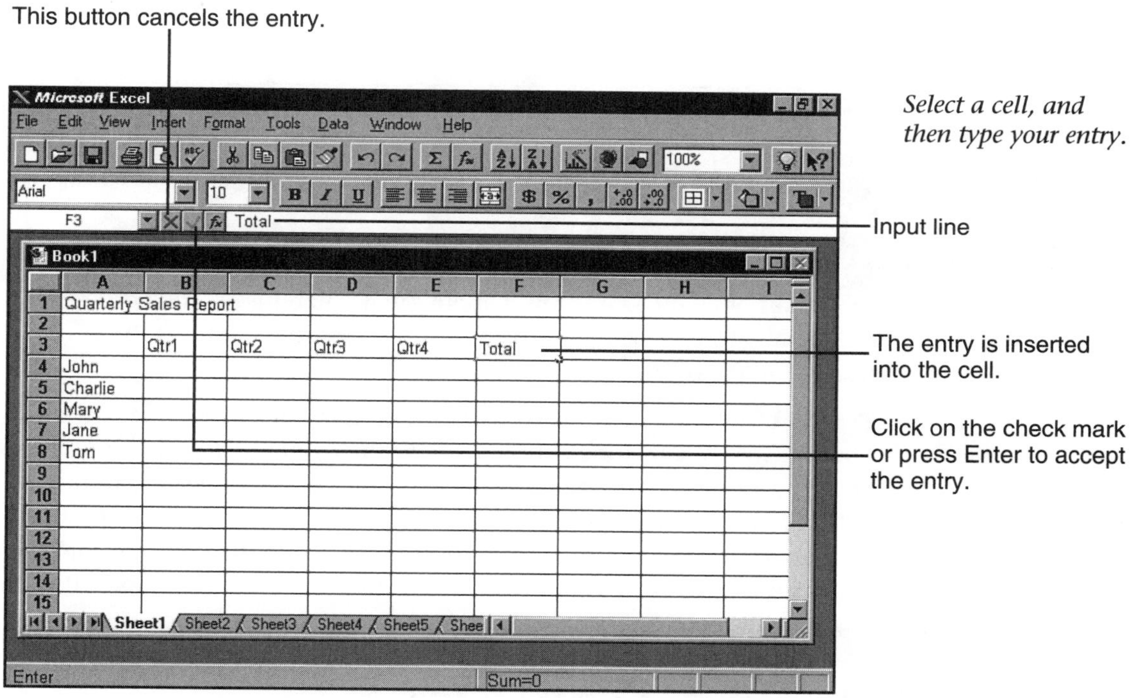

This button cancels the entry.

Select a cell, and then type your entry.

Input line

The entry is inserted into the cell.

Click on the check mark or press Enter to accept the entry.

If an entry is too wide for a cell, it will overlap cells to the right of it...unless the cell to the right has its own entry. In such a case, the entry on the left will appear chopped off (hidden). If you click on the cell, you can view the entire entry on the input line. If you want to see the entire entry in the cell, you can widen the column, usually by dragging the right side of the column header, as shown here.

145

*You can widen
columns by dragging
their borders.*

	A	B	C	D	E	F	G	
1	Quarterly Sales Report							
2								
3		Qtr1	Qtr2	Qtr3	Qtr4	Total		
4	John							
5	Charlie							
6	Mary							
7	Jane							
8	Tom							
9								
10								
11								
12								
13								
14								
15								

Drag the right side of
the column header to
increase the cell width.

Book1 — Sheet1 / Sheet2 / Sheet3 / Sheet4 / Sheet5 / Shee

Step 2 1/2: Editing Your Entries

When you make mistakes or change your mind about what you entered, the best way to make corrections is usually to replace the entry. **Tab** to the cell that contains the entry, type the replacement, and press **Enter**. That's all there is to it.

To edit an entry, click in the cell you want to change, and then click inside the entry in the input line or press a special key, for example **F2**. This puts you in *Edit mode*, and allows you to edit the entry on the Input line. You can then use the arrow keys to move the cursor or insertion point and type your change. Press **Enter** when you're done. Some spreadsheets offer something called *in-cell editing*. Instead of editing the entry on the Input line, you edit it directly inside the cell. To edit an entry, you simply double-click on it, and then enter your changes.

Step 3: Entering Values and Dates

Once you have labeled your rows and columns, you're ready to enter your raw data: the values and/or dates that make up your spreadsheet. As you type your entries, keep the following in mind:

➤ **Values are numbers.** Whenever you type a number, the spreadsheet "knows" it is a value. You don't have to do anything special.

➤ **Don't enter dollar signs or percents.** You can have the program add these symbols for you when you format the cells. Type only the number.

➤ **Type dates in the proper format for your program.** In most programs, you must type the date in the format mm/dd/yy (02/25/96) or dd-mmm-yy (02-FEB-96).

➤ **Dates are handled as numbers.** Although the program displays dates in a format that people understand, it treats a date as a numerical value (for example, the number of days since January 1, 1900). You can then have the program use the date in a formula to calculate when a payment or delivery is due.

➤ ************ Long entries.** If a value you type is too wide for a cell, the program may display a series of asterisks instead of the value. Don't worry—your entry is still there. You can click on the cell to see the entry in the input line, and if you widen the column, the program will display the entire value.

To enter values or labels quickly, many programs let you copy entries into one or more cells or *fill* selected cells with a series of entries. For example, in Excel, you can type January in one cell, and then use the **Fill** command to have Excel insert the remaining 11 months in 11 cells to the right. **Fill** also allows you to duplicate entries. For example, you can type 250 in one cell, and then use the **Fill** command to enter 250 into the next 10 cells down.

Type your first entry.

Drag fill box to right or down.

Excel's Fill feature in action.

The program inserts a series of values.

Step 4: Calculating with Formulas and Functions

At this point, you should have rows and columns of values. You need some way to total the values, determine an average, or perform other mathematical operations. That's where formulas and functions come in. They do all the busy work for you...once you set them up.

What Are Formulas?

Spreadsheets use formulas to perform calculations on the data you enter. With formulas, you can perform addition, subtraction, multiplication, or division using the values contained in various cells.

Formulas typically consist of one or more cell addresses and/or values and a mathematical operator, such as + (addition), – (subtraction), * (multiplication), or / (division). For example, if you wanted to determine the average of the three values contained in cells A1, B1, and C1, you would use the following formula:

(A1+B1+C1)/3

Entering Formulas in Your Spreadsheet

To enter a formula, move to the cell in which you want the formula to appear, type the formula, and press **Enter**. Some spreadsheets assume that you want to type a formula if you start your entry with a column letter. Other spreadsheets require you to start the formula with a mathematical operator, such as an equal sign (=) or plus sign (+).

Some formulas at work.

=E4+E5+E6 gives the total income for the 4th Quarter.

=E10+E11+E12+E13 gives the total expenses for the 4th Quarter.

	A	B	C	D	E	F	G	H	I
1	Hokey Manufacturing								
2									
3	Income	1st Qtr	2nd Qtr	3rd Qtr	4th Qtr				
4	Wholesale	55000	46000	52000	90900				
5	Retail	45700	56500	42800	57900				
6	Special	23000	54800	67000	45800				
7	Total	123700	157300	161800	194600				
8									
9	Expenses								
10	Materials	19000	17500	18200	20500				
11	Labor	15000	15050	15500	15400				
12	Rent	1600	1600	1600	1600				
13	Misc.	2500	2500	3000	1500				
14	Total	38100	36650	38300	39000				
15						Total Profit			
16	Profit	85600	120650	123500	155600	485350			
17									
18									

=E7–E14 subtracts expenses from income to determine 4th Quarter profit.

=B16+C16+D16+E16 totals the four quarter profits to determine total profit.

Most spreadsheets let you enter formulas in either of two ways. You can type the formula directly in the cell in which you want the result inserted, or you can use the mouse to point and click on the cells whose values you want inserted in the formula. To use the second method, called *pointing*, you would use the keyboard and mouse together. For example, to determine the total of the values in B4, B5, and B6, you would type =, click cell B4, type +, click cell B5, type +, and click cell B6.

Check This Out...

Quick Sums

If your spreadsheet application has a toolbar, it probably has a Sum button that looks like Σ. To quickly determine a total, click inside the cell in which you want the total inserted, click the **Sum** button (Σ), and then drag over the cells that contain the values you want to add. When you release the mouse button and press **Enter**, the spreadsheet performs the required calculations and inserts the result.

Using Ready-Made Functions for Fancy Calculations

Creating simple formulas (such as one for adding a column of numbers) is a piece of cake, but creating a formula for the one-period depreciation of an asset using the straight-line method is a chore. To help you in such cases, many programs offer predefined formulas called *functions*.

Functions are complex ready-made formulas that perform a series of operations on a specified *range* of values. For example, to determine the sum of a series of numbers in cells A1 through H1, you can enter the function @SUM(A1..H1), instead of entering +A1+B1+C1+ and so on. Every function consists of three elements:

➤ The @ or = sign indicates that what follows is a function.

➤ The **function name** (for example, SUM) indicates the operation to be performed.

➤ The **argument** (for example A1:H1) gives the cell addresses of the values the function will act on. For example, =SUM(A1:H1) determines the total of the values in cells A1 through H1.

Although functions are fairly complicated and intimidating, many spreadsheets have tools to help. For example, Microsoft Excel offers a tool called the Function Wizard, which leads you through the process of inserting functions. It displays a series of dialog boxes asking you to select the function you want to use, and pick the values for the argument. The following figure shows Function Wizard in action.

Select a type of function.

Tools such as Function Wizard make it easier to work with functions.

| Function Wizard - Step 1 of 2 | ? ✕ |

Choose a function and press Next to fill in its arguments.

Function Category: Function Name

Most Recently Used	DB
All	DDB
Financial	FV
Date & Time	IPMT
Math & Trig	IRR
Statistical	MIRR
Lookup & Reference	NPER
Database	NPV
Text	PMT
Logical	PPMT
Information	PV

Select the desired function.

PPMT(rate,per,nper,pv,fv,type)

Returns the payment on the principal for an investment for a given period.

| Help | Cancel | < Back | Next > | Finish |

Step 5: Performing a Test Run

When your spreadsheet is complete and you're fairly sure it will work, perform a test run to verify that the spreadsheet works. Most spreadsheets automatically calculate formulas as you enter them, but some programs require that you enter a Calculate command. After you enter the **Calculate** command (if your program uses it), look for the following problems:

Crazy results   If your formulas or functions produce results that you know can't be correct, make sure you entered the formulas correctly and that the cell addresses are referring to the right cells.

Narrow columns   If a column is too narrow, you may end up with a label that is chopped short or a value that appears as a series of asterisks. Change the column width to accommodate the longest label or value.

Wrong order of operations   Make sure each formula performs its calculations in the right order. You can change the order of calculations by using parentheses. For example, if you entered =C3+C4+C5/3 to determine the average of C3+C4+C5, the program will divide the value in C5 by 3 and then add it to C3+C4. =(C3+C4+C5)/3 would give you the correct result.

My Dear Aunt Sally

Use this mnemonic to remember the order in which a spreadsheet performs mathematical operations: My (Multiplication) Dear (Division) Aunt (Addition) Sally (Subtraction). To change the order of operations, use parentheses. Any operation inside parentheses is performed first.

Forward references   If you use formulas that rely on other formulas for their calculations, make sure that no formula uses the formula in a later cell. In other words, a formula cannot use a value that has not yet been calculated.

Circular references   A circular reference occurs when a formula uses its own results as part of a calculation. The spreadsheet goes around in circles trying to find the answer, but never succeeds.

If something doesn't work, go back and correct it; then perform another test run until the spreadsheet works.

Step 6: Making the Cells Look Pretty

Once you have the basic layout of your spreadsheet under control, you can *format* the cells, to give the spreadsheet the desired "look." The first thing you might want to do is change the column width and row height to give your entries some breathing room. You may also want to format the values—tell the program to display values as dollar amounts or to use commas to mark the thousand's place.

In addition, you can change the type style and type size for your column or row headings, change the text color, and align the text in the cells. For example, you may want to center the headings or align the values in a column so that the decimal points line up. To improve the look of the cells themselves, and to distinguish one set of data from another, you can add borders around the cells and add shading and color to the cells.

Many newer programs have an Autoformat feature that allows you to select the look you want your spreadsheet to have. The program then applies the lines, shading, and fonts to give your spreadsheet a makeover, as shown in the following figure.

What's Formatting?
Formatting cells means to improve the look of the cells or cell entries without changing their content. Formatting usually includes changing the type style and size of type, adding borders and shading to the cells, and telling the program how to display values (for example, as currency or in scientific notation).

151

The program displays a sample. ──── Click OK to apply the look to your spreadsheet.

Some programs can format your spreadsheet for you.

AutoFormat

Table Format:
Simple
Classic 1
Classic 2
Classic 3
Accounting 1
Accounting 2
Accounting 3
Accounting 4
Colorful 1
Colorful 2
Colorful 3

Sample

	Jan	Feb	Mar	Total
East	7	7	5	19
West	6	4	7	17
South	8	7	9	24
Total	21	18	21	60

OK
Cancel
Options >>

You select the look you want.

Step 7: Getting It in Print

When you finally have all your numbers entered and the spreadsheet has performed the calculations, you may want to print the spreadsheet to send to someone else or to file with your records.

The problems you are most likely to encounter when printing a spreadsheet occur because a spreadsheet is too wide for the paper on which you want to print. If you print a spreadsheet that's too wide, you end up with several pages that you have to tape together. Most spreadsheet programs offer various ways to solve this problem:

➤ **Automatic font reductions.** You can tell some programs to fit the spreadsheet on the page no matter how small it has to make the type.

➤ **Landscape printing.** You can print your spreadsheet sideways on a page to fit more columns across the page. However, you must have a printer that can print in landscape mode (most printers can handle landscape printing).

➤ **Partial printing.** You can select the section of the spreadsheet you want to print and then print only that section.

➤ **Hiding columns.** You can enter a command to hide some of the columns in the spreadsheet. When you print the spreadsheet, the hidden columns are omitted.

Instant Graphs (Just Add Data)

People, especially management types, like to look at graphs. They don't want to have to compare a bunch of numbers; they want the bottom line. They want to see immediately how the numbers stack up. Most spreadsheet programs offer a graphing feature to transform the values you entered into any type of graph (aka *chart*) you want: bar, line, pie, area, or high-low (to analyze stock trends). The steps for creating a graph are simple:

1. Drag with the mouse over the labels and values that you want to include in the graph. (Labels are used for the *axes*.)

2. Enter the **Graph** or **Chart** command. (This command varies from program to program.)

3. Select the type of graph you want to create.

4. Select the **OK** option. The program transforms your data into a graph and inserts it into the spreadsheet, as shown here.

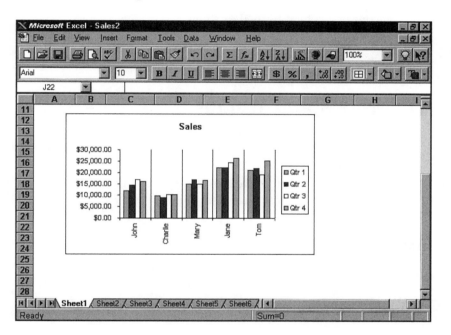

Most spreadsheet programs can quickly throw together any type of graph you need.

Five Cool (and Not-So-Cool) Things You Can Do with a Spreadsheet

I already mentioned a couple practical uses for spreadsheets: averaging grades and balancing your checkbook (although a personal finance program, such as Quicken, works much better). I sat around awhile and thought up some other practical things you can use spreadsheets for:

Schedules   Use a spreadsheet to keep track of your various projects. You can use a separate row for each project and a separate column for each stage in the project.

Invoices   Create an invoice that lists the parts delivered, the number of parts, and the price per part. The invoice can calculate the total due for each part, the subtotal of all parts, the amount of sales tax due, and the grand total (total plus tax).

Loan amortization   If you are purchasing a house or car or taking out a loan to start your business, you can use a spreadsheet to determine how much interest and principal you will be paying on various loans.

Home or business inventory   Use a spreadsheet to keep track of each item you own and how much it is worth. Such a record is invaluable in the event of a fire or theft. (Assuming the record doesn't get burned or stolen.)

Tic-Tac-Toe. Those little boxes are just begging for some Xs and Os. You can crank up your font size and have a ball playing tic-tac-toe on-screen.

Dropping a Few Spreadsheet Names

The big three names in spreadsheets are Quattro Pro, Lotus 1-2-3, and Excel. Quattro Pro is the easiest of the lot, but offers fewer features than either Excel or Lotus 1-2-3. The choice between Lotus 1-2-3 and Excel is a toss-up. If you use Lotus 1-2-3 at work, you might want to stick with it at home as well. If you're looking for a popular spreadsheet that provides plenty of tools for simplifying tasks, Excel is your best bet.

The Least You Need To Know

This chapter has given you a glimpse of the spreadsheet's power. When you get the opportunity to work with some of the spreadsheet applications that are on the market, you'll be amazed at how much work they can save you and how fast they perform their chores. Until you get that chance, make sure you understand the basics:

➤ A spreadsheet is a grid consisting of rows and columns that intersect to form cells.

➤ Each cell has a unique address that's made up of a letter (representing the column) and a number (representing the row).

➤ A cell can contain any of the following entries: a row or column heading, a formula, a function with an argument, or a value.

➤ Formulas perform calculations on the values in the cells. Each formula consists of one or more cell addresses and a math operator.

➤ A function is a ready-made complex formula that performs calculations on a range of values.

➤ Before you begin using your spreadsheet, perform a test run and work out any bugs.

➤ You can format the cells in a spreadsheet to control the text size and style, and to add lines or shading to cells.

Chapter 13

Using a Database To Become an Information Superpower

By the End of This Chapter, You'll Be Able To:

➤ Tell the difference between a database and bouillabaisse

➤ Create a fill-in-the-blank form that you can use to shovel information into your database

➤ Sort your database entries and make your computer hunt them down

Picture this. It's the year 2020. Frank Gifford has moved to FOX TV and is color man for Super Bowl LIV. It's the Cowboys against the Bills (yes, again), and you're in the booth with Frank. You purchased exclusive rights to the only sports trivia database on the planet, making you the most powerful (and highest paid) data broker in history. The Gif turns to you and says, "What was the last team to have lost 4 consecutive Super Bowls in a row?" You overlook the mild redundancy, type **Losses = 4**, and press the **Enter** key. A list of all the teams that lost 4 Super Bowls pops up on your screen, showing the dates of the losses. You say, "The Buffalo Bills, Gif! Super Bowls XXV through XXVIII."

You have instant access to the most valuable information: pass completions, interceptions, and third down conversions. Ahhhh, power!

A database gives you such power by placing information at your fingertips. With a simple command, a database can search through thousands of records in a matter of seconds (no matter how useless and insignificant the information) to pick out just the data you need. In this chapter, you'll learn how such a database works and how to create a database to manage your own information.

The Making of a Database: Behind the Scenes

Before you get mired in all the gory details of what it takes to create a database, take a look at the overall process. It consists of two steps:

By the Way... I bet you're dying to know the difference between a database and bouillabaisse. Bouillabaisse (pronounced booya-base) is a highly seasoned fish stew made with at least two types of fish. A database has no fish, but it can list all the types of fish you might find in a bouillabaisse.

1. **Create a fill-in-the-blanks form.** Forms simulate, on the computer screen, the paper forms you fill out with a pen or pencil, for example, an insurance claim, a tax return, or a Rolodex card. To create a form, you must enter *field names* to indicate where each piece of information should be typed. These names are equivalent to what you see on paper forms: Last Name, First Name, MI, SSN, and so on.

2. **Fill-in-the-blanks.** Once you have a form, you can fill in the blanks with information (or place an ad in the paper for a data-entry operator). The blanks, in this case, are referred to as *fields*. By entering information into the fields, you create a *record*, as shown in this picture. A database file is a collection of records.

A database can be compared to a Rolodex file.

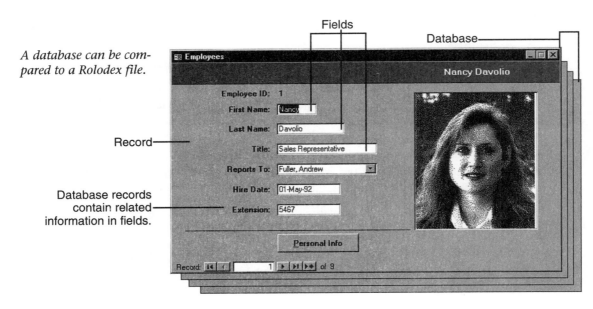

Step 1: Designing the Perfect Form

The best way to start designing a form is to follow the paper system you're currently using—your Rolodex, phone book, calendar, list of employees, accounts receivable, inventory list, or whatever. Think up field names for each piece of information you'll need (or just lift the field names from the existing paper form). Weed out any unnecessary information—you don't want to turn your database into a junkyard. When you're designing the form, keep a few guidelines in mind:

> **What's a Record?** A *record* is a collection of information about a single person, animal, or other animate or inanimate object; it may contain the specifications for a gear, or the name, address, and accounting information for a client. A collection of records makes up a database.

➤ **Use form numbers.** If you're using the database to store information such as invoices or purchase orders, include a field that gives each record a unique number. This lets you find records easily.

➤ **Be logical.** Your form should present information in a natural flow, from left to right and top to bottom, in the order that you use it.

➤ **Leave space to the right.** Leave blank space for entering data to the right of the field name, not below it. Leave sufficient space for your entries. (Many database programs allow you to make a field expandable, so it will automatically stretch to accommodate long entries.)

➤ **Use brief field names.** Keep field names just long enough to explain the entry that follows. Long field names take space away from your entries.

➤ **Use examples.** If an entry can be typed a number of ways, include an example of how you want it—for example, Date (mm/dd/yy). It is likely that someone besides you will enter information into the database. By giving an example of how to format entries, you'll ensure that they are consistent.

➤ **Break certain entries into parts.** If you place each piece of data in a separate field, it will be easier to pull individual pieces of data from your database later. For example, if you need to record a name, create separate fields for the person's title (Mr./Ms./Mrs.), first name, last name, and middle initial.

Newer, top-of-the-line database applications can help you create your own database. For example, when you start Microsoft Access, a dialog box appears, asking if you want to create a new database using the Database Wizard. The wizard leads you through the process of entering your field names, and even allows you to start with an existing form (for example, an address book, recipe list, or home inventory record).

As shown here, the database may display your fields as a form or as a table (sort of like a spreadsheet). In most database applications, you can switch between form and table view, and use whichever view is easiest for you to type your entries.

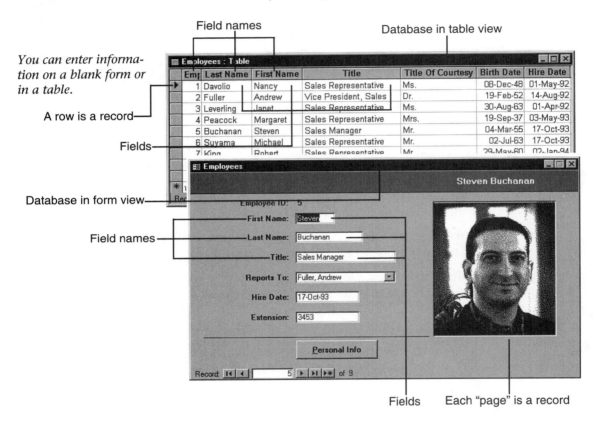

Field names

Database in table view

You can enter informa-tion on a blank form or in a table.

A row is a record

Fields

Database in form view

Field names

Fields   Each "page" is a record

Step 2: Filling in the Blanks

When you start filling out your forms, you'll feel as though you're spending eternity in a doctor's office. Here's where you enter all the information that you want to include in the database: names, addresses, company contacts, part numbers, prices, and inventory lists. Try to get some flunky to do this for you...maybe a relative who owes you a favor. If you have to do it yourself, here's what you do:

1. Type an entry in the first field.

2. Move to the next field, usually by pressing **Tab** or click*ing* inside the field with the mouse pointer.

160

3. Type your entry. (Some programs allow you to import pictures in fields. If you have a picture field, you won't type in the field. Instead, you must enter the Import Picture command and choose the desired picture file.)

4. Repeat steps 2 and 3 until you've typed an entry in each field. (Although you can leave a field blank, doing so may make it more difficult to search and sort records later.)

5. Enter the command to go to the next record or to display a new record. The program saves the record you just entered and displays a blank form for your next record.

Drag-and-Drop Data Entry
Most Windows applications allow you to drag data from one document into another. So, if you already have typed the data somewhere else (for example, if you created a list of addresses with your word processor). You can drag the data from that document into your database.

6. Repeat steps 1–5 until you've entered all your records.

7. Save the database file when you're done.

Type entries here.

Type an entry into each field, and then go to the next record.

Click here to display a blank form for creating a new record.

Ferreting Out Information in a Database

Now that you have this oversized filing cabinet sitting in your computer, how do you go about getting at those records? You have at least three options. You can browse through

161

the records one at a time. You can list the information in every record according to field name. Or you can search for a specific record or range of records.

Just Browsing, Thanks

Browsing consists of flipping through the electronic pages of your database. Browsing is fairly slow and is useful for finding a record only when you don't know what record you want to find. If you have even a vague notion of which record you need, you're better off using one of the other two methods.

Gimme the List

Instead of displaying each record on a single screen, the List (or table) option displays each record on a single line (from left to right across the screen). Although some of the information for each record will be off the right of the screen, you will be able to see a small portion of each record.

In Search of a Single Record

The fastest and easiest way to search a database is to look for a specific record. You start by entering a command telling the database to search, and it responds by asking what you want to search for.

In most databases, you must specify the field in which you want to search and the information you want to find in that field. The entry you type is referred to as *search criteria*. For example, to find out how many sales your representative Alan Nelson made in March, you would ask your database to show you his March record by entering the following search criteria:

➤ Search the Month field for March.

➤ Search the Last Name field for Nelson.

➤ Search the First Name field for Alan.

Only one record matches the search criteria, so Alan Nelson's March sales record appears on the screen. You can review it to determine his total sales for the month.

Searching for a Range of Records

In addition to searching for an individual record, you can tell the database to search for a group of records. For example, to search for purchase order numbers 10013 to 10078, or companies with outstanding invoices of $300 to $1500, you enter the specific range in the field you want to search. The following table shows some sample search entries.

Table 13.1   Searches Within a Specific Range

Search Criteria	Finds
K>W	Words beginning with K through V, but not A through J or W through Z
<=50	Numbers 50 or less
>=3/16/1991<=3/31/1991	Any record from March 16th to March 31st of 1991

Don't Know What You're Looking For?

After you've entered a hundred or a thousand records, no one can seriously expect you to remember the exact spelling of every entry in every field. You'll forget a few, and you need some way of finding these records. That's why most database programs let you use *wild cards* to search for records. (Wild cards stand in for characters you can't remember.)

There are two types of wild cards. One kind represents any single character in the same position. This wild card is usually represented as a question mark (**?**). The other kind represents any group of characters in the same position. This wild card is usually represented by either asterisks (*****) or ellipses (**...**), depending on the program. For example, to search for any entry that ends in "age," you might type **...age**.

Organize! Sort Your Records

As you enter records into your database, the database stores the records in the order that you enter them. If you entered a stack of records in no particular order, your database is a mess. Whenever you call up a list of records, they appear in no logical order. Luckily, the database can *sort* your records in whatever order you specify and present you with a neat, orderly stack.

Like the Search feature, the Sort feature requires you to enter criteria that tell the program how to sort your records. You have to specify two things: the sort field and the sort direction.

When you specify the sort field, you are telling the database the field by which you want the list arranged. For example, if you want your list sorted by postal code, you must tell the program to sort the records according to the entries in the Postal Code field. You can also specify a second sort field that the database would use if the first field was the same for two records (a phone book is sorted by last name and then by first name). The sort direction tells the program whether to sort in ascending order (A B C... or 1 2 3...) or descending order (Z Y X... or 10 9 8...).

Field to sort second (in case there is a tie)

Field to sort first

In Microsoft Access, you can enter sort instructions for 1 or more fields.

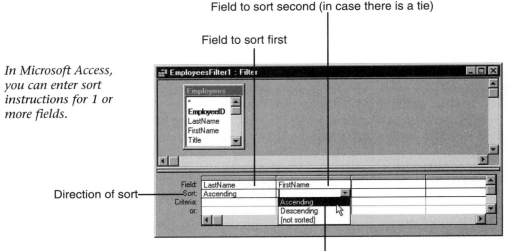

Direction of sort

In Microsoft Access, you can select fields and sort instructions from lists.

Creating Form Letters and Mailing Labels

You've seen how much power the field names give you in searching and sorting your records, but that's not the half of it. You can also use field names to yank information out of your records and to consolidate it in a single location. This allows you to create form letters, reports, invoices, mailing labels, and much more.

For example, to create a form letter, you would use your word processing application to type a generic letter. In place of a specific name and address, you type field names such as:

<Title> <FirstName> <LastName>
<Address>
<City>, <State> <Zip>

Then, you merge your letter with your database. The merge process looks up information in your database and inserts it in the form letter, creating a separate letter for each selected record in the database.

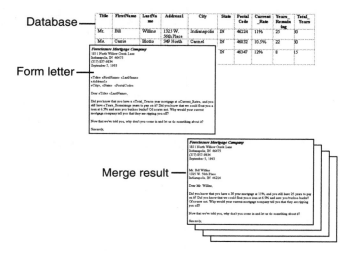

Database

Form letter

Merge result

You can merge your database with a document created in your word processing program to generate a series of personalized letters.

Analyzing Data with Queries

In addition to pulling data out of a database, you can combine data from two or more database files to show trends and analyze the data. For example, say you have one database file that contains a list of products, their ID numbers, and their prices. You have another database file that contains a list of customers and the quantity of each type of product they ordered each month. You want to find out which product is bringing in the most money.

Using a *query*, you could combine the data from the two database files. The query would add the number of each item ordered, multiply it by the price of each item, and then list the totals from largest to smallest.

You can also use queries, to simply pull data from various database files into a single file. The next example shows a query that pulled the product name out of one database file, and the supplier and phone number from another database file. This created an alphabetical list of products with the names and phone numbers of their suppliers.

This database supplies the product names.

This database contributes the suppliers' names and phone numbers.

You can use queries to pull information together in various ways.

The query table contains data from two or more databases.

Choosing the Right Database for You

Database programs vary in how they structure the database and in the special features they offer. That's not to say that one is better than another. You just need to find the one that's right for your needs and budget. Following is a list of popular full-featured databases:

➤ **Act!** is a specialized database designed for keeping track of business contacts and contracts. If you're in sales, you manage contract workers, or you are in some other field in which you have to keep track of people, Act! is the database for you.

➤ **Approach** is Lotus Corporation's award-winning *relational* database applications. (*Relational* means that the application lets you combine data from two or more databases.) Approach is powerful, easy to use, and (as of the writing of this book), the least expensive full-featured database application on the market.

➤ **Access** is Microsoft's relational database program. Like Approach, it is both full-featured and easy to use.

➤ **askSam** (are you wondering why the names of all database applications start with "A"?) is a *free-form database*. It mimics the random pile of notes you might find cluttered on a desk. When you search for data, the program searches the *entire* database—not just a specified field.

Maybe You Already Have a Database!

Many nondatabase programs contain a primitive database program or a way to create a database. For example, your word processing program may allow you to type names and addresses into a document file and then use it as a database. Spreadsheet programs, including Excel and Quattro Pro for Windows, allow you to create databases using the basic spreadsheet structure. Microsoft Windows 3.1 comes with an address book that you can use for phone numbers and addresses (this program was left out of Windows 95). Don't go out and buy an expensive database program if you don't need one.

The Least You Need To Know

A database can be a complicated tool that takes a long time to master. Fortunately, you don't need to know very much to start and take advantage of basic database features. To sort it all out, keep the following information in mind:

➤ A database consists of several records containing field entries.

➤ To create a database, you create a form and then fill out the form to create records.

➤ When you save a record, you're storing information in your database.

➤ You can search your database by browsing page by page, by displaying a list of records, or by entering search criteria for a specific record or range of records.

➤ Field names give you the power to pull information from your database and insert it into a document. This lets you generate comprehensive reports, personalized letters, and mailing labels.

➤ Knowledge is power. Power is corrupt. Therefore, knowledge is corrupt. —Socrates

Chapter 14

Getting Graphical... Even If You're Not Artistic

By the End of This Chapter, You'll Be Able To:

➤ Add prefab pictures to your letters, résumés, and spreadsheets

➤ Create an on-screen slide show using a presentation program

➤ Create graphs and organizational charts without a ruler

➤ Draw a circle, rectangle, or line in any graphics program

➤ Use a scanner to use pictures other people have drawn

In this age of information overload, most of us would rather look at a picture than wade through a sea of words. We don't want to read a newspaper column to find out how many trillions of dollars we owe as a nation. We want a graph that shows how much we owed in 1995 and how much we'll owe in the year 2000, or maybe a map that shows how much of the nation could have built $100,000 homes given the amount of our debt. Maybe even a picture of a tax dollar that shows how much of the dollar goes to pay off the interest on the national debt. We want *USA Today*.

But what about your presentations and the documents you create? Are you as kind to your audience? Do you use pictures to present information more clearly and succinctly? Do you *show* as well as *tell*? After reading this chapter, you will know about several types of programs that will help you answer "Yes" to all of these questions.

Clip Art (for the Lazy and Untalented)

Before we get into the nitty-gritty of graphics programs, I want to warn you that you may not need a graphics program. If you want to add graphics to your newsletters and other documents, you can buy collections of computerized clip art, sketches that some person born with artistic talent created using a graphics program.

Here's the scenario: You're creating a newsletter and you want to spruce it up with some pictures. Nothing fancy, maybe a picture of a birthday cake for a company newsletter or a picture of a baseball player to mark upcoming games for the softball league. You create the newsletter and then enter a command telling the program to insert a piece of clip art. You select the piece you want, click the **OK** button, and voilà, instant illustration, no talent required!

Get It Where You Can: Sources of Clip Art

Some programs (desktop publishing, word processing, business presentation, and drawing programs) come with a collection of clip art on disk. Some of this "free" clip art is very good—but some isn't fit for open house at the local kindergarten. The next figure shows a small portion of the clip art that comes with PowerPoint (a presentation graphics program for Windows). Just for reference, this is some of the good stuff.

These are the individual pieces of clip
art in the Cartoons category.

Many programs come with a collection of clip art.

Each category groups a collection of clip art.

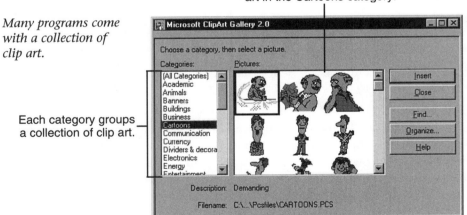

You can also purchase separate clip art libraries on disk, just as you would purchase a program. These libraries typically include hundreds or even thousands of clip art images that are broken down into several categories: borders and backgrounds, computers, communications, people and places, animals, productivity and performance, time and money, travel and entertainment, words and symbols, you name it.

Clip Art Shopping Savvy

Before you plop down 50 bucks for a clip art library, make sure your word processing or desktop publishing program can handle the graphic format of the clip art. For example, if you have a word processing program that can't use PCX files (art created using a program called PC Paintbrush), don't buy a clip art library that consists of PCX images.

Pasting Clip Art on a Page

Now that you have a bushelful of clip art, how do you get it from the bushel into your documents? Well, that depends. Sometimes, you have to open the library, cut the picture you want, and paste it onto a page. Other times, you *import* or *insert* the image by specifying the name of the file in which the image is saved (it's sort of like opening a file). No matter how you do it, the program inserts the clip art in a box as shown here. You can then use your mouse to shove the image around, stretch it, or squeeze it.

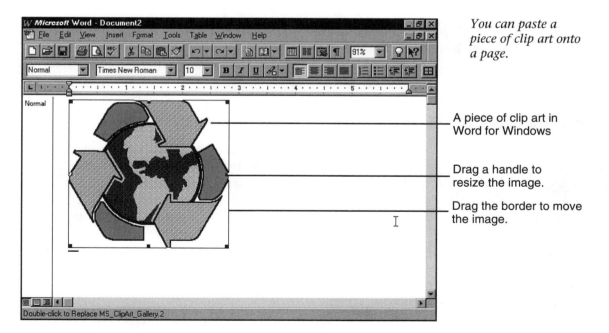

You can paste a piece of clip art onto a page.

A piece of clip art in Word for Windows

Drag a handle to resize the image.

Drag the border to move the image.

Making Slide Shows, Overhead Transparencies, and Handouts

Even if you are not in sales or marketing, you have probably seen a business presentation sometime in your life—probably on TV or in a movie. A sales or marketing representative stands up in front of the board of directors or some other group and shows a series of slides that pitch a new product or show how profitable the company is. How did that person create this presentation? Probably by using a presentation graphics program. Most presentation programs let you create the following:

➤ **On-screen slide shows**   You can create a slide show that can be displayed on a computer screen. If you have the right equipment, you can project the on-screen slide show onto a projector screen or wall, or play it on a TV. (This is the coolest way to go.)

➤ **35mm slide shows**   You can transform your presentation file into 35mm slides for viewing with a slide projector (great for getting uninvited guests to leave early). You can send your presentation to a company that converts presentations into slides.

➤ **Overhead transparencies**   Most printers will print your slide show on special transparency sheets instead of paper (or you can send them out to have them done). You can then display them with an overhead projector. (When printing transparencies, be sure to get transparency sheets that are specifically for printers; otherwise, you'll be sucking molten plastic out of your fancy laser printer.)

➤ **Audience handouts**   Many business people use presentation graphics programs to create audience handouts, which can be used alone or in conjunction with slide shows.

Where Do I Start?

Charts and Slides   Some presentation graphics programs refer to each "page" in a presentation as a *chart*. Other programs call each "page" a *slide* and refer to the presentation as a *slide show*.

Presentation programs are not all alike. With some programs, you first select the type of chart you want to use: pie chart, organizational chart, bar graph, and so on. The chart becomes the central element on the slide. You can then add other elements such as titles, labels, pictures, and sarcastic comments.

With other presentation graphics programs, you start with an overall look. For example, you might select the colors and layout you want to use for all the slides in the slide show. You can then add a chart, bulleted list, title, picture, and other elements to each slide you create. The following sections give you an overall idea of how to create a slide show in a typical presentation program.

Step 1: Pick a Look, Any Look

You can usually start a presentation by picking the colors and layout you want to use for all the slides in your presentation. Most programs come with a collection of professionally designed *templates*. By selecting a template, you ensure that all the slides in your presentation will have a consistent look and that no colors will clash (well, theoretically at least). The next picture shows a list of templates that come with Microsoft PowerPoint and a preview of one of the templates.

Template files

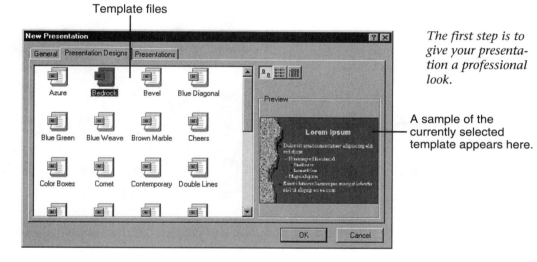

The first step is to give your presentation a professional look.

A sample of the currently selected template appears here.

Controlling the Master

Most presentations have a *master slide* on which you can add elements such as your company logo, your name, the date of the presentation, and the slide number. Any elements you place on the master slide appear on all the slides in the presentation.

Step 2: Adding Pictures, Graphs, and Text on a Slide

Once you have set the look for your slide show, you can start concentrating on individual slides. In most programs, you can add one or more of the following elements

173

to a slide: graphs, titles, bulleted lists, organizational charts, flow charts, and clip art (or your company logo). Each element you add is considered a separate *object*, which you can move around on the slide. Graphs and bulleted lists are the meat and potatoes of any presentation program. If you can do graphs and bulleted lists, you are a prime candidate for marketing manager in a Fortune 500 company.

To add a graph, select the type of graph and then enter your data.

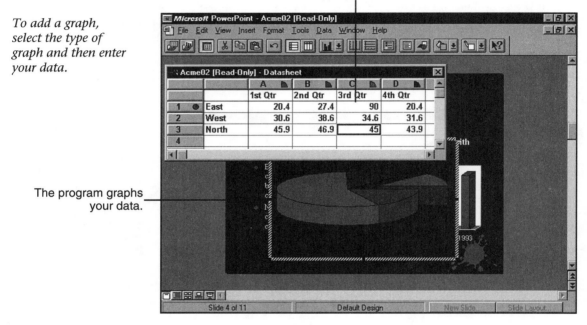

You type your data here.

The program graphs your data.

In most presentation graphics programs, you create one slide at a time. When you are done with one slide, you enter a command to insert a new slide. The new slide has the same design and color as the slide you just created. You can then start plopping *objects* on the new slide.

Step 3: Shuffling Your Slides

Your presentation program should provide a tool that enables you to rearrange the slides in your presentation. Usually, the program displays a screen that shows miniature versions of all the slides. You just drag the slides around wherever you want them.

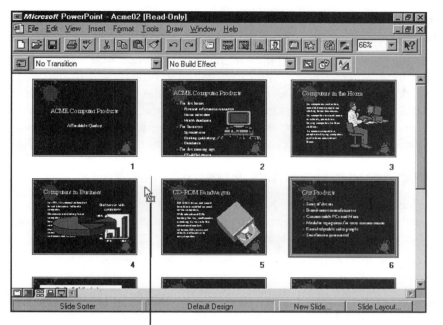

You can display miniature versions of your slides in order to sort them more easily.

Drag a slide from one position to another.

Step 4: Adding Some Fancy Touches

If you're creating an on-screen slide show, you may be able to add some special effects:

➤ **Sounds:** If your computer has a soundboard (such as SoundBlaster), you can plug in a microphone and record your voice, music, or other sounds that will play when you move from one slide to the next.

➤ **Transitions:** These are animated effects that control the movement from one slide to the next. For example, the current slide may open like vertical blinds, revealing the next slide.

➤ **Builds:** This animation effect adds items to the slide while the audience looks on. For example, instead of displaying an entire bulleted list at once, a build would add one item at a time while you're giving your presentation.

Step 5: Transforming a Presentation into Something Useful

After you've created a chart or a series of charts, you need to transform your creation into some usable form. For example, you may want to print the charts, convert them to

175

transparencies so you can use them on an overhead projector, or create a slide show that you can display on-screen.

If you want to create slide shows or overhead presentations but you don't have the equipment for making slides and overheads, you can usually send the files to an outside vendor to have the work done. These vendors can transfer your files to 35mm slides, film, transparencies, or a VHS tape. Many vendors offer overnight service. Many users simply print their presentations on paper, make copies, and use the presentation as a handout. Be careful; this allows the audience to walk out early.

Is a Business Presentation Graphics Program for You?

Many programs offer basic graphics features. For example, several spreadsheet programs (Quattro Pro, Excel, and Lotus) can translate spreadsheet data into graphs. If that's all you need, you would do better purchasing a spreadsheet program.

If you need the advanced features of a business presentation graphics program, however, there are several good ones out there:

➤ **Microsoft PowerPoint**, featured in this chapter, comes with several sample presentations and templates that help you get up and running in a hurry.

➤ **Astound** is a lesser known presentation program that's easy to use and allows you to quickly transform your presentations into World Wide Web pages (to present the presentation electronically on the Internet).

➤ **ASAP**, by Software Publishing is a simple, very affordable presentation program. It doesn't offer the advanced tools of PowerPoint or Astound, but you'll be able to quickly learn the program.

Paint and Draw Programs: For Those with Artistic Talent

So you think you're Leonardo da Vinci or Georgia O'Keefe. If you have even a smidgen of artistic talent, you can create your own computer art. To create art from scratch, you can use either of two types of graphics programs: a paint program or a draw program.

Computerized Graffiti: Painting on Your Screen

Remember the old Lite Brite toy? It consisted of a box with a light bulb in it, a peg board, and a bunch of colored, translucent pegs. You stuck the pegs in the board in various patterns to create pictures. The same principle applies to paint programs. You turn on a bunch of on-screen dots to create a picture.

You already have a paint program, called Paintbrush (in Windows 3.1) or Paint (in Windows 95). From now on, I'll refer to both of them as Paintbrush. In Windows 95, you can find Paintbrush on the Accessories submenu. In Windows 3.1, it's in the Accessories group. Run Paintbrush to display the following screen.

Drawing and painting tools

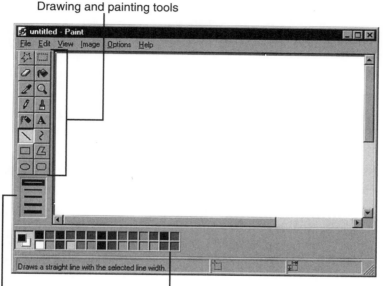

Paintbrush is a paint program that comes with Windows.

Line thickness list   Color palette

Take the following steps to try out some of its drawing and painting tools:

1. From the line thickness list (in the lower left corner), click the desired thickness of the line you want to draw.

2. In the color palette, click the color of the line you want to draw.

The selected color appears here.—

Click the desired color.

3. Click the line or shape you want to draw.

Click a line or shape.—

177

4. Move the mouse pointer where you want one corner or end of the object to appear, hold down the mouse button, and drag the pointer to the opposite corner or end.

5. Release the mouse button. The object appears on the screen.

6. Repeat steps 3 through 5 to draw a circle or rectangle that's not filled in. (You'll fill the shape with color in the next couple steps.)

7. Click the **Fill** tool (it looks like a paint roller in Windows 3.1 or like a paint bucket in Windows 95), and then click the color you want to use to fill the shape.

8. Move the mouse pointer inside the shape, and click. The Fill tool pours color into the shape.

9. Now, draw a shape that's filled with color. In the tool list, click one of the shapes that's filled in (in Windows 3.1). In Windows 95, click a shape, and then click the filled shape in the line thickness list.

10. Click the color you want to use for the inside of the shape, and then right-click the color you want to use for the line that defines the outside of the shape.

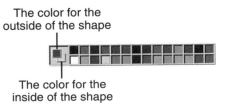

The color for the
outside of the shape

The color for the
inside of the shape

11. Now, drag the mouse pointer across the screen to draw the shape. (Tip: Hold down the **Shift** key while dragging, to draw a perfect square or circle or a perfectly straight line.)

12. Once you have a few objects on the screen, click the **Eraser** tool, and then drag it over parts of your drawing to see how it works. You may need to right-click on the background color.

13. The **Airbrush** tool (looks like a can of spray paint) lets you spray paint the screen. Click the tool, click a color and line thickness, and drag the mouse pointer across the screen.

14. You can cut and copy portions of drawings. Click one of the **Select** tools. And then drag the mouse pointer to select a portion of your drawing.

15. Open the **Edit** menu and select **Cut** or **Copy** to place the selection on the Windows Clipboard. You can now paste the selection.

Click here to select an irregular area. ———

Click here to select
a rectangular area.

16. Open the **Edit** menu and select **Paste**. Drag the pasted selection from the upper-left corner of the screen to where you want it.

You can do much more in Paintbrush, including adding text to your drawing, editing individual pixels (dots) on the screen, and using the color eraser to replace one color with another. However, these steps give you a pretty clear idea of how a paint program works.

Check This Out...

Pixels

Your computer screen is essentially a canvas made up of 150,000 to 700,000 tiny lights called *pixels*. Whenever you type a character in a word processing program, or draw a line with a paint or draw program, you activate a series of these pixels so that they form a recognizable shape on-screen.

Playing with Shapes Using a Draw Program

A draw program lets you create drawings by putting together a bunch of shapes. For example, you might draw a city-scape by putting together a bunch of rectangles of various sizes and dimensions. Of course, you can do this with a paint program, too, so what's the difference? Look at it this way:

➤ In a drawing program, each shape is treated as a separate object. Think of each shape as being formed out of a pipe cleaner (you know, those fuzzy, flexible wire things). If you lay one shape on top of another, you can easily lift the shape off later, without disturbing the other objects.

Check This Out...

Object-Oriented Graphics Draw programs are often called *object-oriented* graphics programs, because they treat objects as individual units rather than as a collection of pixels.

➤ In a paint program, each shape is made of a collection of dots. Think of each shape as being formed out of marbles. You can't just lift one shape without disturbing the marbles that make up the other shapes.

179

In a draw program, you can layer several objects to create a complex drawing.

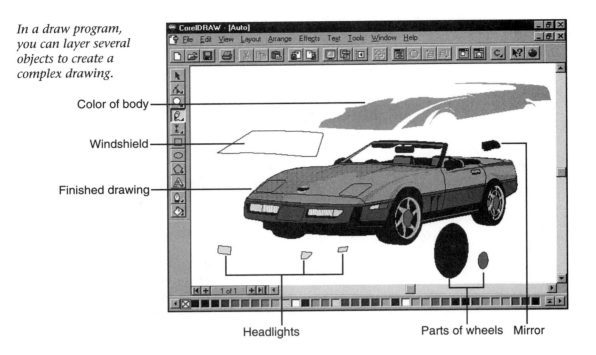

Color of body

Windshield

Finished drawing

Headlights　　　　　Parts of wheels　Mirror

Getting a Handle on Graphics Objects

Once you've drawn an object, handles appear around the object. You can then drag the object anywhere on-screen or change the object's shape, size, or orientation without affecting surrounding objects. To move an object, move the mouse pointer over the center of the object (not on any of the handles). Hold down the mouse button and drag the object to the desired location.

To change an object's size or dimensions, move the mouse pointer over one of the handles and hold down the mouse button (this is commonly called *grabbing* a handle). Drag the handle toward the center of the object to make it smaller or narrower; drag the handle away from the center to make it larger or wider.

Shapes, Together and Apart

In a paint program, if you lay a circle on top of a square, the circle and square become one. Wherever their lines cross, they are linked like Siamese twins. In a draw program, objects retain their autonomy. If you lay a circle on a square, you can later pull the circle off the square just as if it had been drawn on a separate piece of paper.

However, you do have the option of treating the objects as a unit. To group several objects, you usually draw a selection box around the objects. You can then move, copy, or delete the group of objects as if it were a single object.

What About Text?

Although paint and draw programs are not designed to handle huge blocks of text, they do let you add labels and draw arrows to point out important areas of an illustration.

The Trouble with Text

Paint programs handle text as a series of pixels, making the text very difficult to edit. The process may require you to cut a portion of the text and paste in a revised portion. Aligning the revised text can be extremely frustrating. Draw programs offer much more flexibility when dealing with text. The text is contained in a separate box, and you can edit the text just as if you were using a word processing program.

Paint and Draw Programs You Should Consider

If you don't want to shell out a lot of money, and you need to create some simple drawings, Paintbrush (which comes with Windows) probably has all the features you need. However, if you need high-quality art for advertisements, covers, posters, and professional publications, check out the following graphics applications:

➤ **CorelDraw** is the easiest to use full-featured graphics program on the market. CorelDraw 6 comes with a drawing program, a photo-enhancer, a program for 3D imaging, an animation program, morphing capabilities (so you can transform Vanna White into Porky Pig), and a business presentation program. CorelDraw is a must for anyone who's serious about computer graphics.

➤ **Visio** is an inexpensive graphics tool, which is ideal for business use. If you need to create organizational charts, flow charts, floor plans, or schematic drawings, Visio is the program for you. And it's affordable.

➤ **MicroGrafx** is a less expensive full-featured graphics program that offers many of the same features as CorelDraw. However, you'd do better shelling out the extra money for CorelDraw.

➤ **Fine Artist** is a great graphics program for kids. It offers a paint studio, where kids can fling paint onto the screen, rolls of stamps (animals, cars, people, and other beings), sounds, cartoon strips, and much more to keep your kids interested.

Adding Photos and Figures to Your Masterpiece

If you have a photograph or a drawing on paper, and if you have the right equipment, you can turn your existing photos into pixel versions to display on your computer screen. To do this, you need a digitizer or a scanner that converts the image into a series of dots and stores it on a disk. You also must have a graphics program that supports a scanner (the scanner usually comes with a program). Once the image is in your system, you can edit it in your favorite paint program.

In addition, most graphics programs (such as CorelDraw) offer a tracing utility that can convert a scanned image into a collection of shapes, colors, and shades. You can then play with the shapes and colors to create some wild effects.

The Least You Need To Know

Graphics can get as complex as you like. With an advanced graphics program, you can create three-dimensional, life-like drawings that look like sleek color photos in a magazine ad. But for now, just make sure you know the basics:

➤ A business presentation graphics program allows you to create an on-screen slide show, 35mm slide show, overhead transparencies, or audience handouts.

➤ To create a slide show, you pick a template that gives the presentation a consistent look, and then you add graphs, pictures, and text to each slide.

➤ Clip-art images are small pieces of ready-made art that you can include in your presentations and publications.

➤ A paint program allows you to create freehand sketches and other intricate drawings.

➤ In a paint program, you have full control over each pixel on the screen.

➤ A draw program treats each object on-screen as an individual element.

➤ In a draw program, you assemble shapes to create an illustration.

➤ Draw programs are usually used to create floor plans, technical illustrations, and other drawings that consist of regular, geometric shapes.

➤ If you have no artistic talent, do what I do: stick with clip art, and get yourself a good scanner.

Chapter 15

Publish It with Desktop Publishing

By the End of This Chapter, You'll Be Able To:

➤ Make your own greeting cards, banners, and brochures

➤ Stick pictures and text on the same page

➤ Create shaded sidebars that call attention to important text

➤ Squeeze and stretch pictures to make them fit

You've probably gotten computer greeting cards or invitations from friends showing off what they can do with their computers. (They probably just went down to the kiosk at the local drugstore and fed the machine a couple bucks for a customized greeting card.)

Now that you have a computer (and hopefully a color printer), you too can create your own greeting cards, invitations, brochures, business cards, calendars, newsletters, and any other fancy documents. In this chapter, you'll learn the basics of using a desktop publishing program to publish your own works.

Desktop publishing integrates text and graphics.

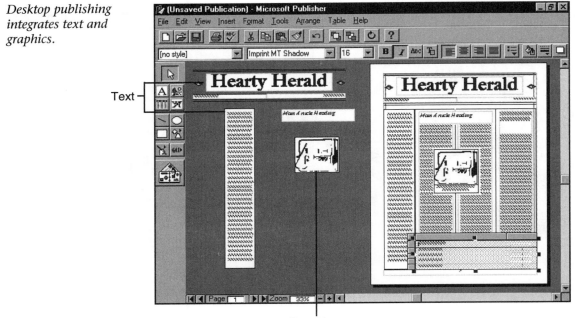

Text

Graphics

But Can't I Just Use My Word Processor?

If you have a top-of-the-line word processing program, such as Word or Word Pro, you can use it to combine text and graphics on a page. You can create brochures, newsletters, and even your own letterhead. So, what makes a desktop publishing program so different from a word processor? Here are some of the major differences:

➤ A word processor comes with advanced tools for creating content (such as a spell- and grammar-checker). Most desktop publishing programs do not offer these tools.

➤ Desktop publishing programs are designed to give you greater control of text and graphics on a page.

➤ A desktop publishing program can flip text and graphics upside-down, allowing you to easily create greeting cards and invitations that fold.

➤ In a desktop publishing program, you can flow text from a column on one page to a column on another page. This makes it much easier to create newsletters.

➤ Most desktop publishing programs let you crop (cut off) sections of a graphic right on a page. In a word processor, you can resize the graphic, but you usually can't crop it.

In short, if you frequently create complex publications such as brochures, greeting cards, and newsletters, you'll find that a desktop publishing program can save you a lot of time and frustration.

Using Automated Features for Simple Projects

If you're interested in creating simple pamphlets, greeting cards, and other small, commonly used publications, many desktop publishing programs offer several automated features you'll probably want to use.

Get a Quick Start with Publishing Wizards

The newest breed of desktop publishing programs (including Microsoft Publisher and Print Shop) include publishing *wizards*, which make it easy to start churning out your own publications quickly. For example, when you start Microsoft Publisher, a window appears, displaying icons for creating sixteen publications, including a card, résumé, brochure, sign and letterhead. There are even icons for paper airplanes and origami (Publisher prints fold lines on the paper).

You double-click the icon for the desired publication, and Publisher starts one of its award-winning *wizards*, a series of dialog boxes that leads you through the process. For example, with the Greeting Card Wizard, you select a picture and greeting for the front of the card, you enter the message that you want to appear on the inside, and you can even place your own logo on the back of the card.

Page Layout for the Stylistically Impaired

Many desktop publishing programs offer the following features to help you lay out pages more consistently and accurately and to help you design publications:

Templates   Some programs come with templates for common publications, such as greeting cards, brochures, newsletters, and business cards. You simply open the template, type in your own information, change the pictures used in the template, and then print.

Master pages   A *master page* contains a collection of elements (company logo, page number, chapter title) that will appear on every page in the publication. When you print the publication, these elements are printed on every page in the same location. If you do not want the text or graphics from a master page to appear on all pages, you can turn it off for certain pages.

Grids   A *grid* is like a transparent piece of graph paper that allows you to align text and graphics precisely on a page. Many programs include a *snap-to* grid. When you

185

move text or graphics on the grid, the snap-to feature snaps the object to the nearest grid line for consistent alignment (hence the name).

Starting from Scratch

If you publish only pamphlets, greeting cards, and other small documents, you will find all you need in Publisher's wizards or in Print Shop's selection of publications. However, if you need to publish a book, or you're creating something requiring a little more creativity, you may want to start from scratch, with a blank page. Although the page may be blank, you'll see several items on-screen:

Paste-up board You can use the space around the page to temporarily store scraps of text and pictures. For example, if you want to move a picture from one page to the next, you can drag the picture off the page and set it on the paste-up board. Turn to the page on which you want the picture to appear; then drag the picture from the paste-up board onto the page.

Rulers Horizontal and vertical rulers appear around the perimeter of the paste-up board. You can use the rulers to help you align text and graphics more precisely. Some programs let you drag the rulers right to where you are aligning objects.

The desktop publishing program gives you an electronic paste-up board.

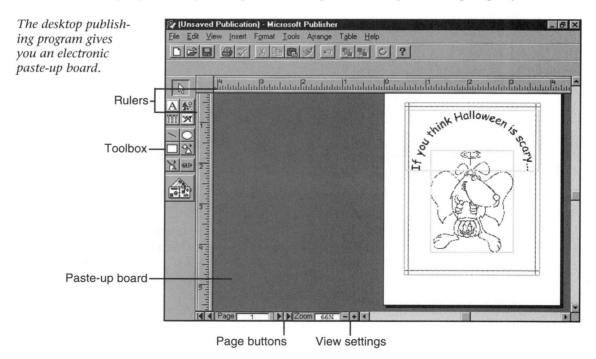

186

Toolbox or toolbar   Nine out of ten programs provide a toolbar that contains buttons for entering commonly used commands. For example, the toolbar may contain a button for placing a picture on a page or drawing a line.

Page buttons   The page buttons let you flip from page to page in your publication.

View settings   Sometimes, you want a bird's-eye view of a page. Other times, you want to see a close-up view of a given area. The View buttons or View commands let you zoom in or zoom out on a page.

Bringing in the Text

When you run a word processor, you can start typing immediately. A desktop publishing program is a little different. To begin typing, you first must create a *text box*. You can then type text into the box or import text that you've already typed in your word processor. To create a text box, take the following steps:

1. Click the **Text Box** button, or select the option from one of the menus.

2. Move the mouse pointer to where you want the upper-left corner of the text box to appear.

3. Hold down the mouse button while dragging down and to the right, until the box is the desired size and dimensions (you can easily resize it later).

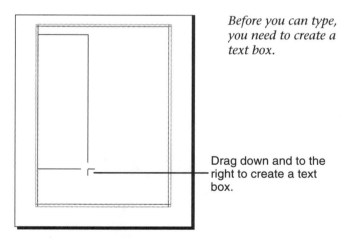

Before you can type, you need to create a text box.

Drag down and to the right to create a text box.

4. Release the mouse button. The text box appears, and an insertion point appears inside the text box.

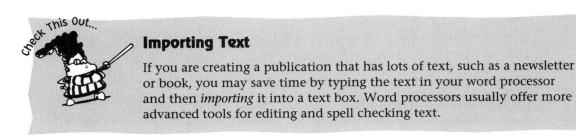

Importing Text

If you are creating a publication that has lots of text, such as a newsletter or book, you may save time by typing the text in your word processor and then *importing* it into a text box. Word processors usually offer more advanced tools for editing and spell checking text.

Taking Control of the Text Box

Once you have a text box on the page, you can start typing. However, if you're in full page view, it will look as though you're typing on the head of a pin. Try zooming in at 100% while you type. Here are a few other tips for working with text boxes:

➤ You can change the type style and type size of the text just as you can in a word processor. Drag over the text, and then choose the type style and type size you want to use.

➤ To change the size or shape of a text box, click its border, and then drag one of the handles (small black boxes).

➤ To move a text box, drag its border.

➤ If the text box is too small to fit all the text, you can reduce the size of the text. Most desktop publishing programs also let you flow the text to another text box, which can be on the same page or on another page.

➤ You can usually add a border around the text box to set it off from surrounding text.

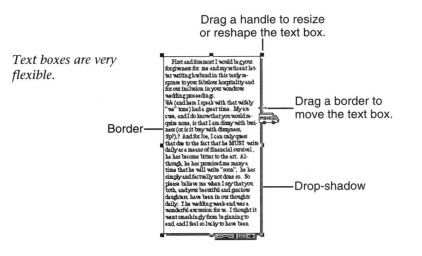

Text boxes are very flexible.

Drag a handle to resize or reshape the text box.

Border

Drag a border to move the text box.

Drop-shadow

Making Your Text Sing

When you bring text into a document, it looks fairly drab—nothing like the elaborate print you see in *Cosmo*. In order to breathe some life into your text, you have to *format* it. Here's a quick list of the formatting you can apply to your text:

➤ **Fonts**   You can use different fonts to emphasize text or set headings apart from the body text. Here are some examples of fonts:

Helvetica 12-point

Times 9-point

➤ **Enhancements**   Unlike fonts, which control the essential quality of text, enhancements act as text makeup. When you apply an enhancement, the typestyle and size remain the same, but the look of the text changes. Some common enhancements are:

Bold	*Italic*	**Shadow**
Condensed	SMALL CAPS	~~Strikethrough~~
Superscript^P	Subscript$_B$	Underline

➤ **Color**   If you have a color printer, you can color your text to create full-page color ads or brochures.

➤ **Alignment**   You can center your text, align it left or right, or fully justify it (so it looks like the text in newspaper columns).

➤ **Line spacing and leading**   You can set line spacing at single or double spacing and increments thereof. (Spacing is determined by the text size you are using.) You can add space between lines of text (called *leading*) to control spacing more precisely. For example, if your résumé is coming up short, you might want to add 2 points of leading between all the lines. Trust me, no one will notice.

➤ **Kerning**   Kerning allows you to close up the space between two characters. For example, if you have a headline that says "Washington Takes a Bath," the Wa in Washington may appear to be farther apart than other character pairs. You can kern the characters to remove the extra space.

Some programs offer additional tools for styling text. For example, Microsoft Publisher has a tool called WordArt, which treats text as a picture, giving you much more control over its appearance. You enter the command to insert a WordArt object, you type the text you want to use, and then select the options to make the text appear the way you want it to.

WordArt lets you insert text as art.

Select an overall look for the text.

Type your text here.

Click outside the box when you're done.

What About the Graphics?

Although you will spend loads of your time playing with your text, the real power of a desktop publishing program is that it also lets you place graphic elements on the page. What kind of graphic elements? There are numerous graphic elements you can put on a page:

➤ If you have a paint or draw program, you can create an illustration and import it into your document.

190

➤ If you think your own artwork leaves something to be desired, many desktop publishing programs come with a collection of clip art you can use to accent your publications. You can also purchase clip art separately.

➤ If you have a scanner, you can scan an image or photo from paper, save it as a file, and import the scanned image into your document. Flip back to Chapter 14 for more information on using graphics in your documents.

➤ Most desktop publishing programs have tools for drawing basic shapes such as lines, circles, and rectangles. These objects let you provide visual devices for dividing the text on a page.

Irreconcilable Differences

Chances are, your desktop publishing program can use files that have been saved in any of the more standard graphic file formats: .PCX, .TIFF, and .BMP. If your desktop publishing program does not support a particular format, you will not be able to import a file that has been saved in that format.

Importing Clip Art and Drawings

To place a picture on a page, enter the **Insert Picture** or **Import Picture** command. The command will vary from program to program. You'll get a dialog box asking which graphics file you want to import. Select the drive, directory, and name of the graphics file you want to import. (You may also have to specify a file format.) Click **OK**. The program slaps the picture somewhere on the screen, usually inside a graphics box that surrounds the picture. You can then use the graphics box to move, resize, or crop the picture, as explained in the next section.

A graphics box can be a tricky thing to deal with. Some desktop publishing programs let you create the graphics box *before* you import the picture. This can distort the picture, because the picture might not have the same dimensions as the box. For example, if you have a picture of a tall, thin man and you import him into a short, wide box, you end up with a picture of a short, fat man. In other words, the box makes the man. If you try to insert a picture into a box of different dimensions, many programs will give you the option of fitting the picture to the box (which can cause distortion) or fitting the box to the picture. Or you can simply resize the box to reverse the distortion.

You have to specify which picture you want to use.

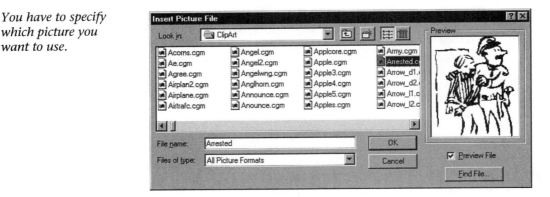

Squeezing and Stretching the Picture

Remember playing with Silly Putty? You can press it against your favorite Sunday cartoon, and then stretch it to twist the face all out of proportion. You can do the same thing with your on-screen pictures. When you click the image, handles appear around it. You can then drag the image to move it, or drag a handle to resize it. If you're resizing an image, and you don't want the Silly Putty effect, you may have to hold down the **Shift** or **Ctrl** key while dragging to prevent distortion.

In addition to resizing and reshaping an image, many desktop publishing programs let you crop the image. For example, if you have a picture showing an entire dog, and you only want to show the dog's face, you can crop off the dog's body. To crop a picture, you usually enter the **Crop** command and then drag one of the handles.

Dropping the Picture on Some Text

When you drop a picture on some text, the text usually has enough sense to get out of the way. The program automatically wraps (shifts) the text, so it flows around the picture. However, in some of the less powerful programs, you have to enter a command to wrap the text.

192

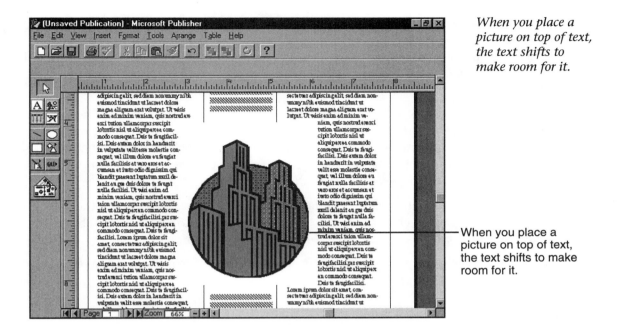

When you place a picture on top of text, the text shifts to make room for it.

When you place a picture on top of text, the text shifts to make room for it.

Stacking and Unstacking Objects

When you lay objects on a page, you eventually get overlapping objects, like a stack of pancakes. With pancakes, you can't eat the one on the bottom unless you move it to the top or move the other pancakes off it. The same is true with text and graphics objects on a page. If you try to click an object that's on the bottom of the stack, you end up selecting the object on top.

To get at the lower strata, you generally have to click the topmost object and then enter a **Send to Back** command that tells the object where to go. Some programs even offer on-screen buttons to make the process easier.

What's The Best Desktop Program for You?

If you don't want to invest the time and money learning to use a desktop publishing program, try a full-featured word processing program, such as WordPerfect, Microsoft Word for Windows, or WordPro. These advanced word processing programs support several fonts and typestyles, allow you to import graphics, let you preview pages, and provide line drawing tools for accenting your documents.

If you're an artist and you need to add stylized text to your drawings (to create ads or magazine covers, for instance), shop for a good graphics program, instead. CorelDraw has text styling tools that are much more advanced than the tools you'll find in any desktop publishing program. Corel can also help you create calendars, greeting cards, brochures, and other small publications.

If you need the features of a desktop publishing program, think carefully about how you will use it most often before you buy; desktop publishing programs differ in the number of features they offer. Some programs are great for designing single pages for brochures and newsletters, but they lack the comprehensive features required for publishing long documents with repetitive page layouts, such as books.

If you want to create greeting cards, résumés, newsletters, business cards, and other short publications, programs such as Microsoft Publisher and Print Shop offer enough basic features to get the job done without overwhelming you with complexity.

For more intensive work, a program like PageMaker or QuarkXPress provides more features for refining the appearance of your pages.

The Least You Need To Know

In this chapter, you learned a great deal about desktop publishing, including some advanced information about typesetting. Although all this information is vitally important (yeah, right), some facts are more important than others:

➤ Desktop publishing programs let text and graphics rub elbows.

➤ Although desktop publishing programs do let you type text and create graphic images, their main purpose is to *manage* the text and graphics that are created in other programs.

➤ When you import text into most desktop publishing programs, the text is placed in a text box.

➤ When you import a graphic image into a desktop publishing program, the image appears in a graphics box.

➤ When you buy groceries, the bagger puts your groceries in a grocery bag (or sack, depending on where you live).

➤ You can move an object on-screen by dragging it with the mouse.

➤ When you select an object, handles appear around it. You can drag a handle to change the size and dimensions of the object.

➤ If you have a good word processing program or a good graphics program, don't waste your money on a desktop publishing program.

Chapter 16

Managing Your Money (and Uncle Sam's)

By the End of This Chapter, You'll Be Able To:

➤ Use your computer to write and print checks, and automatically update your balance

➤ Keep track of your cash flow—to make sure you have as much flowing in as is flowing out

➤ Plot a course for your financial future

➤ Use your computer to do your taxes

The whole concept of money was supposed to simplify things, to make it easier to exchange goods. Instead of trading a fox pelt for a lobster dinner, you could sell the pelt to someone who wanted it and then take the money to the local seafood restaurant and pay for your lobster dinner.

Somewhere in history things got all fouled up. We now buy and sell money, store our money in banks and use checks to get at it, and even have chunks of our money removed from our paychecks before we've even touched it. To help manage your money in these trying times, you can use two types of programs: personal finance (or check-writing) programs and tax programs.

Getting Personal with Your Finances

The only thing personal about finances is that you have to take a personal interest in them to keep from going broke. Few people actually enjoy balancing checkbooks and figuring budgets. However, personal finance programs can help make these jobs a little less painful.

Personal finance programs are often called *check-writing* programs, because their main purpose is to help you keep a balanced checkbook. However, these programs are becoming more diverse. You can use some personal finance programs to manage the finances of a small business, and others (such as Quicken and WealthStarter) contain tools for teaching you how to manage your money intelligently.

Automated Check Writing

The problem with writing checks by hand is that you have to enter a lot of duplicate information. You write the date on the check, the name of the person or business the check is for, the amount of the check (both numerically and spelled out), and a memo telling what the check is for. Then you flip to your check register and enter all the same information again. If you happen to make a mistake copying the amount from your check to your register, you'll have lots of fun balancing your checkbook at the end of the month.

With a check-writing program, your computer enters the date automatically. You enter the name of the person or business to whom you're writing the check, the check amount (only once), and a memo telling what the check is for. The program spells out the check amount on the check, enters the required information in the check register, and calculates the new balance. This eliminates any discrepancies between what is written on the check and what appears in the register. It also eliminates any errors caused by miscalculations.

Do You Really Want To Print Checks?

Printing checks sounds good until you realize how much work it takes: you have to get special checks that fit in your printer, and some printers require you to print a full page of checks (up to three) at a time. And if you go grocery shopping, you have to tear a check off the page. Many users continue writing checks by hand; they use the check-writing program to record the checks, balance their checkbooks, and manage their budgets.

When you write a check, the information is automatically entered in the register.

The program enters the check amount in the register and determines the new balance.

Enter the amount of the check.

The program spells out the amount.

Optional entries

Category keeps track of budget information.

Enter the name of the person to whom you're writing the check.

Balancing Your Checkbook in the '90s

Back in the old days, balancing a checkbook was an exercise in frustration. You calculated and recalculated till you started seeing double. With a check-writing program, you simply mark the checks that have cleared, mark the deposits on the bank statement, and enter any service charges. The program takes care of the rest, determining the total according to the register.

If the total on your register does not match the total on the bank statement, the program lets you know. If you have to correct an entry in the register, the program automatically recalculates the total, saving you the time of doing it over.

Mark checks that
have cleared.

Mark cleared bank
deposits.

*Your register can
virtually reconcile
itself.*

Cir	Date	Chk #	Payee	Amount		Cir	Date	Chk #	Payee	Amount
			Reconcile Bank Statement: Joe's Checking						Go To Options Help Iconbar	

Reconcile Bank Statement: Joe's Checking

Mark New Edit Delete Info... Help Close

		Payments and Checks					**Deposits**		
Cir	Date	Chk #	Payee	Amount	Cir	Date	Chk #	Payee	Amount
✔	2/20/96	0	IQuest	-15.00	✔	2/ 8/96		Audio Tran...	450.00
✔	2/28/96		Waddell & ...	-160.00	✔	2/13/96		Contract D...	960.00
✔	2/28/96		Waddell & ...	-200.00					
	11/15/95	1047	Escrow to RFS	-410.00					
✔	2/14/96	1073	Computer Li...	-16.94					
✔	2/ 8/96	1074	Direct Deliv...	-17.00					
✔	2/13/96	1075	Blockbuster...	-483.43					
✔	2/14/96	1076	Marsh Visa	-423.50					
✔	2/20/96	1077	Bayne Acc...	-215.00					
✔	2/26/96	1078	Jaynes Plu...	-80.46					
	3/ 8/96	1079	Direct Delivery	-18.00					

9 checks, debits	-1,611.33		2 deposits, credits	1,410.00

☐ Sort by Date

Cleared Balance:	532.04
Bank Ending Balance:	532.04
Difference:	0.00

Finished   Finish Later   Cancel

The program determines the balance.

Creating Cash and Credit Card Accounts

Although personal finance programs originally focused on checking accounts, they can
now help you manage all your accounts: savings, credit cards, cash, and so on. You
simply enter a beginning balance for each account, and then enter the transactions. This
allows you to keep track of all your money.

*You can create
accounts for all of
your transactions.*

Create New Account

Checking   Savings

Credit Card   Cash

Money Market   Investment

Asset   Liability

Help   Cancel

Taking Control of Your Financial Destiny

Before you can take control of your finances, you have to figure out where all your money is going. For instance, you can't decide if you are spending too much on car repairs unless you know exactly how much you are spending. Would you save money by buying a new car instead? Is there any way you can set aside money for investments? With accurate budget information, you can make financially sound decisions.

With most personal finance programs, you can have the program keep track of each expense for you. Many programs come with a set of home or business expense categories you can use when recording your transactions. If an expense is not listed, you can create your own expense category. Whenever you record a transaction (check, cash, credit card), you specify the category of the expense. At the end of the month, you tell the program to generate a budget report.

The program compares actual spending to your budgeted amounts.

The program shows if you are over budget or under budget for each item.

Fancy Finance Features

Check writing and budget reports are the bread and butter of any personal finance program. However, several programs offer additional features that you might find useful:

Recurring entries   If you have a monthly bill that is the same each month (a mortgage payment, rent, or budgeted utility payment), a recurring entry feature can save you some time and prevent errors. The program issues the same payment each month.

Bill planning   You enter the information for all the bills you have to pay for the month and then mark the bills you currently plan to pay. The program compares the total amount with your current checking account balance to determine whether you have enough money. You can then prioritize your bills.

Electronic bill paying   If your computer has a modem, you may be able to pay your bills without writing a check. You must subscribe to a service that connects you to your mortgage company, bank, utility company, and others that you have to pay. If you owe money to a person who is not connected to the system, the service will issue them a paper check.

Reminders   A Reminder feature automatically tells you when a bill is due. You specify the number of days in advance you want to be notified. When you start your computer, the program displays a message letting you know if any bills are due.

Income tax estimator   Compare how much you are actually paying in taxes to how much you should be paying to determine whether you are on track for the year.

Investment manager   Now that you have a budget and are saving loads of money, you may decide to invest that money. If you do, an Investment Manager feature can help you keep track of how your investments are doing.

Financial advice   Some personal finance programs, such as WealthStarter, offer financial advice to help you if you need life insurance or are contemplating how much you should be saving each month to send Junior to college.

Loan calculator   Most personal finance programs come with a loan calculator that you can use to determine loan payments and figure out just how much interest you will pay. You enter the principal of the loan (how much money you want to borrow), the annual interest rate, and the term, and the program figures out the payment, how much goes toward paying off the principal, and how much you pay in interest.

If you're shopping for a personal finance program, try Quicken for Windows. If you have a CD player, get the CD edition. It comes with interactive financial advice (including video clips), an online financial course called Finance 101, a mutual fund finder, investment advice, and much more.

Although other finance programs don't quite stack up to Quicken, Microsoft Money and Managing Your Money are both fairly good programs.

This refinance calculator can help you determine if it would pay for you to refinance.

Taxes? Taxes? We Don't Need No Stinking Taxes

Speaking of personal finances, you can also get programs for doing your taxes. In TurboTax, for example, you enter your name, the amount of money you made, the number of deductions you can claim, and so on. The program determines which forms you need to fill out and how much money the IRS owes you or how much money you owe the IRS. And because all the forms are linked, you enter a piece of information only once; TurboTax copies the information to the appropriate forms. For example, you enter your name and social security number only once, and it is placed at the top of every form and schedule.

If you used a finance program, such as Quicken, during the year, you can import information (such as your salary, business deductions, and contributions) from your Quicken file. This saves you from having to retype the information.

Fill out your 1040 on-screen.

TurboTax leads you through the process with an on-screen interview.

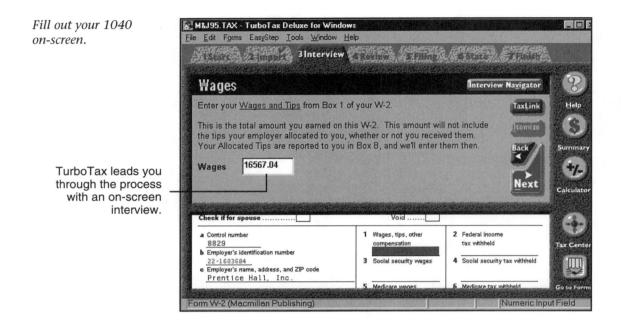

Tax Advice and Mock Audits

Unlike paper tax forms, your electronic form allows you to play with the numbers. In fact, tax programs offer suggestions on how you can save money. For example, the program might suggest tax deductions you haven't thought of, or it might find that you are eligible for earned income credit. Whenever you're done filling out the form, simply enter the command telling the program to analyze it and suggest additional tax savings.

If you're afraid that your tax return will be audited for some reason, have the program do a mock audit for you. The mock audit checks for obvious omissions (such as social security numbers for children), and it determines if there are any numbers on your return that might raise a red flag. For example, the IRS might question that $10,000 sack of clothes you donated to Good Will last year.

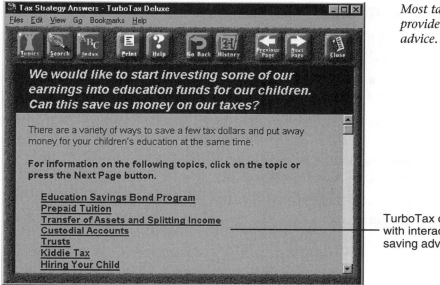

Most tax programs provide useful advice.

TurboTax comes with interactive tax saving advice.

Filing Electronically for an Early Refund

If your computer has a modem, you might be able to file your return electronically, and receive your refund in less than two weeks! You usually have to pay a fee to file electronically, because you can't just send your tax return to the IRS. No, that would be too easy. Instead, you have to send the return to a company that sends it to the IRS. You also have to mail a paper copy of the return (signed and dated, of course) to the same company, so it can keep the complete return on file.

If all this sounds appealing to you, file the return electronically. Otherwise, just print it out on paper, sign it, and mail it to your local IRS office (before April 15).

Popular Tax Programs

The most popular (and widely considered the best) tax program is TurboTax. It is easy to use and offers the help you need to find the deductions you're entitled to. You might spend a little more for TurboTax than you would for other tax programs, but you'll more than make up the money in your refund.

Other good tax programs include Kiplinger's TaxCut (running a close second to TurboTax), Simply Tax (which seems to get better every year), and Personal Tax Edge.

The Least You Need To Know

Whether you're a financial wizard or a blue-collar worker just trying to stay solvent, you can benefit from check-writing and tax programs. Just keep the following points in mind:

➤ There are two basic types of money-management programs: personal finance programs and tax programs.

➤ Personal finance programs keep track of income and expenses and help you budget your money as an individual.

➤ Many personal finance programs come with financial tools, including a loan calculator and an investment manager.

➤ Tax programs can help you fill out your 1040 form, provide tax-saving advice, and even perform a mock audit.

Chapter 17

Give Me the Works: Integrated Software and Suites

By the End of This Chapter, You'll Be Able To:

➤ Tell the difference between a Swiss army knife and an integrated program

➤ Use two types of programs together to work more efficiently

➤ Decide whether an integrated program is right for you

➤ Name the three most popular integrated software packages

Integrated software is the Swiss army knife of software packages. In a single integrated package, you usually get a word processing program, a spreadsheet and/or database program, a communications program (for your modem), and a graphics program—often for one low introductory price. In this chapter, you learn how to determine if such a package is right for you.

An integrated package offers several programs.

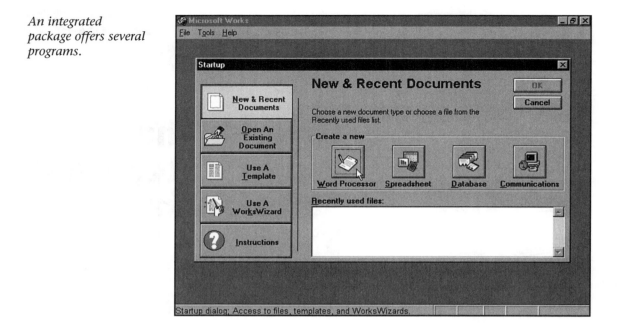

Works Versus Suites and Offices

By the Way...

The names of integrated programs usually end with the word *Works*, *Suite*, or *Office*: Microsoft Works, Microsoft Office, Lotus SmartSuite, Corel PerfectOffice, and PFS: WindowWorks.

Software manufacturers offer two types of integrated packages. The first type, whose name typically ends in "Works," provides a collection of less advanced programs that you can use together to create simple letters, spreadsheets, databases, graphics, and other documents. These programs are very inexpensive (usually under $100), but the applications in the package do not offer advanced features. For example, Microsoft Works contains a less advanced version of the Microsoft Word word processing application.

Suites and Offices, on the other hand, consist of collections (bundles) of advanced, stand-alone applications. For example, PerfectOffice Professional contains the full version of WordPerfect (word processing), Quattro Pro (spreadsheet), Paradox (database), Presentations (business presentation), and GroupWise (personal information manager and electronic mail). You pay anywhere from $400 to $600 for an Office or Suite, but that's about one third the price if you purchase all the applications individually.

Why Go Integrated?

Integrated programs have three basic advantages. First, they are *easy to learn*. All programs in the group have a consistent look and feel, making it easy to learn each program and to shift between them. Once you learn to print a file in one program, you know how to print a file in all the other programs.

Second, they work together. The file formats used in all of the programs are *compatible*, so you can cut and paste data from one file into another. That's not to say that ALL freestanding programs have compatibility problems. Many free-standing programs (especially Windows programs) are compatible with others to some degree, but it's a hit-and-miss proposition; you don't know that two programs work together until you try to use them together. An integrated package gives you some peace of mind.

Finally (and perhaps most importantly), integrated programs are *cheap* (or should I say *inexpensive*?). You get several programs for the price of one or two.

Why Not Go Integrated?

Going integrated may not be the best solution for everyone. Integrated packages have a few disadvantages. First, in an integrated package, you may not get the advanced features you get in a high-end stand-alone program. For example, the word processor that's part of Microsoft Works does not have a tables feature, autoformatting, and many other features that are available in Microsoft Word (the full-featured word processor). However, if you purchase Microsoft Office, you do get the full version of Microsoft Word (but you pay more money).

Second, you may not need some of the programs that are included in the integrated package. If you don't need a database or spreadsheet program, why pay for it? If you don't need a spreadsheet program, but you do need an advanced word processing program for working on books or reports, your money is better spent on a more advanced word processing program. If you plan on using *at least two* applications in an Office or Suite, it's usually a pretty good deal.

Reaping the Benefits of Integrated Software

Because all the applications in an integrated software package work as a team, you can usually do more with them than you can with individual programs. The following sections describe some ways you can use two or more programs together to work smarter.

Pulling Addresses Right Out of Your Address Book

Check This Out...

Integrated Databases

Although most advanced word processing programs provide a way to create a simple database and to merge it with a document, it's usually easier to create a database using the database program in an integrated software suite.

Most integrated packages include a database and a word processing program. You can create a database to keep the names and addresses of all your relatives, clients, and business contacts.

Whenever you need to write a letter to someone whose name is in the database, you can enter codes in the letter that will pull the necessary pieces of information from the database. You then *merge* the database and letter to copy the specified information from the database into the letter. You can use this merge feature to create a single letter or to send letters to anyone listed in the database.

You can merge your address book with a letter to pull information from the address book into the letter.

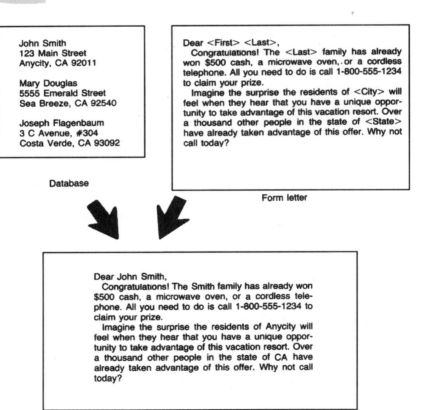

John Smith
123 Main Street
Anycity, CA 92011

Mary Douglas
5555 Emerald Street
Sea Breeze, CA 92540

Joseph Flagenbaum
3 C Avenue, #304
Costa Verde, CA 93092

Database

Dear <First> <Last>,
　　Congratulations! The <Last> family has already won $500 cash, a microwave oven, or a cordless telephone. All you need to do is call 1-800-555-1234 to claim your prize.
　　Imagine the surprise the residents of <City> will feel when they hear that you have a unique opportunity to take advantage of this vacation resort. Over a thousand other people in the state of <State> have already taken advantage of this offer. Why not call today?

Form letter

Dear John Smith,
　　Congratulations! The Smith family has already won $500 cash, a microwave oven, or a cordless telephone. All you need to do is call 1-800-555-1234 to claim your prize.
　　Imagine the surprise the residents of Anycity will feel when they hear that you have a unique opportunity to take advantage of this vacation resort. Over a thousand other people in the state of CA have already taken advantage of this offer. Why not call today?

Adding Spreadsheets to Your Letters and Reports

If you work with numbers, you can use the spreadsheet to perform all your number crunching for you. Then, when you need to use the numbers to make a point in a letter or report, you can plop the numbers from the spreadsheet right into your document. Because the spreadsheet works along with the word processing program, you don't have to worry about reformatting the spreadsheet or printing it on a separate page.

Sending Letters over the Phone Lines

If you have a modem, and the integrated package comes with a communications program, you can create a letter in the word processing program and send it by way of modem to your colleague or friend.

It Takes Two to Modem

To send a letter by modem, your colleague or friend must have a computer with a modem, and the modem must be turned on and waiting to receive your letter. Or you can send the letter by way of an electronic mail service or an online service. (Refer to Part 5.)

Have Your PC Place the Call

Some integrated programs have a dialing feature that can dial any phone number displayed on-screen. To use this feature, you must first connect a phone to your modem. (Look at Part 5, "Reaching Out with a Modem," for all the messy details about modem communications.)

Use your address book database to find the phone number you want to dial, then have the telecommunications program dial the number through your modem. When the phone on the other end starts ringing, pick up your phone.

Making Your Point with Graphs

If your integrated program contains both a word processing program and a graph or charting program, you can create a letter or report in the word processing program and insert a graph anywhere in the document. This is especially useful for sales reports, annual stockholder reports, and other business-related documents.

Saying It Artfully

If your integrated package comes with a collection of clip art and/or a drawing program that lets you create your own art, you can insert art into your documents to create your own customized letterhead, newsletters, and business cards. You can even add small pictures and eye-catching borders to your resumé to give it a personal touch.

Popular Integrated Packages and What They Offer

Not all integrated packages are created equal. Some are more like utility programs (programs that help you manage your computer system and files) that are strong on utilities and weak on everything else. Others contain powerful word processing and spreadsheet programs, but no database or graphics. Here's some information about a few of the more popular integrated programs:

Microsoft Works for Windows   This package includes a word processor with mail merge, a spreadsheet with business graphics, a database manager with report generator, and a telecommunications program. In addition, because this package works in Windows, you can use Paintbrush to create illustrations for your documents.

PFS: Windows Works   In addition to the usual programs (word processor, database, spreadsheet, and telecommunications), Windows Works offers a graph tool, a calculator, and file management tools that allow you to create directories, and copy, move, and delete files more easily than you can from the DOS prompt.

Lotus SmartSuite   SmartSuite is one of the best business application suites for networked computers. It offers Word Pro (perhaps the best word processor on the market), Lotus 1-2-3 (spreadsheet), Organizer (for keeping appointments and contact information), Approach (award-winning database application), and Freelance (business graphics).

Microsoft Office   The original, and most popular, integrated office suite for businesses, Microsoft Office offers Microsoft Word (word processing), Excel (spreadsheets), Access (database), PowerPoint (presentations), Schedule + (appointment keeper), and Binder (for organizing your documents).

PC Tools   PC Tools is best known as a utility program (for maintaining your computer). However, PC Tools contains an integrated program called Desktop Accessories. The integrated program contains a database, a word processor, a telecommunications program, a set of calculators, a calendar program, a clipboard (for transferring data between documents), and a macro editor. Although it's not the best integrated program listed here, it may be the best buy of the lot.

Sharing Data (Even If Your Programs Are Not Integrated)

Windows and most Windows applications support a data-sharing technology called OLE, which is pronounced "Oh-lay" and stands for *Object Linking and Embedding*. OLE not only allows you to copy data from one document and paste it into another, but it also allows you to link the data in two documents. With linked data, whenever you edit the data in the original document, the data is automatically updated in any other documents that contain a link to that data.

You can usually share data simply by copying it from the document you created in one application to the document you created in another. But just how is the data between the two documents related? If you change the data in one document, will it automatically be changed in the other one? The answer is, "That depends." It depends how the two applications are set up to share data, and it depends on how you insert the copied data. You can share data in any of the following three ways:

Link If you're using two applications that support OLE, you can share data by creating a *link*. With a link, the file into which you pasted the data does not actually contain the linked data; the link is stored in a separate file on the disk. Whenever you edit the linked file, any changes you make to it appear in all other documents that are linked to the file. For example, say you insert an Excel graph into a Word document as a link. Whenever you change the graph in Excel, those changes will appear in the Word document.

Embed With OLE, you can also *embed* data from one file into another file. With embedding, the pasted data becomes a part of the file into which you pasted it (the link between the files is broken). However, the pasted data retains a connection with the program that you used to create it. If you double-click on the embedded data, Windows automatically runs the associated program, and lets you edit the data.

Paste You can paste data in any number of ways (including pasting the data as an embedded or linked object). However, not all applications support OLE. For those applications that do not support OLE, you can still share data between programs by copying and pasting the data. However, the pasted data will have no connection with the application or document where the original data was stored.

To copy data from one document to another, you first select the data you want to copy from the *source document*. You then open the **Edit** menu and select **Copy**. This places the selected data on the Windows Clipboard. Next, switch to the document into which you want to place the copied data (this can be in the same application or another application). Move the insertion point where you want the data inserted, open the **Edit** menu, and select **Paste**.

...your changes automatically
appear in the linked file.

*With links, pasted
data is automatically
updated.*

W Microsoft Word - BullDog				
File Edit View Insert Format Tools Table Window Help				

Quarterly Sales Report

Product	Qtr 1	Qtr2	Qtr3	Qtr 4
T-Shirts	56,000	53,150	53,850	186,750
Sweatshirts	38,650	38,950	39,500	136,350
Shorts	37,100	37,305	38,225	131,425
Sweatpants				
Other				
TOTAL	$ 19			

X Microsoft Excel - BullDog					
File Edit View Insert Format Tools Data Window Help					

G21

	A	B	C	D	E	F
3						
4	Product	Qtr 1	Qtr2	Qtr3	Qtr 4	Total
5	T-Shirts	56,000	53,150	53,850	186,750	349,750
6	Sweatshirts	38,650	38,950	39,500	136,350	253,450
7	Shorts	37,100	37,305	38,225	131,425	244,055

Sheet1 / Sheet2 / Sheet3 / Sheet4

Ready   Sum=0

When you edit data in the original file...

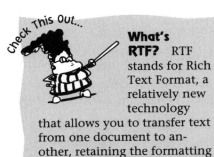

Check This Out...

**What's
RTF?** RTF
stands for Rich
Text Format, a
relatively new
technology
that allows you to transfer text
from one document to an-
other, retaining the formatting
of that text.

To create a link between two documents, use the **Edit,
Copy** command as previously explained. Switch to the
document into which you want to paste the data, and
move the insertion point where you want the data placed.
Now, open the **Edit** menu and select **Paste Special**. This
opens a dialog box, asking how you want the data pasted.
Choose the format in which you want to paste the data
(for example, as a picture or as RTF text), make sure **Paste
Link** is selected, and click **OK**.

To embed a selection from one file into another, first copy
the selection, as explained earlier. Then, switch to the
document into which you want the selection pasted, and move the insertion point to the
desired location. Open the **Edit** menu and select **Paste Special**. Make sure the **Paste**
option (not Paste Link) is selected. In the As list, click the option that has "Object" at the
end of it, and click **OK**.

To edit linked or embedded data, simply double-click it. This runs the application used to
enter the data; you can then edit it using the application. If you edit linked data, the data

is changed in its source file and in the file in which it is pasted. If you edit embedded data, the original data remains unchanged. Only the pasted data changes.

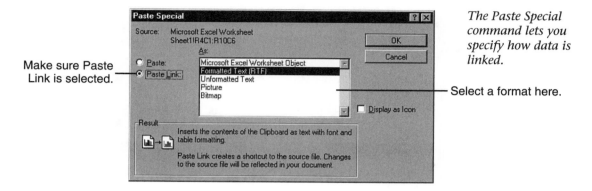

Make sure Paste Link is selected.

The Paste Special command lets you specify how data is linked.

Select a format here.

The Least You Need To Know

Once you know about the individual programs that make up an integrated software package, there's not much more you need to know. That's why this chapter is so short. However, if you are considering purchasing an integrated program, keep the following points in mind:

➤ Integrated software offers three major benefits: the individual programs are easy to learn, they work together, and they are inexpensive.

➤ Integrated software has two major drawbacks: the package may include programs you won't use, and the individual programs may not be as powerful as a comparable program you can buy separately.

➤ Integrated software allows you to use two or more programs together to work smarter, faster, and more efficiently.

➤ When shopping for an integrated package, compare the programs and tools offered by each package.

Chapter 18

Games and Educational Programs

By the End of This Chapter, You'll Be Able To:

➤ Blast spaceships out of the sky

➤ Play pinball, Tetris, and other arcade games on your computer

➤ Stick a set of encyclopedias in your CD-ROM drive

➤ Name a few programs that can help young children get a start on the basics

➤ Learn Spanish from your PC

A computer isn't all business. Slap a joystick on it, and it's a two-thousand dollar, 32-bit game system. For another 40 bucks, you have a personal chess master, who will not only play chess with you for 24 hours a day, but can also teach you some tricks and strategies. Slap a CD-ROM encyclopedia disk in the CD drive, and you have complete set of encyclopedias on your desktop, complete with sound, pictures, and video clips. In this chapter, you'll learn about some of the fun and educational software that can keep you entertained and intellectually fulfilled.

Having Fun with Computer Games

I've seen it happen. I've seen friends and relatives with good intentions buy computers to "do work at home" and "get organized." Two weeks later, they're asking me to help them hook up a joystick and find a copy of Mech Warrior II. The next time I see them, their eyes are glazed over, their thumbs are twitching, and they can't speak in complete sentences. In the following sections, you'll learn about the various types of games that can turn even the most well-disciplined worker into a computer game junkie.

Exploring with Adventure/Role-Playing Games

Although computer games have recently become more diverse, adventure games are still the staple. In adventure games, you usually take on the persona of some hero, maybe Mario or Indiana Jones. You are then sent on some mission, such as stopping the Nazis from obtaining a new secret weapon or saving a kingdom from destruction.

In Myst, one of the most popular games to hit the computer screen, your job is to help this creator, called Altrus, find out who's destroying all the cultural hot spots he has created. He suspects one of his sons. (My guess is that the old man was too busy creating things to give his sons any quality time.) At any rate, the graphics and sound are great, and the game is a challenge for even the sharpest mind. This game is mostly for older kids and adults.

Myst is one of the most popular computer games ever.

Shoot 'Em Up Arcade Games

If you're into mind-rot computer games, where you coast around toasting on-screen robots or blasting away alien ships, you might want to buy a joystick and shop for one of the many action games. Mech Warrior II is one of the most popular of this genre. In it, you assemble your own robot, choosing the basic structure, armor, and weapons you want to use. After a brief training session, you wander off blasting other robots, and trying not to get blasted yourself.

Another fine action game called Fury is specially designed to take advantage of the Windows 95 32-bit technology. (32-bit means the sound and graphics are awesome, and the controls are smoother.) In Fury, you're in the cockpit of a futuristic spacecraft, as you fight your way through eight different worlds, blasting everything in your path. I read somewhere that this program was used to train fighter pilots in the Cuban air force.

Getting Some Virtual Exercise with Sports Games

You may be familiar with sports games on Nintendo or Sega Genesis. Well, similar games are available for PCs. For example, in Front-Page Sports Football and NFL Challenge, you get to play head coach for your favorite football team. Pick your players, and call your own offensive and defensive plays. You can purchase programs for almost any sport, from individual sports, such as golf and tennis, to team sports, such as baseball and basketball. Although these games don't provide the 30 minutes of aerobic exercise you need, they may keep you from eating so many doughnuts.

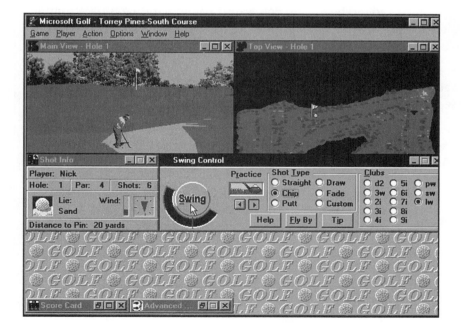

Golf is a little less frustrating on a computer.

Planning a City

Check This Out...

The Classics
In addition to the fancy new computer games, you can use your computer to play such classics as chess, solitaire, bridge, and rummy.

Ever wonder what it's like to plan a city? In SimCity, you get to do just that when the citizens of SimCity elect you mayor. You lay out roads and highways, attract professional ball clubs to your city, and build industrial plants and recreational areas. See the effects of your decisions on such problems as crime, pollution, and inflation. If the citizens of your fair city are happy with your decisions, you can sit back and watch them prosper. Make the wrong decisions, and you can watch them depart, leaving you with no city to govern.

Before You Buy a Game

Shopping for computer games may just be the most frustrating computer activity you will encounter. The box might show monsters and spaceships lunging at you from the sales rack. When you get the program home, your screen shows monsters that look like they're built out of Legos. The best way to shop for a game is to try it out first. If that's not an option, use the following checklist:

➤ **Video**   If you have a VGA or SVGA monitor, make sure the game supports that monitor. If you buy a game that offers only CGA support, the on-screen pictures will look blocky.

➤ **Sounds**   If you have a sound board and you want a game that creates nifty sounds, make sure the program includes sounds, and that it supports the type of sound board you have. (See Chapter 26 for more details about sound boards.)

➤ **Controls**   Some games do not allow you to use a joystick. If you're flying the latest in futuristic aircraft, you don't want to have to fumble around with a mouse and keyboard. (See Chapter 26 to learn about joysticks.)

➤ **CD-ROM**   Because compact discs can store gobs of data, game makers can add all sorts of neat sounds, animation, and video clips to games on CD-ROM to bring them to life. If you have a CD-ROM drive, look for CD versions of your favorite games.

Education in the '90s

Now that Bill Clinton has promised to have a computer in every classroom by the year 2000, we will soon be dumping knowledge and wisdom into young minds by the truckload. Well, maybe not. However, computers, coupled with the right software, can be a valuable teaching tool. Educational software typically presents information in a colorful, entertaining medium that is more engaging than most lectures, and provides students with immediate feedback.

The following sections briefly show some of the available educational and reference software. Because the market is flooded with educational software, there's really no way to cover this type of software thoroughly.

Ask Your Kids for Suggestions
Before you buy an educational program, ask your kids what they want. Take them to the store with you; they might get to try out the program before you buy it. Kids won't learn anything from a program that they won't play with.

Check This Out...

Before you go shopping for educational software, do some research. Check out computer magazines for reviews, ask teachers, and ask other parents. Most software stores are reluctant to accept returns on software products, so find out all you can about a program before you buy it.

Getting a Jump on Reading

One of the greatest pleasures of parenthood is watching your child start to read. However, it may be a very frustrating experience as well. You just don't know what kind of exercises your child needs, and even when you do know, you may not have the patience to work through those exercises as often as needed. To help, you can purchase any of many reading and reading readiness programs for your child.

Three of the more popular reading programs on the market are Reader Rabbit, Reader Rabbit 2, and Reader Rabbit 3, which contain several games to help develop early reading and writing skills, including phonics. In Reader Rabbit 2, for example, the child can play four games to help acquire and sharpen his reading skills. In one game (the Phonics Pond), the child is challenged to catch fish that match a specific phonics rule.

Disney's Animated StoryBook is also a good program for beginning to intermediate readers. Children can follow along as Grandmother Willow reads the story of Pocahontas.

The program also contains several games you can play with the various movie characters. The animation, graphics, and sounds are terrific.

Globetrotting with Carmen Sandiego

Chances are you have heard reports about the average high-school student not being able to point out Washington, D.C. on a United States map, and how the country is going to crumble because of it. If you're overly concerned that your kids may not be able to pinpoint Washington, D.C. or Baghdad, consider getting them a game called Where in the World Is Carmen Sandiego?

Carmen Sandiego makes learning Geography fun by making you solve a mystery. At the beginning of the game, Carmen or one of her fellow V.I.L.E. agents has committed a crime. It's up to you to solve the crime and find and arrest the criminal. Throughout the game, you receive clues from various people. For example, a bank teller may say, "I last saw the culprit driving away in a limousine flying a red and green flag." Or "The person you are looking for exchanged all the dollars for rubles." You must make the connection between the clue and where on the globe that clue refers to.

Mastering Math

Most beginning math programs on the market are designed to help kids learn counting, equalities and inequalities, and the four mathematical operations: addition, subtraction, multiplication, and division. What differentiates these programs, however, are the games they use to teach the basics.

One of my favorite beginning math programs is Math Blaster, which offers four games. One of the more interesting games makes you choose the correct answer for the problem that is shown at the top of the screen. You have to shoot the little rocket man into the right spaceship to score.

Dealing with the More Creative Side

Although there are computer programs for almost every academic subject a child might encounter in school, there are also programs for the more creative, less academic subjects, such as creative writing and art. One of the most popular programs to help kids channel their creative energies is Fine Artist. Fine Artist comes with several shapes and drawing tools that kids can use to create their own pictures and story boards. Kids can also use the program to make their own signs, greeting cards, and cartoon strips. The CD that comes with this book has a working version of Creative Writer, Fine Artist's sister program.

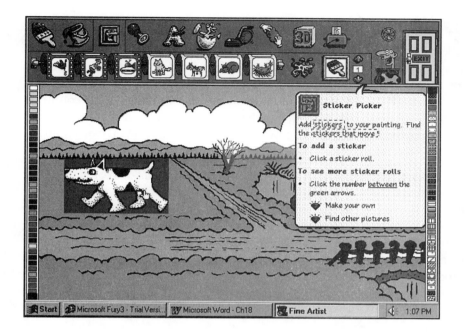

Fine Artist provides all the tools needed for a budding artist.

College and Continuing Education

Young children are not the only ones who can benefit from educational programs. College students and adults who want to improve their minds can benefit as well. Here's a sampling of what the software market has to offer the older student:

➤ Typing tutorials can help you tell the difference between your home keys and your house keys. A program called Typing Tutor even comes with an arcade style game that increases your typing speed as you play.

➤ Standardized test programs can help you prepare for the ACT, SAT, GRE, GMAT, LSAT and college boards. Once you have worked through the sample questions, you'll be more comfortable and confident when it comes to taking the real thing.

➤ Foreign language programs can help drill you on vocabulary, sentence structure, verb tenses, and the other basics you'll need to become fluent. For Spanish, try the Learning Company's Learn to Speak Spanish program.

➤ Science programs, such as Body Works, ChemistryWorks, and Orbits can help you through beginning level anatomy, chemistry, and even astronomy.

Encyclopedias on a Disc

How would you like to have a 26-volume set of encyclopedias on a single disc? Encyclopedias that can play snippets of Mozart's symphonies, show full-color pictures on your screen, and let you look up an article just by typing a portion of its name? How about a world atlas that provides a view of the globe along with information about each country? Or maybe you would like a book of mammals that lets you hear lions roar and monkeys chatter and lets you view the animals moving in their natural habitats? You can get all this and more with a CD-ROM player and the right discs.

For example, say you want to know a little bit about the life and music of Wolfgang Amadeus Mozart. In the old days, you would flip through the encyclopedia to Mozart, and then read the article and look at the pictures. As for his music, the encyclopedia was of no help. With a CD-ROM encyclopedia, you stick the disk in the drive, choose **Find**, type **Mozart**, and press **Enter**. A list of titles appears, one of which is for Mozart. Click **Mozart**, and you can find out all about the composer, and you can even listen to snippets of one of his compositions.

An Encyclopedia on CD-ROM gives you instant access to the information you need.

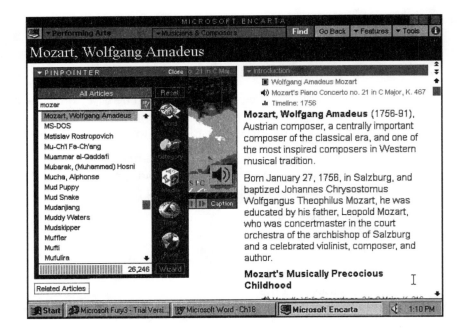

A Complete Reference Library

If you do any writing for school, for business, or for pleasure, you probably use several reference books to help you develop your work. For example, you might use a dictionary to look up spellings and a thesaurus to find synonyms. With Microsoft Bookshelf on CD-ROM, you get several reference books on a single disc. Bookshelf contains the following six reference books that you can use for home, office, or school:

➤ *The American Heritage Dictionary*   Contains definitions for over 66,000 words. To find a definition, you select American Heritage Dictionary from the **Definitions** menu, type the word you want to look up, and press **Enter**. No more flipping pages.

➤ *Roget's Electronic Thesaurus*   Need another word for *lazy*? Simply press **Alt+E**, type **lazy**, and press **Enter**. The thesaurus gives you a list of suggestions. You can then choose a word from the list to view a list of that word's synonyms.

➤ *1991 World Almanac and Book of Facts*   This electronic book contains a hodgepodge of information about the world, including census figures, U.S. economics figures, Employment figures, off-beat news stories, scientific achievements for 1990, and much more.

➤ *Barlett's Familiar Quotations*   If you like snappy quotes and insights from famous poets, politicians, and other visionaries, you'll love this book. In addition to offering the famous quotes from the paper version of the book, the CD-ROM version makes it easy to look up quotes, either by author or by using a word from the quote.

➤ *Concise Columbia Book of Quotations*   This book offers 6,000 quotes that are appropriate for speeches and presentations. The quotes are organized by subject, so you can look up quotes for subjects such as War, City Life, and even Living Together.

➤ *Concise Columbia Encyclopedia*   This encyclopedia offers 15,000 pages of articles about historical topics, including everything from Greek mythology to the Iran-Iraq war.

Don't Forget the Information Superhighway

Although this chapter focused on educational programs, keep in mind that online information services also provide learning resources. You can take college courses online, search for information in online encyclopedias, read newspaper and magazine articles, and converse with some very intelligent people from all over the world. Part 5 will provide more information about online services and the Internet.

The Least You Need To Know

Once you get a hold of a few nifty games and educational programs, you'll find yourself spending less and less time doing anything productive, and more time playing and browsing. While you're at it, keep the following points in mind:

➤ Computers owe their increasing popularity to the fact that they provide a user with a personal video arcade.

➤ Don't expect the game to look like the picture on the box.

➤ Before you shell out a pocketful of money for a game, make sure it can keep up with your system, and that your system can keep up with the game.

➤ In early learning, computers can help children practice critical tasks and express their creativity.

➤ Encyclopedias and other reference materials on compact discs make it easy to look up information.

➤ With a computer and a good collection of educational software, you can start your own magnet school. You can then play Mech Warrior while your education software turns your students into geniuses.

Part 4
Managing Disks, Directories, and Files

You're a slave to your computer. You install applications where it tells you to. You save your document files to the default drive and directory. And even when you stop using a program, you leave its files on your hard drive, afraid that any deletion will bring your system to a grinding halt.

In this section, you'll learn how to take control of your disks, directories, and files. You'll learn how to format floppy disks, create your own directories (called "folders" in Windows 95), rearrange files, and even remove some of the vagrant files that are cluttering your hard disk. And you'll learn how to do all this in DOS, Windows 3.1, and Windows 95.

Formatting and Copying Floppy Disks

In addition to acting as second-rate Frisbees and first-rate drink coasters, floppy disks store files and enable you to transfer files from one computer to another. Before you can use them in this capacity, however, you need to know how to format the disks (prepare them to store data) and copy disks.

Making a Floppy Disk Useful

You get a brand new box of disks. Can you use them to store information? Maybe. If the disks came *preformatted*, you can use them right out of the box. If they are not formatted, you'll have to format them, with the help of DOS or Windows.

Formatting divides a disk into small storage areas and creates a *file allocation table* (FAT) on the disk. Whenever you save a file to disk, the parts of the file are saved in one or more of these storage areas. The FAT functions as a classroom seating chart, telling your computer the location of information in all of its storage areas.

Format Once

You normally format a disk only once: when it is brand new. If you format a disk that contains data, that data is erased during the formatting process. Before you format a disk, make sure the disk is blank or that it contains data you will never again need.

Before You Begin

Before you start formatting disks, ask yourself a couple questions:

➤ **What kind of floppy disk drives do I have?** What capacity is each disk drive? Is it high-density (1.2MB or 1.44MB) or double-density (360K or 720K)? The documentation that came with your computer will tell you whether you have high- or double-density drives. If you have DOS 6.0 or later, enter **msd** at the DOS prompt; this runs the Microsoft Diagnostics program, which tells you the floppy disk drive types you have.

Low-density Is Obsolete
Low-density drives are rare. If you have a new computer, you can safely assume that you have high-density drives. However, low- or double-density *disks* are still common.

➤ **What kind of floppy disks do I want to format?** Do you have high-density or double-density disks? Check the disks or the box in which the disks came.

Why does this matter? There are two reasons. First, you can't format a high-density disk in a double-density disk drive. For example, you cannot format a 1.2MB disk in a 360K drive. Second, you *can* format a double-density disk in a high-density drive if you tell your computer specifically to do that. For example, you can format a 360K disk in a 1.2MB disk drive, if you know what you're doing.

Formatting Diskettes in Windows 95

In Windows 95, you can format disks using either My Computer or Windows Explorer. I prefer using My Computer, because it's lying there on my desktop. Here's what you do:

1. Insert a blank disk in drive A or B, and close the drive door, if necessary.

2. Double-click the **My Computer** icon. A window appears, displaying icons for all the drives on your computer.

3. Click the icon for the drive you're using to format the disk: A or B. (DO NOT double-click the drive icon; Windows 95 cannot format a disk whose contents are displayed.)

4. Open the **File** menu and select **Format**. The Format dialog box appears, as shown here.

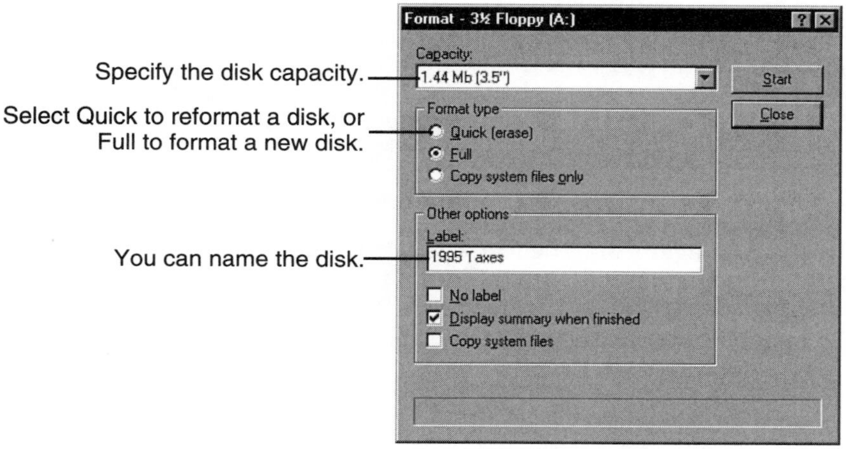

Specify the disk capacity. ─────

Select Quick to reformat a disk, or
Full to format a new disk.

You can name the disk. ─────

*Enter your format-
ting preferences.*

5. Open the **Capacity** drop-down list, and select the capacity of the disk. For example, for a high-capacity 3 ¹/₂" disk, you would select **1.44MB (3 ¹/₂")**.

6. If you are formatting an unformatted disk, click **Full** under Format type. If you are reformatting a formatted disk (to refresh it), click **Quick (erase)**.

7. (Optional) Click inside the **Label** text box, and type a label for the disk (up to 11 characters). If you add a disk label, the label will appear next to the drive's icon in Explorer and in My Computer.

8. (Optional) Click any of the following options to turn them on:

   No label tells Explorer not to add a label to this disk.

   Display summary when finished displays a dialog box at the end of the format operation indicating how much storage space is available on the disk and whether the disk has any defects.

   Copy system files makes the floppy disk bootable. That is, you can stick it in drive A and start your computer with it.

229

Quick Formatting To quickly format an unformatted disk in Windows 95, simply insert the disk, and then double-click its icon. Windows displays a series of dialog boxes to lead you through the process.

9. Click the **Start** button. My Computer displays a dialog box, showing the format progress. If you turned on **Display summary when finished**, a dialog box appears when the formatting is complete.

10. Wait until the formatting is complete, then click the **Close** button. You're returned to the Format dialog box, where you can format another floppy disk.

11. Click the **Close** button.

Formatting Diskettes in Windows 3.1

Formatting disks in Windows 3.1 is almost as easy as doing it in Windows 95. Here's what you do:

1. Start Windows and double-click the **Main** group icon.

2. Double-click the **File Manager** icon. The File Manager window appears.

3. Insert a blank disk in drive A or B, and close the drive door, if necessary.

4. Open the **Disk** menu and select **Format Disk**. The Format Disk dialog box appears.

The Format Disk dialog box.

Specify the letter of the drive.

Specify the disk capacity.

230

5. Click the arrow to the right of the **Disk In** option, and select the drive that contains the blank disk.

6. Click the arrow to the right of the **Capacity** option, and select the capacity of the disk.

7. Click **OK**. The Confirm Format Disk dialog box appears, warning you that formatting will erase any data on the disk and asking if you want to proceed.

8. Click **Yes**. File Manager formats the disk. When done, File Manager displays a message asking if you want to format another disk.

9. Click **No** to quit or **Yes** to format another disk.

Get Your Capacities Straight Disk capacity, not drive capacity. If you are formatting a double-density disk (360K or 720K) in a high-density drive (1.2M or 1.44M), make sure you select the capacity of the *disk*, not the drive.

Using the DOS FORMAT Command

If you picked up your computer at a garage sale, and you don't have either version of Windows yet, you can still format disks with DOS. Insert the new, blank disk you want to format in the floppy drive, and then perform one of the following steps:

➤ If the disk and drive capacities match, type **format a:** (if the disk is in drive A) or **format b:** (if the disk is in drive B), and press **Enter**. Follow the instructions that appear on the screen.

➤ If you're formatting a double-density disk in a high-density drive, use the /F switch to specify the disk capacity. For example, to format a 360K disk in a 1.2MB drive, type **format a: /f:360** and press **Enter**. To format a 720K disk in a 1.44MB drive, type **format b: /f:720** and press **Enter**.

Always Specify a Drive Letter Format plus drive letter. Always follow the FORMAT command with the letter of the drive you want to use. With some versions of DOS, if you enter the FORMAT command without specifying a drive letter, DOS may attempt to format drive C, your computer's hard drive. This could destroy your hard drive data.

Reusing Disks without Losing Data

Once you've formatted a floppy disk, you usually don't have to format it again. If you want to reuse the disk, make sure you no longer need the files it contains, and then delete those files, as explained in Chapter 21, "Copying, Moving, and Deleting Files."

231

If you start having problems with a disk, you might be able to fix it by reformatting the disk. Perform the same steps given earlier to format the disk in Windows or DOS. Keep in mind that formatting destroys any data on the disk, so if the disk contains files you need, copy those files to another floppy disk or your hard disk before reformatting.

Disk Errors

Several factors might cause disk errors. The read/write head inside the disk drive might go out of alignment over years of use, storage areas on the disk might start to go bad, or the data on the disk may have become corrupted by dirt or some magnetic field. If you get disk errors with several floppy disks, have the disk drive repaired or replaced. If you're having trouble with a single disk and reformatting doesn't seem to help, trash the disk.

Copying Disks for Friends and Colleagues

Although illegal, the main reason people copy floppy disks is to pirate software. For ten bucks, you can make Christmas presents for the entire family! I'm not going to lecture you on the evils of this practice. You know it's wrong, and if you thought there was any way you might get caught, you'd probably stop. However, I will say that the only reason you *should* copy floppy disks is so you can put the original program disks in a safe place and use the copies for installing and using the program. Having done my duty for the software industry, let us proceed.

Get Some Blank Disks

To copy disks, first obtain a set of blank disks that are the same *size* and *density* as the program disks you want to copy. You cannot copy low-density disks to high-density disks or vice versa. And you can't copy a $5^1/_4$-inch disk to a $3^1/_2$-inch disk either. Don't worry about formatting the disks; your computer can format the disks during the copy operation. However, the copying will go faster if the disks are formatted.

While you're at it, write-protect the *original* disks (the ones you want to copy, not the blank disks). This prevents you from accidentally copying a blank disk over an original disk and ruining it.

Copying Disks in Windows 95

If you're using Windows 95, you can copy disks using either My Computer or Windows Explorer. In My Computer, take the following steps:

1. Insert the original disk you want to copy into one of the floppy disk drives.

2. Double-click **My Computer**.

3. Click the icon for the drive that contains the disk.

4. Open the **File** menu and select **Copy Disk**. A dialog box appears, asking which drive you want to copy from and which drive you want to copy to.

If you have only one floppy disk drive, you must use the same drive for the source and destination disks.

Windows 95 asks which drives you want to use.

5. Click the same drive letter in the **Copy from** and **Copy to** lists.

6. Click the **Start** button.

7. Wait until a message appears telling you to insert the destination disk.

8. Remove the original disk and insert the destination disk.

9. Click **OK**, and then wait until the copying is complete.

> **Dual Drive Copy** If you have two floppy disk drives of the same size and capacity, insert the original disk in drive A and the blank disk in drive B. In the **Copy from** list, click drive A, and in the **Copy to** list, click drive B.

Copying Disks in Windows 3.1

To copy disks in Windows 3.1, use File Manager. The procedure you follow is about the same as the Windows 95 disk copy procedure, although it's equally uninteresting. Here's what you do:

1. Open the **Main** program group window, and double-click the **File Manager** icon.

2. Insert the original disk in drive A or B, and close the drive door if there is one.

3. Open the **Disk** menu and select **Copy Disk**. If you have two floppy drives, the Copy Disk dialog box appears, asking you to specify the source drive and destination. If you have only one floppy drive, skip to step 7.

233

4. From the **Source In** list box, select the letter of the drive that contains the original disk.

5. Select the same drive from the **Destination In** list box. (Don't worry, File Manager will tell you to switch disks at the appropriate time.)

6. Select **OK**. The Confirm Copy Disk dialog box appears.

Windows asks you to confirm the disk copy operation.

Click Yes.

7. Select **Yes** to continue.

8. When you are instructed to insert the Source diskette, choose **OK** since you already did this in step 2. The Copying Disk box appears, and the copy process begins.

9. When you are instructed to insert the destination disk, remove the original disk from the drive and insert the blank disk. Then choose **OK** to continue. The Copying Disk box disappears when the process is complete.

Copying Disks with DOS

Once you have the blank disks, making copies is easy (but not very interesting). Here's what you do:

1. Type **diskcopy a: a:** (or **diskcopy b: b:**) and press **Enter**.

2. Insert the original program disk into the drive you specified (a: or b:), and close the drive door if there is one.

3. Press any key. DOS reads the information from the disk and stores it in memory.

4. When DOS prompts you, insert one of the blank disks in the specified drive and press any key. DOS writes the information stored in memory onto the blank disk.

5. Follow the on-screen messages, swapping disks into and out of the disk drive as instructed, until you've created a copy of each program disk.

Copying Programs from Your Hard Drive

New computers always come with a bunch of software on the hard disk. The manufacturer may also include a CD or diskettes containing the same software, just in case anything happens to the program on your hard disk...or, he might not.

Can you copy a program from the hard drive to a set of floppy disks? Usually not. When you install most Windows programs, the installation utility typically places files in the Windows folder, the Windows/System folder, and any other folders you'd never think of looking in. Unless you're a super sleuth, you'll never find all the files that make up a program. Another problem is that most programs can't fit on a single floppy disk.

Some small DOS programs install all their program files in a separate directory on your hard disk. To copy a program such as this to a floppy disk, simply use My Computer or File Manager to copy the files, as explained in Chapter 21, "Copying, Moving, and Deleting Files."

The Least You Need To Know

Few people use floppy disks anymore. They buy everything on CD-ROM and store all their data on the hard disk. When you can't avoid working with a floppy disk, keep the following important points in mind:

➤ You can't use a new floppy disk until you've formatted it.

➤ Formatting destroys any data on the disk, so avoid reformatting disks.

➤ To format or copy disks in Windows 95, run **My Computer**, open the **File** menu, and select the **Format** or **Copy Disk** command. Follow the on-screen instructions.

➤ To format a disk with DOS, insert the disk and enter **format a:** or **format b:**.

➤ To format or copy disks in Windows 3.1, run **File Manager** and find the appropriate command on the **Disk** menu.

➤ Copies of your favorite software make affordable Christmas presents, but they're illegal.

Chapter 20

Making and Deleting Directories (or Folders)

By the End of This Chapter, You'll Be Able To:

➤ List the similarities between a landfill and a hard disk

➤ Jump from directory to directory in Windows or DOS

➤ Make your own directories for storing files

➤ Wipe out entire directories with a single command

➤ Name a directory after your favorite actor

Right now, you might be thinking of your hard disk as a data landfill. Each time you install an application, you can almost hear the dump truck beeping as it backs up to your disk, your hard disk grinding under the added burden. You start to wonder where future generations are going to dump their files.

Without directories, this image might be accurate. But directories help organize the files into logical groups, making them much easier to find and manage...assuming you know what you're doing.

Climbing the Directory Tree

Check This Out...

What's a Path? A path is a map to the desired drive and directory. For example, in the figure, the path to the MEGHAN directory is C:\HOME\MEGHAN. Backslashes (\) are used to separate the directory names.

Before you lay your fingers on any directories, you should understand the basic structure of a directory tree. Shake that landfill analogy out of your mind, and start thinking of your disk as a big, sterile filing cabinet, stuffed with manila folders. Each folder represents a directory that stores files and/or additional directories.

The structure of a typical hard disk is shown here. The monkey at the top of the tree, **c:**, is the *root directory*; other directories branch off from the root. In the figure, the HOME directory branches off from the root directory (C:\) and includes four *subdirectories*: MEGHAN, RYAN, MEDICAL, and TAXSTUFF. Each of these subdirectories contains files. (And don't ask me why the root is at the *top* of the tree; that's just the way it is.)

A typical directory tree.

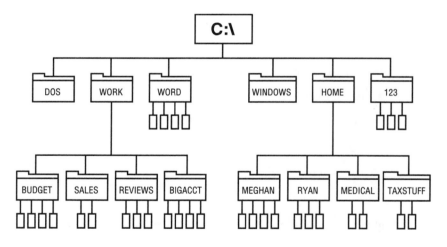

Do-It-Yourself Directories

You rarely have to create your own directories. When you install an application, it usually makes the directories it needs or uses existing directories. However, you will need to make directories for your own data files, so they don't get mixed up with all your program files.

When creating directories, try to follow one rule: *keep the directory structure shallow.* If you bury a file eight subdirectories deep, you're going to have to do a lot of digging to get it out. On my drive, I have one directory for everything everyone in the family creates. It's called DATA. Under it, I have a subdirectory for each book I write, a subdirectory for my personal files, a subdirectory for tax records, and a subdirectory for the files that my kids and wife create. Most of the files are buried only two levels deep.

Directory Name Rules and Regulations

In Windows 3.1 and DOS, you can't use just any name for a directory. A directory name can consist of up to eight characters with a three-character extension (just like a file name). You can use any characters except the following:

" . / \ [ ] : * < > | + ; , ?

And don't use the extension—it'll just complicate things later.

Windows 95 is much more flexible with its naming conventions. Directory names can be up to 255 characters (although I can't imagine why you would want a directory name that long). You can't use any of the following characters:

\ / : * ? " < > |

> **Folders and Directories**
> Windows 95 calls directories *folders.* Same thing, different name.

Making Folders in Windows 95

In Windows 95, you can create folders all over the place: in My Computer, Windows Explorer, or even on the Windows desktop. Give it a shot; try creating a new folder on drive C. You can always delete the folder later, if you don't need it. Take the following steps:

1. Double-click the **My Computer** icon.

2. Double-click the icon for drive C. A window opens showing all the folders currently on drive C.

3. Right-click on a blank area inside the window to display a shortcut menu.

4. Rest the mouse pointer on **New**, and then click **Folder**. Windows creates a folder on drive C called **New Folder**.

239

In Windows 95, a new folder is a right-click away.

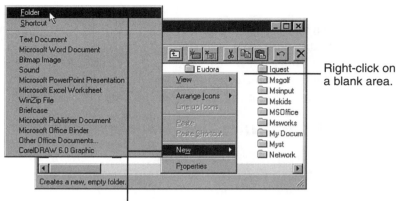

Right-click on a blank area.

Point to New, and click on Folder.

Desktop Folders If the Windows desktop becomes too crowded with shortcuts and other icons, you can create folders to help organize the desktop. Right-click on a blank area of the desktop, point to **New** and click **Folder**.

5. Type a name for the folder 255 characters or fewer. As you start typing, the New Folder name is deleted and is replaced by what you type.

6. Press **Enter**.

You can also create folders inside folders (subfolders). To do that, first double-click on the folder in which you want the new folder placed. This displays the contents of the folder. Then follow the same steps given above to create a new folder.

Grafting Directories in Windows 3.1

Although Windows 3.1 doesn't give you the same flexibility with folders that you get in Windows 95, the procedure for creating folders is equally simple. Here's what you do:

1. Run Windows, and open the **Main** group window.

2. Double-click the **File Manager** icon. The File Manager window appears.

3. Hold down the **Shift** key while clicking the drive letter icon for the drive on which you want the new directory. This displays all the directories and subdirectories on the selected drive.

4. Click the directory under which you want the new directory, or click the drive letter at the top of the directory tree (to make the directory under the root directory).

240

5. Pull down the **File** menu and select **Create Directory**. The Create Directory dialog box appears.

6. Type the name of the new directory in the dialog box, and then click **OK** or press **Enter**.

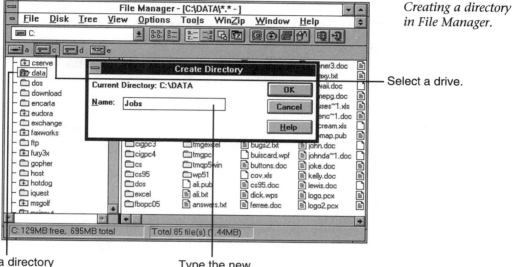

Creating a directory in File Manager.

— Select a drive.

Select a directory under which you want the new subdirectory.

Type the new directory's name here.

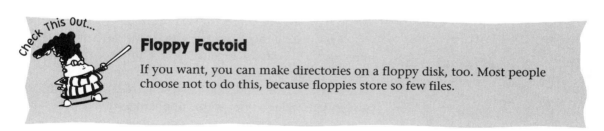

Floppy Factoid

If you want, you can make directories on a floppy disk, too. Most people choose not to do this, because floppies store so few files.

Making Directories with DOS MD

Making directories with DOS is like trying to get dressed in a dark closet (not that I've ever done that). DOS doesn't display a directory tree, so you pretty much have to know your existing directories' names in order to get the job done. Here, try it:

1. Change to the disk on which you want the new directory. For example, type **c:** and press **Enter**.

241

2. Change to the directory under which you want the new directory. For example, type **cd \dos** and press **Enter** to change to the DOS directory. To create a directory under the root (first) directory, type **cd ** and press **Enter**.

Display the Directory Tree To display a list of directories under the current directory, type **dir /a:d** and press **Enter**.

3. Type **md** *dirname* where *dirname* stands for the name of the new directory. For example, type **md mylife** and press **Enter**. DOS creates the new directory, but it won't show you it unless you ask.

4. To change to the new directory, type **cd** *dirname* (where *dirname* is the name of the new directory) and press **Enter**.

If you ever get really good at this, you can stop using the CD command. Just type something like **md c:\dos\mylife\taxes** and press **Enter**. This creates the subdirectory TAXES under the MYLIFE directory.

Nuking Directories

Directories are like federal spending programs; they're easy to make, but tough to get rid of. In DOS, for example, you first have to delete all the files and subdirectories before DOS lets you zap the directory. Once you've done that, you change to the directory that's above the one you want to delete, type **rd** *dirname*, and press **Enter**. (Remember to type the directory name in place of *dirname*.)

The Dangerous DELTREE Command If you have DOS 6.0 or later, you can delete directories that contain subdirectories or files. Change to the directory above the one you want to delete, type **deltree** *dirname*, and press **Enter**. You'll get a warning message; type **Y** to confirm or **N** to cancel.

If you try to delete a directory that contains files, DOS displays an error message saying that you can't delete the directory. This often happens if a directory contains hidden files (files whose names you can't display). In most cases, the files are hidden for a reason; these are usually system files, which you're not supposed to delete. However, if you know that you can safely delete the files, use Windows to display their names and delete them.

In Windows 95, it's almost too easy to delete a directory (er, folder). You simply drag the folder over the Recycle Bin icon, release the mouse button, and respond to a couple confirmation messages. Or you can just click the folder and press the **Del** key. Either way, the directory and its contents go to La La Land, and you can continue playing Doom.

Windows 3.1 makes it easy to delete directories, too, but because Windows 3.1 doesn't have a Recycle Bin for undeleting directories, you have to be more careful. Delete the wrong directory, and you'll find yourself in deep doo-doo. To delete a directory, run File Manager, click the directory you want to delete, and then press the **Del** key (or open the **File** menu and select **Delete**). You'll get a series of confirmation boxes; just follow the instructions and make your picks.

Renaming and Moving Directories or Folders (Windows Only)

DOS doesn't offer any easy ways to rename directories. You basically have to make a new directory, copy all the files from the old directory to the new one, and then delete the old directory and all its files. In Windows or Windows 95, renaming is a snap.

Don't Rename Program Directories Windows uses the names of program directories to find the program files it needs to run the programs. If you rename a program directory, Windows usually throws a fit and won't run the program for you.

➤ In Windows 95, click the icon for the folder you want to rename. Then, click the name of the folder and type the new name.

➤ In Windows 3.1, run File Manager, and click the directory you want to rename. Open the **File** menu and select **Rename**. Type a new name for the directory, and click **OK**.

Moving Directories or Folders (Windows Only)

In Windows 3.1 and Windows 95, you can quickly move directories or folders to reorganize your hard disk. In both Windows 95 and Windows 3.1, you can move a directory or folder simply by dragging it over the directory or folder icon where you want to move it. Before we go into the step-by-step instructions on how to move folders or directories, read the following list for some important hints:

➤ If you drag a directory to another disk drive, Windows assumes you want to copy the files to that drive. If you want to move the files, hold down the **Shift** key while dragging.

➤ If you drag a directory to another directory on the same disk drive, Windows assumes you want to move the directory into the destination directory. If you want to copy the files, hold down the Ctrl key while dragging.

➤ To move a directory to another disk drive, hold down the **Shift** key while dragging the directory icon over the icon for the drive. The directory is placed inside the currently active directory on that drive. (This is good for copying a group of files to a floppy disk.)

➤ You can move a directory into another (destination) directory. Drag the directory you want to move over the icon for the destination directory.

➤ In Windows 95, you can move a folder to the Windows desktop by dragging it from My Computer or Windows Explorer onto a blank area on the desktop.

This dragging thing sounds easy, till you try to do it. It's tough trying to get the two icons you need to work with on the same screen at the same time.

In Windows 3.1, the best way to accomplish this feat is to display two directory tree windows in File Manager. Open the **Window** menu, and select **New Window**. Then, open the **Window** menu and select **Tile**. With two windows on the screen, you can easily display the two icons, and simply drag the directory you want to move over another drive or directory icon.

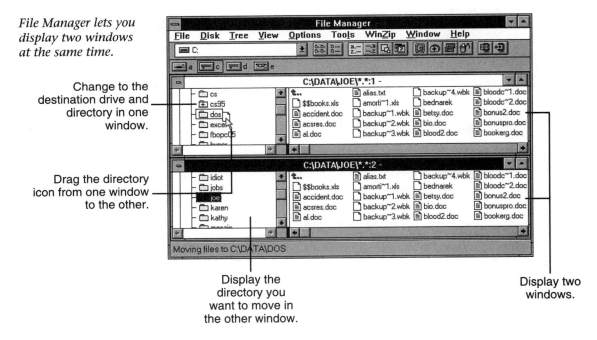

File Manager lets you display two windows at the same time.

Change to the destination drive and directory in one window.

Drag the directory icon from one window to the other.

Display the directory you want to move in the other window.

Display two windows.

In Windows 95, the process is a bit more complicated. The easiest way I have found to move a folder is to cut and paste it. Right-click the icon for the folder you want to move, and click the **Cut** command. Now, change to the drive or folder in which you want the cut folder placed. Right-click the drive or folder icon (or in its contents window), and click the **Paste** command. Here are a couple other convoluted ways to move folders in Windows 95:

➤ Run Windows Explorer (**Start, Programs, Windows Explorer**). In the **Contents** list (on the right), display the icon for the folder you want to move. In the **All Folders** list (on the left), make sure you can see the icon for the destination drive or folder. Drag the icon for the folder you want to move over the icon for the destination drive or folder, and release the mouse button.

➤ Use My Computer to display two windows: one that contains the icon for the folder you want to move, and another that displays the contents of destination drive or folder. Drag the folder you want to move over a blank area inside the destination window, and release the mouse button.

In Windows Explorer, it's tough to display the source and destination.

Drag the folder over the destination icon.

Make sure you can see the icon for the destination drive or folder.

Display the folder icon you want to move.

The Least You Need To Know

Consider this chapter basic training for Chapter 27, where you'll use your directory and file management skills to optimize your hard disk. Until then, here are a few of the more important points:

➤ Your disk *is* a big data landfill; it's just a little better organized.

➤ Hard disks and CDs typically group files in directories or folders to make them more manageable.

➤ Directory (or folder) names are the same as file names, except you don't usually add extensions.

➤ You can delete directories or folders in Windows by clicking the directory or folder and pressing the **Del** key.

Copying, Moving, and Deleting Files

By the End of This Chapter, You'll Be Able To:

➤ Pick a peck of files in DOS or Windows

➤ Duplicate files on hard disks or floppies

➤ Move files from one disk or folder to another

➤ Find misplaced files and other interesting relics

To take control of your computer, you have to deal with files. To share a file, you might have to copy it to a floppy disk. To reorganize files, you have to move them to different drives or directories. And to do any of these file management tasks, you have to find the files in the first place. If all this sounds fun to you, you probably enjoy whacking your funny bone on your armrest, too. However, these chores are essential if you want to share files and rid your disks of useless trash.

Pick a File, Any File

If you're copying, deleting, or moving a single file, picking a file is about as easy as picking a losing lottery number. In DOS, you just enter the desired command followed by the file's name. In Windows, you click on the file. If you want to work with a group of files, however, things start to get a little tricky. In the following sections, you'll learn how to handle the complexities.

Poke and Pick in Windows

Windows makes it easy to select one file; you click on it (in File Manager, Windows Explorer, or My Computer). You would think if you clicked on another file, you'd select that one, too, but it doesn't work that way. Picking another file unpicks the first one. This can be maddening to anyone who doesn't know the tricks for selecting groups of files:

What's Contiguous Mean?
Contiguous is a fancy name for "neighboring." Files that are next to each other in a list are said to be *contiguous*. Neighboring storage areas (sectors) on a disk are also said to be contiguous. Not to be confused with "contagious."

➤ To select neighboring (contiguous) files, click on the first file, and then hold down the **Shift** key while clicking the last file in the group.

➤ To select non-neighboring files, hold down the **Ctrl** key while clicking the name of each file.

➤ To deselect a file, hold down the **Ctrl** key while clicking its name.

➤ In Windows 95, you can drag a box around the files you want to select. When you release the mouse button, all files in the box are highlighted.

Shift+click to select a group of neighboring files.

Ctrl+click to select nonneighboring files.

You can select neighboring or non-neighboring files.

![Exploring - Data window screenshot showing file selection]

13 object(s) selected   75.5KB

If you're selecting groups of files, it often helps to change the way the files are sorted or arranged. In both Windows 95 and Windows 3.1, you can open the **View** menu and choose to sort files by name, by type (using their file name extensions), by size, or by date. For example, you can sort files by type to list all the document files (which end in .DOC) together.

In Windows 95, you can also arrange the icons by opening the **View** menu and selecting one of the following options:

➤ **Large Icons** is good if you want to select only a few files.

➤ **Small Icons** displays tiny icons. Folders (directories) appear at the top of the window, and files at the bottom. In this display, you can drag a box around files down and to the right.

➤ **List** displays tiny icons (just like Small Icons view), but folders (directories) are listed on the left, and files are listed on the right.

Small Icons vs. List

In Small Icons view, if you click a file in one column, and then **Shift+Click** on a file in another column, you select a rectangular block of files, just as if you had dragged a box around them. In List view, files snake up and down a page like newspaper columns. If you click a file in one column and then **Shift+click** on a file in another column, you select all the files between the two files you selected.

Using DOS Names and Wild Cards

To select a single file in DOS, you follow a command with the name of the file you want the command to act on. To select multiple files, you use wild-card entries (see Chapter 8). Here are some examples, so you won't have to flip back to Chapter 8:

➤ ***.com** specifies all files whose names end in .COM. For example, this may include WINDOWS.COM, FORMAT.COM and EDIT.COM.

➤ **chpt??.doc** specifies all files that start with CHPT, have two or fewer additional characters, and end in .DOC. This may include CHPT01.DOC, CHPT14.DOC, and CHPT4.DOC.

➤ **g*.???** specifies all files that start with G and end in three characters or fewer. This may include GO.BAT, GERSHWIN.DOC, GAGGLE.BK, and GLOO.M.

Merely typing a wild-card entry at the DOS prompt won't do anything; you need a command to go with it. For example, you might enter **copy *.com a:** to tell DOS to copy all files that have the .COM extension to the disk in drive A. Later in this chapter, you'll learn more about combining wild-card entries with commands.

Using Wild Cards in Windows 3.1

If you love working with wild-card entries, File Manager provides that service as well. Change to the drive and directory that contains the files you want to select. Then, open the **File** menu and choose **Select Files**. Type your wild-card entry, click the **Select** button, and then click **Close**. Windows 95 does not allow you to select files using wild cards.

Cloning Files

Your computer moonlights as a high-speed copy machine. Does your friend or colleague need a file? Simply drag it from your disk to a floppy disk. Do you need to modify a file without changing the original? Just copy the file under another name or in a different directory. You can even copy entire drives or directories.

Dragging Files in Windows 95

In Windows 95, you can copy files in any number of ways, using My Computer, Windows Explorer, or both. The most popular way to copy files is to drag the files from one disk or folder (the source) to another (the destination). However, because it's somewhat difficult to display both the source and destination on the same screen at the same time, it's often easier to copy and paste the files:

1. Run **Windows Explorer** or **My Computer**, and select the files you want to copy.

2. Right-click one of the selected files to display a shortcut menu, and click **Copy**.

3. Change to the drive and folder in which you want to paste the copied files. This displays the contents of the selected drive or folder.

4. Right-click inside the window that displays the contents of the destination drive or folder, and click **Paste**. Windows copies the files to the destination.

If you don't like the copy and paste approach, there are plenty of other techniques for copying files:

➤ In **Windows Explorer**, select the files you want to copy in the **Contents** window, and display the icon for the destination drive or folder in the **All Folders** window. Hold down **Ctrl** while dragging one of the selected files over the icon for the destination drive or folder.

➤ In **My Computer**, display two windows: one for the files you want to copy, and one for the destination drive or folder. Hold down **Ctrl** while dragging one of the selected files into a blank area of the destination window.

➤ To copy files from your hard disk to a floppy, select the files you want to copy, and then right-click one of the selected files. Point to **Send To**, and click the drive to which you want to copy the files. (Make sure there's a disk in the drive.)

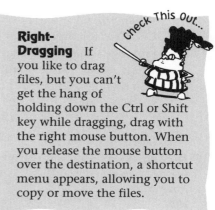

Right-Dragging If you like to drag files, but you can't get the hang of holding down the Ctrl or Shift key while dragging, drag with the right mouse button. When you release the mouse button over the destination, a shortcut menu appears, allowing you to copy or move the files.

You only have to hold down the **Ctrl** key when you're copying files from one folder to another on the *same* disk. If you don't hold down the Ctrl key, Windows moves the files. If you are dragging files to a different disk drive, Windows assumes you want to copy them.

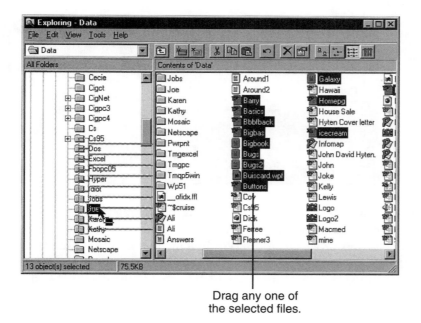

You can drag files to the destination drive or folder.

Drag any one of
the selected files.

Copying Files in Windows 3.1

To copy files in Windows 3.1, you run File Manager and then drag the files from one drive or directory to another. If you are copying the files to a different directory on the same disk, hold down the **Ctrl** key while dragging.

When you release the mouse button, File Manager displays a confirmation dialog box. Click **Yes** to confirm, and File Manager copies the selected files. If the destination contains a file that has the same name and extension as one of the files you are copying, you'll get a warning box that asks if you want to overwrite the existing file. Click **No** to skip this file and proceed copying the other files, or click **Yes** to overwrite the existing file with the copy.

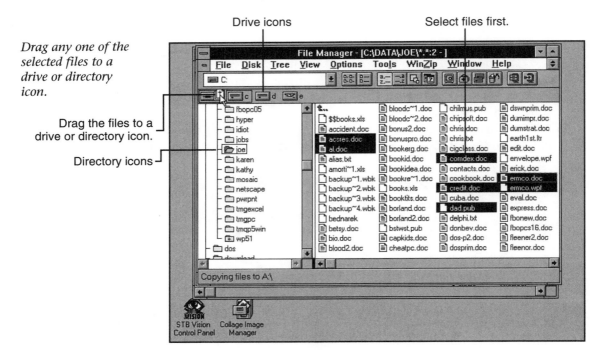

Drag any one of the selected files to a drive or directory icon.

Drive icons

Select files first.

Drag the files to a drive or directory icon.

Directory icons

Some people prefer to create two windows in File Manager and drag the files from one window to the other. To create a new window, double-click a drive icon; File Manager creates a new window for this drive. Open the **Window** menu and select **Tiled** to display both windows. In the source window, select the files you want to copy. In the destination window, change to the drive and directory into which you want the copies placed. Then, drag the files from the source to the destination window.

Copying Files at the DOS Prompt

To copy files with DOS, first change to the drive and directory that contains the files you want to copy. Then type

copy *file1.ext d:\directory*

where ***file1.ext*** is the name of the file you want to copy, and ***d:\directory*** is the drive and directory to which you want the file copied. (See the examples listed in Table 21.1.) Press **Enter**. DOS copies the file(s).

Table 21.1 Sample Copy Commands

Command	What It Does
copy *.doc a:	Copies all files that have the .DOC extension from the current directory to the disk in drive A.
copy chap09.doc b:	Copies only the file named CHAP09.DOC from the current directory to the disk in drive B.
copy *.doc c:\samples	Copies all files that have the .DOC extension from the current directory to a directory named C:\SAMPLES.
copy *.* c:\samples\books	Copies all files from the current directory to C:\SAMPLES\BOOKS.
copy chap09.* c:\samples	Copies all files named CHAP09 (CHAP09.DOC, CHAP09.BAK, etc.) from the current directory to C:\SAMPLES.

Copy Errors

If you try to copy a file to a drive and directory that contains a file of the same name, you'll get a message asking if you want to replace the file. Before answering Yes, make sure the file you are replacing is one you will never need. Otherwise, rename one of the files (as explained later in this chapter) before copying.

A quick way to copy a directory and its contents from one drive to another is to use the XCOPY command. For example, to copy all the files and subdirectories of the C:\DATA directory to drive A, you would type **xcopy c:\data a:** and press **Enter**.

Giving Your Files New Names and Locations

If you need to place a file in the witness relocation program, you can give it a new name and location:

➤ In Windows (3.1 or 95), you move files by dragging them (just as if you were copying them, but don't hold down the Ctrl key). If you want to move files from one disk to another, hold down the **Shift** key while dragging.

➤ To rename a file in Windows 95, click the file's icon, and then click the file's name (the name appears highlighted). Type a new name for the file, and press **Enter**.

➤ To rename a file in Windows 3.1, click the file's name, and then open the **File** menu and select **Rename**. Type the new name you want to give the file, and then click **OK**.

➤ You don't move files in DOS. To move a file, you have to copy it to the desired destination; then delete the original.

➤ To rename a file in DOS, you change to the drive and directory that contains the file, and then use the RENAME or REN command followed by the current file name and the new file name or location. For example, you might enter **ren myfile.doc yourfile.doc**.

Moving the Masses

In DOS, when you need to rename or move a bunch of files, use wild-card entries. For example, you can type

ren *.doc *.old

to change the extension on a group of files from .DOC to .OLD. You can use wild cards in Windows 3.1, too, but Windows 95 doesn't allow it.

Wiping Out Duplicates and Other Useless Files

I'm beginning to think that files procreate. I can't have created all those files that are overpopulating my hard drive; I just don't work that hard. If you get the same feeling about your disks, you might need to do a little housekeeping. Get your shovel, and meet me in Windows:

➤ In Windows (95 or 3.1) simply select the files you want to delete, and then press the **Delete** key (or open the **File** menu and select **Delete**). Answer the confirmation messages, and the files are gone.

➤ In Windows 95, you can drag one of the selected files over the Recycle Bin. Release the mouse button, answer a couple confirmation messages, and you're done.

➤ In Windows 95, you can also click the **Delete** button in the toolbar (the button with the **X** on it). If the toolbar isn't displayed, open the **View** menu and select **Toolbar**.

➤ Still another way to delete files in Windows 95 is to right-click a selected file, and click **Delete**.

➤ To delete files at the DOS prompt, change to the drive and directory that contains the file, and enter the **DEL** command followed by the name of the file you want to delete. For example, you might type **del myfile.doc** and press **Enter**.

Check This Out...

Undeleting Files

You might be able to recover accidentally deleted files. In Windows 95, open the Recycle Bin, right-click the file you want to undelete, and select **Restore**. In DOS, change to the drive and directory that contained the file, type **undelete**, and press **Enter**. In File Manager, open the **File** menu and select **Undelete**. If these commands are unavailable, you have an early version of DOS that does not offer undelete capabilities for Windows 3.1.

The Land of the Lost: Finding Files

If all you have is DOS, you'll have as much luck finding a lost file if you placed a picture of it on a milk carton. You change drives and directories and dig through directory lists trying to find a familiar name. Good luck.

Windows 95 offers the best file finder in the business. If you recently worked on the file, the first place to look is the **Documents** submenu (on the **Start** menu). This submenu lists the last 15 files you worked on. If you can't find the file there, try this:

1. Open the **Start** menu again, point to **Find**, and click **Files or Folders**. The Find dialog box appears, asking what you're looking for.

2. Open the **Look in** drop-down list, and click the drive or folder you want to search.

3. In the **Named** text box, type the file's name (or a portion of it). If you don't know the name, you can click the **Advanced** tab, and specify some unique text that might be contained in the file.

4. Click the **Find Now** button. Windows searches your hard drive and displays a list of files and folders that match the name you typed.

Windows 95 can help you track down lost files.

Type the file's name or a portion of it.

Find: All Files

File Edit View Options Help

Name & Location | Date Modified | Advanced

Named: Jersey

Look in: [C:]

☑ Include subfolders

Find Now

Stop

New Search

The Advanced tab lets you search the contents of a file.

Select the drive or folder you want to search.

Using an Application to Find Files

Most Windows applications keep track of the last four or five files you've worked on in that application. Open the **File** menu, and look at the bottom of the menu for the names of recently opened files.

The Windows 3.1 file finder isn't quite as hi-tech as the one in Windows 95, but it will get the job done. In File Manager, open the **File** menu and select **Search**. The Search dialog box appears, asking for the name of the file you want to find and the drive and directory where you want to search for it. Type the name of the misplaced file, or type a wild-card entry in the **Search For** text box; for example, you can type **read*.*** to find all the README files on the disk. Click **OK**.

Once Windows has found the files you want to work with, you can copy, delete, or move them directly from the window that lists the files.

The Least You Need To Know

Now that you can find, copy, move, rename, and delete files, you have all the tools you need to clean house:

➤ To select several files in Windows, click on the first file; hold down the **Ctrl** key while clicking on files to select more.

➤ To copy files in Windows, hold down the **Ctrl** key while dragging any one of the selected files to a drive or directory icon.

➤ To move files in Windows, hold down the **Shift** key while dragging.

➤ To find files in Windows 95, click the **Start** button, point to **Find**, and click **Files or Folders**.

➤ To find files in Windows 3.1, run File Manager, open the **File** menu, and select **Search**.

Part 5
Reaching Out with a Modem

How would you like to play a computer game against a friend in another town? Get the latest news, weather, and sports without taking your fingers off the keyboard? Connect to an online encyclopedia, complete with sounds and pictures? Order items from a computerized catalog? Send a letter and have it arrive at its destination in a matter of seconds? Or even transfer files from your computer to a colleague's computer anywhere in the world?

In this section, you'll learn how to do all this and more. You'll learn how to buy a modem that can keep up with traffic on the Internet (and how to install it). You'll get a taste of the big three online services. And you'll get a quick tour of the Internet. With this section, a modem, and the right software, you'll be well primed to master the information age.

Chapter 22

Buying, Installing, and Using a Modem

Okay, I admit it, the section opener was a tease. I wanted to tell you all the neat things you could do with a modem, so you would start thinking that you simply can't live without one. I conveniently left out all the complicated information about shopping for a modem, hooking it up, and figuring out what software you need. Now that I've sucked you in, I'll hit you with the hard stuff.

Shopping for a Modem

Before you start shopping for a modem, you need a brief lesson in modem-ese, the language of modem ads. Do you think I'm exaggerating? Then read the following ad I lifted from my favorite computer catalogue:

v.34 BOCA 28.8Kbps Modem External

If it's speed you need, nothing beats the BOCAMODEM 28.8Kbps. It meets Rockwell's new V.34 standard. You'll transmit data at 28,800bps up to 115,200bps with data compression and send and receive faxes at 14,400bps. You'll lower your phone bills and increase productivity with quicker connect times and super-fast delivery of large files. The Boca V.Fast modem is backward-compatible with lower speed V.32bis, V.32, and V.22bis modems. Includes a high-speed, buffered 16C550 UART on-board in the internal.

If you're in shock, try to calm down. You'll be able to translate this gobbledygook by the time you finish this section. Take it slow, and read on.

Inside or Out? Internal and External Modems

Modems come in two types: *internal* and *external*. An internal modem is a board that plugs into an expansion slot inside your computer. Yeah, you have to flip the hood on your system unit, and plug the thing in. It's not all that difficult to do, but if you've never done it, get a knowledgeable friend to walk you through it for the first time.

An external modem plugs into a serial port (a receptacle) on the back of your computer. To use an external modem, you must have an extra serial port. Look at the back of your system unit to see if it has an extra outlet called COM.

Which is better? Internal modems are less expensive, take up less desk space, and require only one connection (the phone line). If you have an open expansion slot inside your computer, get an internal modem. External modems have a couple advantages: they are easy to install, and most come with indicator lights that show you what the modem is doing (these can help you troubleshoot common problems).

16550 UART

You might see 16550 UART tacked on to a modem ad. Is that good? Well, Windows 3.1 has a hard time transferring modem signals in the background. 16550 UART helps Windows do this more efficiently. Most internal modems have their own 16550 UART support built in, so if you go with an internal modem, don't worry about it. However, if you're purchasing an external modem, make sure your serial port uses 16550 UART. (Check the documentation or enter **msd** at the DOS prompt and press **Enter**. Click the **COM Ports** button, and look under **UART Chip Used**.)

Go Hayes-Compatible

The Hayes modem, made by a company called Hayes Technologies, has set the standard in the modem market. Hayes modems use a set of commands that allow you to tell the modem what you want it to do and how you want it to operate. (For example, to dial the phone number 567-1234, you would enter the Hayes command ATDT followed by the phone number.) This set of commands is called the *Hayes command set*. When a modem is advertised as being Hayes-compatible, it means that it understands Hayes commands. Make sure the modem is Hayes-compatible, or you may have trouble running the more popular telecommunications software.

Get a Speedy Modem

Modems transfer data at different speeds, commonly referred to as *baud rates* or *bits per second (bps)*. The higher the baud rate, the faster the modem can transfer data. Common baud rates include 2,400, 9,600, 14,400, and 28,800bps. Although you pay more for a higher baud rate, you save time and decrease your phone bill by purchasing a faster modem. Don't go with anything slower than a 28,800bps modem, no matter how cheap the 14,400bps modem is.

In the ad at the beginning of the chapter, you may have noticed that the modem was said to be *downward-compatible* (or *backward-compatible*). This means that if you connect the 28,800bps modem with a slower modem (say 14,400bps), the two modems can still communicate. Most modems are downward-compatible.

Baud and Bps—What's the Difference?

Baud is the maximum number of times a modem can change the signal it sends per second. *Bits per second* refers to the number of bits of information transferred per second. A modem may send more than one bit of information for each change in the electrical signal. For example, a modem operating at 300 baud may be transferring at 1,200 bps. So if you are comparison shopping, you would do better to compare rates based on bits per second.

V.34bis, V.42bis, and Throughput

Nothing perks up a modem ad like a list of standards: V.34bis, V.42bis, MNP 2–4. You don't know what these standards represent, but you just gotta have them. To understand the standards, keep in mind that they fall in three categories: modulation, data compression, and error correction. (*Modulation* is a way of sending signals; sort of like AM or FM radio signals, but through the phone lines.) The following table lists common standards.

Modem Standards of the Rich and Famous

Category	Standard	What It Does
Modulation	V.22	Transfers up to 1,200bps.
	V.22bis	Transfers up to 2,400bps.
	V.32	Transfers up to 9,600bps.
	V.32bis	Transfers up to 14,400bps.
	V.32terbo	Transfers up to 19,200bps.
	V.34 or V.Fast	Transfers up to 28,800bps.
Error Correction	MNP 1, 2, 3	Checks for phone line noise and corrects transmission errors.
	MNP4	Checks for transmission errors and adapts to phone line conditions.
	LAPM	Prevents transmission errors.
	V.42	Combines MNP 2, 3, and 4 with LAPM.
Data Compression	MNP 5 and 7	Compress data 2:1
	V.42bis	Compresses data 4:1.

Modems that come with data compression can squish data before sending it. This allows the modem to send more data per second. Trouble is, both modems (the caller and receiver) must use the same data compression standard in order for it to work. If you know that you'll be communicating with another modem using a specific data compression standard, make sure you get a modem with a matching standard. For online services, you don't need to worry too much about data compression.

Oh yeah, and don't let the term "throughput" confuse you. Throughput is simply a measure of how much data a modem can transfer given its speed and data compression capability. For example, in the ad I mentioned earlier, the throughput was advertised as 115,200bps *with data compression*. That means that when the modem is operating at maximum speed 28,800bps using V.42 data compression, the modem can transfer data at 115,200bps. Although conditions rarely allow for this high-speed data transfer, it looks good on paper.

What About the New ISDN and Cable Modems?

The trouble with most modems is that they have to use phone lines, which were designed for voice communications, not data communications. (You know how little useful data is transferred during a typical voice conversation.) Voice is carried over the phone lines by analog (wave) signals, which aren't the most efficient carriers of digital information.

Currently, 28,800bps modems push the limits of standard phone lines. Even if you have a 28,800bps modem, you'll usually find that your connection is slightly slower (say 26,400bps or even 14,400bps) because of line noise or some other glitch. If you want to go beyond this speed, you need an ISDN (Integrated Services Digital Network) or cable modem.

ISDN modems use special phone lines to transfer data at up to 128Kbps (128,000bps). That's over four times faster than a 28,800bps modem! In addition, an ISDN phone line is like having two phone lines. You can carry on a voice conversation on one line and connect to the Internet on the other line (although the connection will be half the speed—64Kbps). If you're considering an ISDN modem, check out the following:

➤ Call your phone company first. Ask if they offer ISDN service and find out how much it will cost for connecting and monthly fees. This information alone will usually be enough to convince you that you don't need ISDN service.

➤ Before you buy an external ISDN modem, make sure that you have a super-fast serial port connection or that the modem connects to a parallel port (and you have an open parallel port). Otherwise, the modem will transfer data over the phone lines faster than it can transfer data to and from your computer.

➤ Make sure the modem can handle analog data transfers at 28,800bps. You may still have to establish analog connections with some services.

The newest modems on the market are cable modems, which make a computer "cable ready." They act like the cable connection on your TV set. And like the cable connection on your TV set, they require you to call the cable company and have a person come out to install the cable service. Because these coaxial cables can carry so much information (30MB per second!), they are ideal for video connections and the Internet. The trouble is that TV cables are made to bring information into your house, not out of it. However, cable companies are working hard to update their lines for two-way communication.

Future Outlook The modem and communications industries are moving so fast that the new technologies are going to have to play king of the hill to determine the standard. My advice is to wait until you can pull signals into your computer through an RCA satellite dish.

263

Flash ROM Is Good

Modem manufacturers are constantly developing new technology to increase data transfer rates. Many of these improvements come in the form of the instructions that tell the modem how to compress and decompress data. These instructions are stored in the modem's ROM (read-only memory). A flash ROM allows you to update the instructions to take advantage of the new technology. You obtain the ROM update from the modem manufacturer (either on disk or over the phone lines) and install it in your modem. Without flash ROM, you would have to buy a whole new modem.

To Fax or Not To Fax?

Some modems, called fax modems, come equipped with the added capability either to simply send faxes or to both send and receive faxes. Like fully equipped fax machines, a fax/modem allows you to dial a number and transmit pages of text, graphics, and charts to a conventional fax machine, or to another computer that has a fax/modem. You can also use the fax modem to receive incoming calls.

Shop carefully. Many fax/modems are able only to send faxes, not to receive them. If you want to receive faxes, make sure the fax/modem can handle incoming faxes. Also, make sure your modem supports Class 1 and 2 Group III fax machines. Nearly 90 percent of faxes in use today are of the Group III variety.

Voice Support

If you plan on having your computer answer the phone and take messages, make sure the modem offers voice support. Without voice support, your modem can answer the phone, but it can only make annoying screeching noises...which is useful for making telemarketers back off.

Some modems are also designed to handle video calls, sort of like on *The Jetsons*. However, if modems are too slow to handle simple file transfers, you can imagine how slow they are to transfer video images. Also, you and your friend would both need cameras attached to your computer, to film you while you're talking, and that's just too weird.

Do You Need Another Phone Jack for the Modem?

If you already have a phone jack near the computer, but your phone is plugged into it, you don't need to install an additional jack. Most modems come with two phone jacks: one that connects the modem to the incoming phone line and another one into which you can plug your phone. When you are not using the modem, you use the phone as you normally would. If your modem doesn't have two phone jacks, you can purchase a split phone connector from an electronics store. The split phone connector allows you to plug both your phone and your modem into the same jack.

If your computer is far from an existing phone jack, get a long phone cable, or have an additional phone jack installed. If you're good with a screwdriver and pliers (and maybe a drill, hammer, or other instruments of destruction), you can probably do it yourself in less than an hour.

When the Line Is Busy

If your modem and phone are on the same line, your modem will try to answer the phone when it rings. (This drives my wife crazy.) To get around this problem, you can buy a voice/data switch that routes the call to either your computer or your phone. If the incoming call is one of those high-pitched computer squeals, the switch routes the call to the computer. If the call is a normal phone call, your phone rings so you can pick it up and start talking.

Installing a Modem

Modem installation varies depending on whether you are installing an internal or external modem. With an internal modem, you must get under the hood of your PC, plug the modem into an open expansion slot, and plug the modem into the phone jack. If you're a rank beginner, get some experienced person to coach you through it.

Just about anyone can install an external modem. All you have to do is turn off the computer and make three connections:

➤ **Modem to serial port**   Connect the modem to the serial port (usually marked COM) on your computer using a serial cable.

➤ **Modem to power source**   Plug the modem's power cord into a receptacle on your wall or into your power strip or surge suppressor.

➤ **Modem to phone line**   Connect the modem to the phone jack. This is just like plugging a phone into a phone jack. (You might also want to connect your phone to the modem, as shown here.)

An external modem requires three connections.

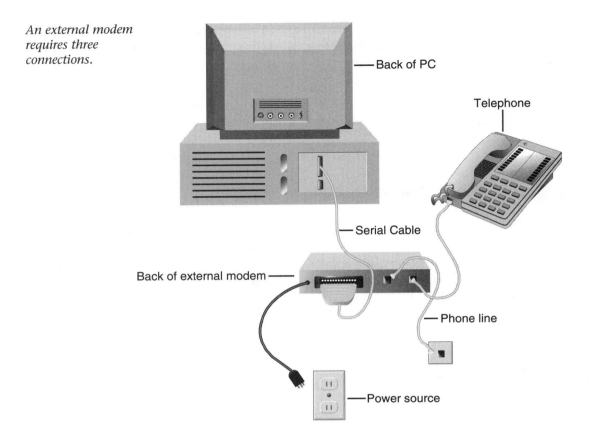

Back of PC

Telephone

Serial Cable

Back of external modem

Phone line

Power source

Before You Call

Before you begin using your modem, you might need some additional software. To determine what software you need, ask yourself what you want to do with the modem. The following paragraphs describe some of the common uses for a modem and the type of program required for each use.

Online information services   If you want to connect to an online service (such as Prodigy or America Online), you have to purchase a special program and pay the subscription price to the service. Skip to the next chapter for details.

Surf the Internet   This is sort of like connecting to an online service (in fact, you can connect to the Internet through an online service). You can also connect (less expensively) by using a local *Internet service provider*. The service provider usually equips you with the software you need and any other instructions you need to get started. See Chapter 24, "Doing the Internet Shuffle."

Games in two-player mode   If you have a game that allows you to play games in two-player mode using a modem, the program probably contains all the tools you'll need to play the game over the phone lines. Refer to the user manual that came with the game.

Transfer files between two computers or connect to a bulletin board system   You will need a communications program. Most modems come with a simple communications program. Windows comes with a program called Terminal (HyperTerminal in Windows 95), which works fine. Your modem probably came with its own communications program, which is usually better than the one in Windows.

Remote computing   Say you have a computer at work and one at home. You can purchase a special remote computing program that lets you control your computer at work from your computer at home and vice versa. Try Norton's pcAnywhere.

"Free" Long Distance Calls   If you heard the buzz about this, that's just what it is. You can't just avoid long-distance charges to your pal across the country by placing the call with your modem. You need special software, and an Internet connection. Your friend needs the same special software and Internet connection. Then, you have to call at the same time, go to a special area on the Internet, and find your pal. This isn't easy.

Bulletin Board System

A bulletin board system (BBS for short) enables a computer to automatically answer the phone when other computers call. The BBS allows the calling computer to copy files to it (*upload* files) and copy files from it (*download* files). Although you can purchase a BBS program to set up your own BBS, most users work with BBSs set up by computer companies and professional associations.

Know Your Telecommunications Settings

If you connect your computer to another computer or to an online service, you must make sure both computers are using the same *communications settings*. Otherwise, errors may result during data transfer. For example, if one modem is talking at 14,400bps and the other is listening at 2,400bps, it's likely that some information will get lost. Common communications settings include the following:

Baud rate   The transfer rate can be only as fast as the *slower* of the two modems allows.

COM port   The COM port setting tells the telecommunications program where to look for your modem. (The COM port setting applies only to your computer; the settings do not have to be the same on both computers.) If you get a message saying that the program cannot find your modem, try changing the COM port setting.

Parity   Tests the integrity of the data sent and received. Common setting is None or No Parity.

Data bits   Indicates the number of bits in each transmitted character. Common setting is Eight.

Stop bits   Indicates the number of bits used to signal the end of a character. Common setting is One bit.

Duplex   Tells the computer whether to send and receive data at the same time (Full), or send data or receive data but not both at the same time (Half). Common setting is Full.

You can change most communications settings using a single dialog box.

The important thing to remember is that the communications settings must be the same on both computers (although your modem and telecommunications program can adjust most of the settings automatically). Once the settings are right, you can enter a command to have the modem call the other computer. The communications program dials the number and establishes the connection between the two computers.

What Went Wrong?

Rarely do modem communications proceed error free the first time. Any minor problem or wrong setting can cause a major disruption in the communications between your computer and the remote computer.

The Least You Need To Know

The most difficult aspects of telecommunications are in picking out a good modem and setting it up. Once you get the modem working for at least one program, the rest is easy. As you struggle, keep the following in mind:

➤ In order for you to use a modem, you need three things: the modem, a communications program, and a connection to your phone jack.

➤ The speed at which a modem transfers information is measured in bits per second (bps). When shopping for a modem, look for one that transfers data at 28,800bps or faster.

➤ Modems that have fax capabilities can transfer faxes to or from a fax machine or another computer that is equipped with a fax modem.

➤ The telecommunications program you need depends on what you want to do. When you subscribe to an online service, you usually get the program you need in order to connect to the service.

Chapter 23

Connecting to an Online Service

> **By the End of This Chapter, You'll Be Able To:**
>
> ➤ Connect to one of the big four online services
>
> ➤ Pick a local access number (to avoid long-distance charges)
>
> ➤ Send and receive mail electronically
>
> ➤ Chat live with friends and strangers
>
> ➤ Get games, pictures, and other files for free

One of the first things most people do with a modem is connect to one of the big four online services: America Online, Microsoft Network, Prodigy, or CompuServe. When you subscribe to the service (usually for about 10 bucks a month), you get a program that allows you to connect locally to the service (assuming you live near a major town), and you get access to what the service offers. This includes electronic mail, news, research tools, magazines, university courses, and much, much more.

What's the Cost?

What's the price you pay for all of this? When you're shopping for an online service, compare subscription rates and consider the focus of each service. Here's a rundown of the four biggies:

Check This Out...

Canceling Your Membership
Online services typically waive the first month's usage fee. If you choose to no longer use the service, be sure you cancel your membership before next month's billing period begins.

America Online charges a flat rate ($9.95) for five hours a month, and $2.95 for each additional hour at any time of the day or night. You can send as many e-mail messages as you like. America OnLine is an online information service for the Me generation. Call 1-800-827-6364 for a startup kit.

CompuServe charges $9.95 for unlimited connect time to many basic services, including news, weather, and business information. Special services cost extra. E-mail charges vary depending on the length of the message and the speed of your modem; however, you can send over 200 pages per month free. CompuServe has traditionally been more technical and business oriented. Call 1-800-487-0588 for a startup kit.

Microsoft Network has two plans. The Standard plan has a monthly fee of $4.95 which includes 3 hours of usage per month. Each additional hour is $2.50. The Frequent User plan charges $19.95 per month for 20 hours of usage ($2.00 for each additional hour). If you have Windows 95, you can double-click the **Microsoft Network** icon and sign up right now.

Prodigy offers two membership plans. The Basic plan gives you 5 hours of usage per month for $9.95 ($2.95 an hour if you go over that). The 30/30 plan gives you 30 hours of usage for $29.95 ($2.95 for each hour over 30). Special services (such as investment brokers and online banking services) also cost extra. Prodigy is a family-oriented online service. Call 1-800-PRODIGY for a startup kit.

When you first connect to any of the online services, keep tabs on your phone bill. If you use a modem to call long distance, your friendly neighborhood phone company charges you long-distance rates—so keep this in mind when you are chatting on the modem. Most online information services, however, provide you with a local number for connecting to the service. You can then communicate with other people in different states by way of the local connection, thus avoiding long-distance charges.

Starting Your Online Account

When you subscribe to an online service, you get a startup kit that includes the software you need to connect to the service, an account number and password, and documentation that teaches you how to start. You install the software just as you install any new software—by running the installation or setup program on the first disk.

The installation program copies the necessary files to your hard disk and then asks you to specify which COM port and type of modem you are using. Some installations test the COM port and modem settings for you, and simply ask for your confirmation.

Extra Charge for Fast Service?
Although most services currently charge the same amount for 14,400bps and 28,800bps service, make sure you don't have to pay more for a higher speed connection.

The installation program then uses the modem to dial a toll-free number that gives you access to local connections in many cities. By selecting a local number, you avoid long-distance charges. Once you select a local number (and usually an alternate number, in case the first number is busy), the installation program disconnects from the toll-free connection and then reconnects you locally.

Once you have a local number to dial, you can sign on to the service and start using it. To sign on to Prodigy or America Online, you simply enter your screen name (user name) and password, and then click the **Dial** or **Connect** button. The service dials the local access number, connects you, and displays an opening screen that lets you start using the service. With CompuServe, you must select a feature (for example, News or Mail) before you sign on; CompuServe then dials the local access number, connects to the service, and takes you immediately to that feature.

When you are done with the service, you hang up. You usually do this by opening the **File** menu and selecting **Disconnect** or **Exit**.

Phone Charges

If you dial a long-distance number, or if your phone service charges for local calls, keep in mind that you will be charged for your modem calls just as you are charged for voice calls.

If you have mail, you can click here to get it.

These buttons take you to the most popular areas in America Online.

The screen that greets you when you sign on to America Online.

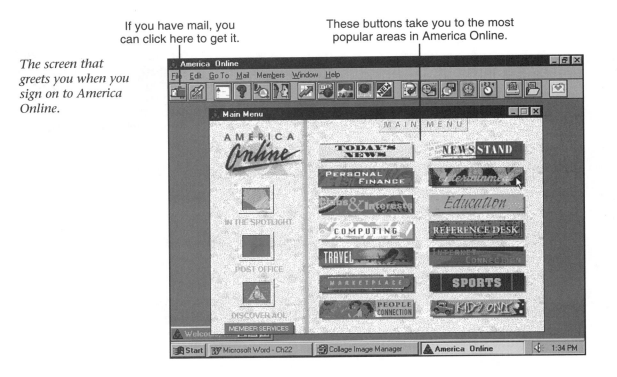

Navigating the Service

Online Help
To get help on America Online, press **Ctrl+K**, type **help**, and press **Enter**. On CompuServe, press **Ctrl+G**, type **practice**, and press **Enter**. On Prodigy, press **Ctrl+J**, type **help**, and press **Enter**.

Although each online service offers different tools for moving around in the service, the tools are very similar. Most services display buttons and menus that allow you to use popular features, such as mail, news, and games. In addition, you can use keywords to quickly access a feature. For example, on America Online, you can press **Ctrl+K**, type the name of the feature you want to use (News, Mail, Help), and press **Enter**. On CompuServe, you can use keywords by pressing **Ctrl+G**; and on Prodigy, you press **F6** (or **Ctrl+J**).

Postage-Free Mail, Same Day Delivery

How would you like to send a letter and have it reach its destination in less than a minute? With electronic mail (*e-mail* for short), you can enjoy warp speed delivery at a fraction of the cost.

To send an e-mail letter, you first enter the **Compose Mail** command (or its equivalent). This brings up a dialog box that allows you to compose and address your correspondence. Type the e-mail address of the person to whom you want to send the message (this is usually the person's screen name, if she is a member of the same service). Click inside the **Description** area and type a brief description of your message. Finally, type your message (or paste it) in the **Message** area and then click the **Send** button. In a matter of seconds (or minutes), the message appears in your friend's mailbox. When your friend connects to the service, your message appears in her mailbox.

Everyone (including you) on your online service has an electronic mailbox. Whenever you sign on, the application indicates in some way if you have mail waiting. To get your mail, you enter the **Get Mail** command or click the **Mail** button. This displays a list of waiting messages. Double-click the message you want to read. The message appears inside a dialog box, which usually contains a **Reply** button, allowing you to respond immediately to the message.

Click here to respond.

Your incoming messages appear on-screen.

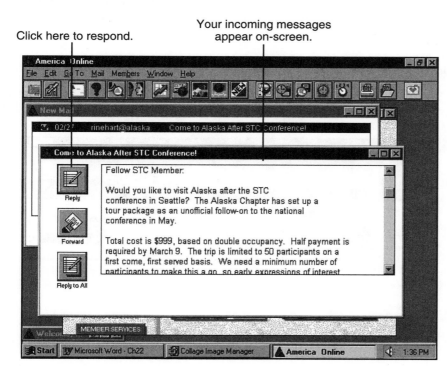

You have your own electronic mailbox.

275

Conversing in Chat Rooms

If you don't like waiting for mail, you can converse with your friends and colleagues in one of the many chat rooms the online service provides. You pick a room in which 20 or so people are hanging out and then start typing. Your messages appear on the screens of the other people in the room, and their messages appear on your screen. To go to a chat area on any of the major online services, do the following:

Sordid Conversations
If you have children who might be using the service, you must be careful with mail and chat rooms. Although most service members attempt to be civil, some members may be a bit unruly. Most services allow you to block access to questionable areas, including chat rooms.

➤ In CompuServe, open the **Services** menu and select **CB Simulator**.

➤ In America Online, press **Ctrl+L**. This takes you to a lobby. You can go to specific chat rooms by clicking the **List Rooms** button, and then selecting the name of the desired room.

➤ In Prodigy, press **Ctrl+J**, type **chat**, and press **Enter**. This displays a list of rooms from which you can choose.

➤ In The Microsoft Network, click the **Categories** button and then double-click the **Chat World** icon. Keep clicking icons until you find the room you want.

Chat rooms let you converse with other members.

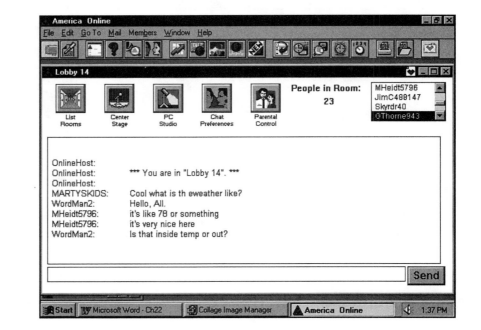

Sharing Common Interests

Online services started as computerized community centers where people could share their ideas, problems, and solutions. This tradition is still alive in online *forums* and *boards*. You can find a forum or board for almost any special interest category—from gardening and parenting to computers and automobiles. If you have a question, you simply post a message on the board. In a day or so, other members post answers in an attempt to help you out. You can get free legal advice, information on how to grow prize roses, and help finding long-lost relatives. Forums and boards are also a great place to talk about your favorite books, movies, and TV shows, although not all users will agree with your tastes.

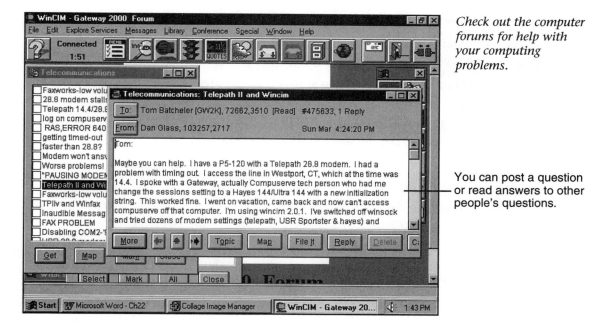

Check out the computer forums for help with your computing problems.

You can post a question or read answers to other people's questions.

Reading Online Newspapers and Magazines

Electronic publishing is big these days. In addition to publishing paper periodicals, publishers are placing their articles in electronic format on online services. You can get the latest headline news, read popular magazines (such as *Time* and *Newsweek*), and search newspapers and magazines for information on specific topics.

Downloading Files and Programs

Online services contain huge vats of files, offering everything from game files and software updates to digitized photographs of famous actors and actresses. You can download (copy) any of these files to your computer using your modem. The procedure is fairly simple:

1. Sign on to the service and go to the area that contains the file you want to download. In America Online, you can go to the Download area (the Software Center). In other services, you normally must enter a special interest forum to download files related to that forum.

2. Enter the command to search for a particular file or application. A dialog box usually appears asking you to specify the type of file you want.

3. Follow the on-screen instructions or prompts to find the file you want to download.

4. Select the file, and then enter the command to download the file. A dialog box usually appears, prompting you to specify a name, drive, and directory for the file.

5. Enter the requested information and press **Enter**. The service sends the file to your computer and stores it in the specified drive and directory. This can take minutes or hours depending on the file size and modem speed.

Nabbing the file is only half the story. You may have to download additional files in order to work with the file you just downloaded. For example, if you downloaded a picture of your friend, and the file's name ends in GIF, you need a program (called a GIF viewer) that can display GIF files. You can usually find the file you need using the same techniques described above.

You might also encounter compressed (zipped) files that end in ZIP. Services commonly store large files in a compressed format, so the files take up less space and require less time to download. If you find one of these files, you'll need a program called PKZip to decompress the file and make it useable.

Decompressing a ZIP File

The easiest tool to use for decompressing ZIP files is called WinZip, and you can download it from most online services. When you download it, you end up with a file called winzip.exe (or something similar), which is a self-extracting ZIP file (it decompresses itself). All you have to do to install the program is to display the winzip.exe file in File Manager, Windows Explorer, or My Computer, and then double-click on the file name. Follow the instructions to complete the installation.

To use WinZip to decompress other compressed files you downloaded, take the following steps:

1. In Windows 95, the WinZip installation places WinZip on the Start menu. Click the **Start** button, point to **Programs**, point to **WinZip**, and then click the **WinZip** option. In Windows 3.1, the WinZip installation creates a program group with program-item icons for running WinZip. Double-click the **WinZip** icon to run WinZip. The WinZip window appears.

2. Click the **Open** button on the toolbar. A dialog box appears, asking you to select the compressed file you want to decompress.

3. Use the dialog box that appears to select one of your compressed files, and then click the **OK** or **Open** button.

WinZip shows you the names
of the files that are contained
in the compressed file.

WinZip handles the decompression for you.

Click the Extract button.

Name	Date	Time	Size	Ratio	Packed	Path
data.pck	05/09/95	21:15	1,603,63	67%	532,230	
badtoys.exe	05/09/95	21:12	144,128	61%	55,666	
regform.txt	05/05/95	20:01	1,817	68%	584	
firm.msg	04/28/95	19:25	506	62%	193	
readme.txt	05/08/95	23:00	1,078	52%	519	
file_id.diz	05/07/95	23:28	274	34%	180	

Selected 0 files, 0 bytes   Total 6 files, 1,711KB

4. Click the **Extract** button in the toolbar. A dialog box appears, asking where you want the decompressed files placed.

5. Select the drive and folder or directory in which you want the unzipped files placed.

6. Make sure to select the **All files** option, so WinZip will unzip all the files in the zipped file.

7. Click the **Extract** button. WinZip unzips the file and stores all the extracted files in the specified directory. (You can then delete the compressed file you downloaded.)

279

If WinZip is unavailable, you can use a program called PKZip to decompress files. To decompress a ZIP file, first copy the ZIP file and the file PKUNZIP.EXE to a directory on your hard disk. Change to the drive and directory that contains the ZIP file. Type **pkunzip** *filename*.**zip** (where *filename* is the name of the zipped file) and press **Enter**. PKUnzip decompresses the file. Delete the ZIP file from your hard disk so it doesn't take up disk space.

Decompressing Self-Extracting ZIP Files

PKZip can also create self-extracting ZIP files that have the EXE extension. You simply copy the file to an empty directory and then run it; it decompresses itself. You can then delete the EXE file from your hard drive.

Other Compression Programs

PKZip is one of the most popular compression programs on the market, but it's not the only one. A different compression program may have been used. If that's the case, you can usually download that compression program (and the documentation for using it) from your online service.

Internet Access

You'll learn all about the Internet in the next chapter. However, before you leave, you should know that most online services offer limited access to some Internet features. Although you won't experience the full, intimidating effect of the Internet, online services do give you a good first encounter. Learn how to access the Internet using online services in Chapter 24.

The Least You Need To Know

Okay, you've read enough. Now, get hold of a couple free online trial membership kits and get connected. As you're cruising your online service, be sure you try everything:

➤ Send an e-mail message to a friend or colleague.

➤ Visit a chat room.

➤ Find the hourly news service.

➤ Read a couple articles from online magazines.

➤ Check out the Internet access.

Chapter 24

Doing the Internet Shuffle

By the End of This Chapter, You'll Be Able To:

➤ Describe the Internet in 25 words or less

➤ Name three ways you can connect to the Internet

➤ Poke around in computers all over the world

➤ View pictures, movies, and sounds

➤ Write a complete sentence using only Internet acronyms

Unless you've set up permanent residence in the New York subway, you've probably heard the terms "Internet" and "information superhighway." The Internet is a massive computer network connecting thousands of computers all over the world, including computers at universities, libraries, businesses, government agencies, and research facilities.

By connecting to the Internet, you can tap many of the resources stored on these computers. You can copy files from them, use their programs, send and receive electronic mail (*e-mail*), chat with other people by typing messages back and forth, get information about millions of topics, shop electronic malls, and even search for a job or a compatible mate.

Finding an Entrance Ramp

Before you can navigate the Internet, you have to find an entrance ramp—a way onto the Internet. You have several options:

Online service connection   The easiest way to connect to the Internet is to use an online service. All the major online services (Prodigy, America Online, CompuServe, and The Microsoft Network) offer Internet access. However, you can usually get a better monthly service rate from a local Internet service provider.

Permanent connection   If your company or university has a network that is part of the Internet and your computer is connected to the network, you have access to the Internet through the network. This is the least expensive (and fastest) way to go. Your network administrator can tell you if you're connected.

Internet service provider   One of the least expensive ways to connect to the Internet is through a local service provider. Most local Internet service providers charge a monthly fee of about $15 for unlimited connect time (or for a huge chunk of time, say 200 hours). You use your modem to connect to the service provider's computer, which is hooked in to the Internet.

I'll explain more about how to access the Internet using an online service or an Internet service, but first, I want to introduce you to the World Wide Web because this is the method you'll use in this book for accessing the Internet.

Browsing the World Wide Web

The easiest way to do the Internet is to connect through the World Wide Web (the *Web* for short). The Web is a collection of "*documents*" stored on computers all over the world. Each computer that has Web documents is called a *Web server*; it serves up the documents to you and other users on request. (The other computer, the *client,* which is your computer, acts as a customer, demanding specific information and complaining about the prices and service.)

What makes these documents unique is that each contains a *link* to other documents contained on the same Web server or on a different Web server (down the block or overseas). You can hop around from document to document, from Web server to Web server, from continent to continent, by clicking these links.

And, when I say "document," I don't mean some dusty old text document like you'd find in the university library. These documents contain pictures, sounds, and video clips, animations, and even interactive programs. When you click one of these multimedia links, your modem pulls the file into your computer, where the Web browser or another (*helper*) application "plays" the file (more about helper applications later in the chapter). All you have to do is tilt your chair back, nibble on popcorn, and watch the show.

To do the Web, you need a special program called a *Web browser*, which works through your service provider to pull documents up on your screen. You can choose from any of several Web browsers, including Mosaic, Netscape Navigator, and Internet Explorer. You also need the *helper applications* that play the picture, sound, movie files, and animation clips. All these helper applications and a browser are provided as part of the "package" when you access the Internet through an online service, such as America Online, or Prodigy. If you choose to use a local Internet service provider, your service provider usually supplies a free Web browser and shareware helper applications.

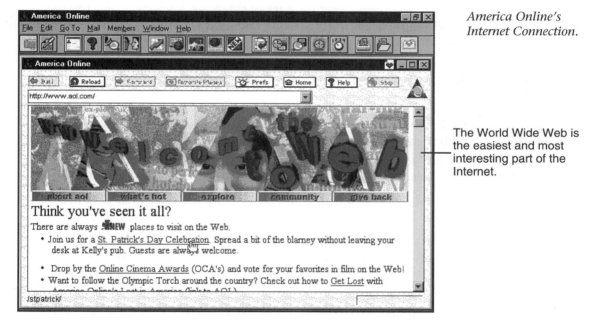

America Online's Internet Connection.

The World Wide Web is the easiest and most interesting part of the Internet.

Connecting Through an Online Service

The easiest way to connect to the Internet is to use an online service. Flip back to Chapter 23, find the list of online service phone numbers, and call for a free trial membership. Install the software, sign on, and then take one of the following steps to tap into the Internet:

➤ In America Online, display the Main menu (it appears when you sign on), and click the **Internet Connection** button. The best way to surf the Internet is through the World Wide Web. Click the **World Wide Web** icon.

➤ In CompuServe, open the **Services** menu and click **CompuServe Mosaic**. This establishes the CompuServe connection and hooks you into the World Wide Web.

➤ In Prodigy, bring up the sign-on screen, and enter your user ID and password. Click the **Web Browser** option; then click the **Connect** button.

➤ To connect with The Microsoft Network, you need another program (called Internet Explorer). Read on.

Internet Explorer is included on the CD at the back of this book. It comes with a nifty program called Internet Setup Wizard, which (if you have Windows 95) leads you through the process of setting up Windows 95 to establish an Internet connection. In short, with Windows 95 and the CD at the back of this book, you can connect to the Internet right now! Simply skip ahead to "Using Microsoft's Internet Explorer," later in this chapter for details.

Using a Local Internet Service Provider

Although an Internet service provider is the least expensive in terms of money, it's a little more complicated than simply signing on to an online service. However, most service providers give you the software you need to connect to the Internet, and they will help you get up and running. If you don't know of any service providers in your area, ask at a computer store or users group in your area, or check in the phone book.

When you call to set up an account, you'll need to supply some information and specify just what you want:

➤ The service provider will want to know the maximum speed of your modem (for example, 14,400bps) and the COM port it is connected to (COM1 or COM2 usually).

➤ The service provider will also ask if you're using a Macintosh or PC, and whether you are running Windows 95 or Windows 3.1.

➤ The service provider will ask if you want a SLIP (Serial Line Internet Protocol) or PPP (Point-to-Point Protocol) connection. PPP is better, especially if you're using Windows 95. Friends don't let friends set up SLIP connections in Windows 95.

➤ If you're using Windows 3.1, make sure your service provider supplies *configured* software. With configured software, the provider enters all the settings required to establish the connection. You simply install the program.

➤ If you're using Windows 3.1, the service provider should supply a program called Winsock—a TCP/IP (Transmission Control Protocol/Internet Protocol) program. It dials into the service provider's computer and establishes the Internet connection. Windows 95 has its own, built-in TCP/IP.

➤ The service provider should also supply a program called a Web browser. This program allows you to tap into most of the features of the Internet. However, the CD at the back of this book contains Microsoft's Web browser, Internet Explorer. For more information, see the earlier section "Browsing the World Wide Web."

Setting Up Your Internet Connection in Windows 95

Some service providers will help you set up the Internet connection in Windows 95. Some expect you to do it on your own, but they will provide you with a list of settings you need. Once you have the connection settings from your service provider, you can use the Internet Setup Wizard (from the CD at the back of this book) to set up connection yourself:

1. Insert the CD Sampler disc into your CD-ROM drive, and follow the instructions at the back of this book to run CD Sampler.

2. Click on the **I.E. 2.0** button. A dialog box appears asking you to confirm the installation.

3. Click **Yes**. The installation utility displays a license agreement.

4. Read the agreement and click **I Agree**. The Browse for Folder dialog box appears, prompting you to select a parent folder.

5. Click on the icon for the drive on which you want Internet Explorer installed (usually the C drive). Then click **OK**. A dialog box appears telling you to restart your computer.

6. Click **OK**, exit all applications (including CD Sampler), and restart your computer.

You should now see an icon on the Windows desktop labeled **The Internet**. Double-click this icon to start the Internet Setup Wizard. If the Internet Setup Wizard does not start, click the Windows 95 **Start** button, point to **Programs/Accessories/Internet Tools**, and click on the **Internet Setup Wizard**.

Setup Wizard displays a series of dialog boxes, asking you questions. The big question is whether you already have a service provider or whether you want to use the Microsoft Network. If you choose Microsoft Network and you don't have a Microsoft Network account, the program will help you establish the account. Respond to the remaining dialog boxes.

The Internet Setup Wizard configures Windows 95 to automatically display a Connect To dialog box whenever you try to run the Web browser (Internet Explorer). This dialog box contains all the information you need to dial into your service provider's computer (or The Microsoft Network) and establish a connection. You simply double-click **The Internet** icon on the Windows desktop. The Connect To dialog box appears. Supply any

285

of the requested information, and click the **Connect** button. If you're using your own service provider, after you connect you should see the following dialog box, and you can use Internet Explorer to start wandering the Web. For details about using Internet Explorer, see "Using Microsoft's Internet Explorer," later in this chapter.

If you see this dialog box, you're connected.

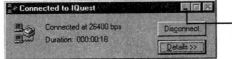

You can click here to remain connected and get the dialog box out of the way.

Setting Up Your Internet Connection in Windows 3.1

Windows 3.1 doesn't come with its own Internet software. Your service provider should give you a copy of Winsock that's configured for your computer. If Winsock is not set up specifically for your computer, you might be able to cheat your way to a quick connection. Try the following steps. If they don't get you connected, you may have to call your service provider for help. Here's what you do:

1. Follow your service provider's instructions for installing Winsock. This should place the program in the Winsock directory.

2. Open Program Manager's File menu and select **Run**. You need to run a program called System Editor to edit one of your startup files.

3. Type **sysedit**, and press **Enter**. System Editor appears, displaying the four system startup files.

4. Change to the Autoexec.bat window, and look for a line that starts with **Path=**.

5. Move the cursor to the end of the **Path=** line, and type **;c:\winsock**. This tells your computer where to look for Winsock.

6. Open the **File** menu and select **Save**.

7. Exit Windows, reboot your computer, and restart Windows.

8. In Windows, double-click the **Winsock** icon. If Winsock is not configured, a dialog box appears, prompting you to enter the connection settings (which your service provider should have given you).

9. Enter the settings, and click **OK**. Many settings are already entered for you. If your service provider did not give you a particular setting, leave the setting as is. Don't worry about what all these settings mean—just enter the settings you have.

10. Open the **Dialler** menu, and click **Login**. This displays a series of dialog boxes, asking you to enter the phone number to dial, your user ID, and your password. In

each dialog box, enter the requested information and click **OK**. (This is the only time you'll be asked for this information.)

A few settings are required.

Enter your service
provider's domain
(name).

Pick the type of
connection you
signed up for.

Trumpet Winsock Setup

IP address	0.0.0.0
Netmask	255.255.255.0
Default gateway	198.70.144.10
Name server	198.70.36.70
Time server	
Domain suffix	iquest.net
Packet vector	00
MTU	576
TCP RWIN	2048
TCP MSS	512
Demand load timeout (secs)	5
TCP RTO MAX	60

☐ Internal SLIP ☒ Internal PPP

SLIP port 1
Baud rate 38400
☒ Hardware handshaking
☐ Van Jacobson CSLIP compression

Online status detection
◉ None
○ DCD (RLSD) check
○ DSR check

[Ok] [Cancel] [Help]

Winsock dials the phone number you entered and tries to connect to the service provider. Watch the screen. If a message appears indicating that the connection has been established, you're in luck. If you see something like "Script aborted," you've run into problems. Call your service provider and cry for help.

Now, You Need To Run Another Program

When you connect to the Internet for the first time, you expect fireworks, but all you get is a dinky dialog box telling you that you're connected. When you dial into the Internet, all you're doing is opening a connection between your computer and the Internet. If you want to do something on the Internet, you need to run a specialized program that taps into specific features of the Internet:

➤ **Web browser** (such as Netscape Navigator or Internet Explorer) lets you tap into the World Wide Web, which is sort of a global multimedia library. You can view pictures, play sounds and video clips, and even view animations. See the next section, "Using Microsoft's Internet Explorer," for details on how to install the Web browser from the CD at the back of this book.

➤ **E-mail program** (such as Eudora) lets you check your electronic mailbox and send mail to anyone in the world who is connected to the Internet.

➤ **Newsgroup reader** allows you to read and post messages in newsgroups (electronic bulletin boards).

➤ **FTP program** lets you copy files and programs from the Internet.

Do-Everything Web Browser
You can tap most of the resources on the Internet using Netscape Navigator or Internet Explorer (both popular Web browsers). It allows you to send and receive e-mail, access newsgroups, copy files, and use Gopher menus. If you were on a deserted planet and you could have only one Internet program, pick a Web browser.

➤ **Gopher program** is a menu system that lets you move around the Internet by selecting items from Gopher menus.

➤ **Telnet program** lets you connect to other computers and use their resources just as if you were sitting at their keyboards.

➤ **Chat program** allows you to connect to chat rooms on the Internet and talk to other people "live."

If your service provider supplied you with any of these programs, follow the instructions to install the program on your hard disk, but don't try running the program until your computer is connected to the Internet. Before using any of these programs, you must connect using Dial-Up Networking (in Windows 95) or your Winsock program (in Windows 3.1), as explained in the previous two sections. Once connected, you can then run one of your Internet programs and start using it to access the Internet.

Using Microsoft's Internet Explorer

In case you haven't heard, Microsoft has recently declared war in the battle over control of the Internet. Its strategy is to make its online service (The Microsoft Network) more of an Internet service provider. Fortunately, Microsoft has made it fairly easy to connect to the Internet with its own Web browser, Internet Explorer.

If you have Windows 95, you can use Internet Explorer to explore the Web. Follow the instructions in "Setting Up Your Internet Connection in Windows 95," earlier in this chapter, to set up your Internet connection and install Internet Explorer. To run Explorer, double-click **The Internet** icon on the Windows desktop. Or click the **Start** button, point to **Programs**, **Accessories**, **Internet Tools**, and click **Internet Explorer**. A dialog box appears, prompting you to connect to a service provider. Complete the dialog box, and click the **Connect** button.

Your modem dials the service provider or Microsoft Network, and establishes the connection. The Internet Explorer window appears, and it loads Microsoft's home page. You can start to wander the Web simply by clicking links (highlighted text or pictures). Click the **Back** button to flip to a previous page, or click **Forward** to skip ahead to a page you've visited but backed up from.

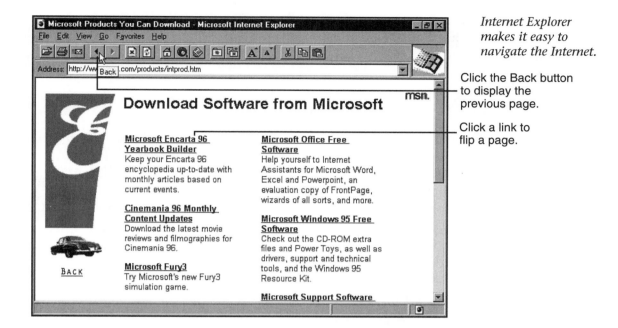

Internet Explorer makes it easy to navigate the Internet.

Click the Back button to display the previous page.

Click a link to flip a page.

Using URLs To Find Specific Pages

You've seen them on TV, in magazines, maybe even in your daily newspaper: bits of odd looking text, such as http://www.whitehouse.gov or http://www.toystory.com. What are these things? They're addresses of specific Web pages. These addresses are called Uniform Resource Locators (or URLs, pronounced "you are ells"). You enter the address in your Web browser, usually in a text box called Location or Go to, at the top of the screen, and your Web browser pulls up the page.

Techno Talk

URLs Dissected

To give you some idea of how these addresses work, let's dissect one. First, all Web page addresses start with http://. Gopher sites start with gopher://. FTP sites start with ftp://. You get the idea. The rest of the address reads from right to left. For example, in the URL http://www.whitehouse.gov, .gov stands for *government*, whitehouse stands for *White House*, and www stands for *World Wide Web*. Addresses that end in .edu are for pages at educational institutions. Addresses that end in .com are for commercial institutions.

All you really have to know about a URL is that if you want to use one, type the URL *exactly* as you see it. Type the periods as shown, use forward slashes, and follow the capitalization of the URL. Any typos and a message will appear telling you that the page doesn't exist.

Using Internet Search Tools

How do you find information on the Web? Many Web sites have search tools that filter through an index of Internet resources to help you find what you're looking for. You simply connect to a site that has a search tool, type a couple words that specify what you're looking for, and click the **Search** button. Here are the URLs (addresses) of some popular search tools on the Web:

> **http://www.yahoo.com**
>
> **http://www.lycos.com**
>
> **http://www.webcrawler.com**

Doing Electronic Mail

Because the Internet connects computers all over the world, it's ideal for transmitting messages electronically. You can sit in front of your computer and jot notes to your friends across town, across the country, or in exotic foreign lands. And these messages arrive in a matter of minutes or hours rather than days.

The procedure for sending messages over the Internet varies, depending on the e-mail program or online service you're using. In most cases, however, you get a dialog box that asks you to enter the person's e-mail address, a description of the message, and the message itself.

The e-mail address typically consists of two parts: the person's *login name* and *domain name*. The login name is the name that the person uses to connect to the Internet. The domain name is the address of the computer the person connects through. Type the address in all lowercase characters, and use an @ sign to separate the login and domain names.

If you're sending messages from a commercial online service, such as PRODIGY or America Online, you have to specify that the message is going to someone outside the service. For example, on CompuServe, you type INTERNET: before the e-mail address.

If you were sending a message from CompuServe to a member of America Online, the address might look something like this:

INTERNET: jsmith@aol.com.

Sending mail with a typical Internet e-mail program.

E-mail address

Type your message here.

Sharing Interests in Newsgroups

A *newsgroup* is a discussion group, an electronic bulletin board on which users exchange messages. For example, you might post a message on a body-art newsgroup asking the best way to remove the tattoo of your ex's name from your left bicep. Another user (more experienced in such matters) will read your message and post a reply, which you can then read.

The Internet supports over 10,000 newsgroups covering everything from gardening to desktop publishing. Whatever your interest, you can find a newsgroup (maybe three or four) where you can swap information with others.

To read newsgroup postings (and post your own messages), you need a newsgroup reader. When you connect to the Internet with the reader, it displays the names of all the newsgroups your service provider subscribes to. After you pick a newsgroup, the reader displays a list of recent postings from which you can choose.

Newsgroups let you read and post messages.

To read a message, double-click on its description.

The contents of the message appears.

---

alt.music.tom-waits (7 articles)

Articles Sort Search

```
> 2091 03/07 FryeDude            15 Keith Richards
n 2092 03/10 PACO 5              7 Re: Time – chopro
n 2094 03/12 Joel               50 *** CDs For Sale –– Take a Look! ***
n 2095 03/11 NEWBOULD DAVID F.   23 Re: lyrics – need help
s 2096 03/12 Aaron              59 Re: Coffee & Cigarettes
s 2097 03/14 johnhenry          10 Re: Tom's TV streetwalking past
s 2098 03/11 Bongo J            11 Re: Big Time
```

Re: Coffee & Cigarettes (71 lines)

File Edit Search View Respond

brempel@cc.umanitoba.ca (Ben Rempel) wrote:

>You can add "Bearskin" to your movie list. Tom plays the lead but
>as I posted earlier, its a dedicated Tom fan who will watch the
>whole thing through (I know, I did) cuz its a bit of a stinker.
>Like to hear more about the Iggy Pop thing too!

Hey, Ben, stop being so harsh about Bearskin!

I saw that film about two years ago, before I became really aware of
Tom's stuff, and personally I think it's definitely worth a look.
Okay, so there's no explosions, no sex, little swearing etc, but it's
an attempt at something different – something at least a bit unusual
and original. It's not my *favourite* film, nor it is as good as Jim
(jarmusch)'s work, but it's a sweet, funny little film.

Bear in mind that, since it's the closest Tom has had to top billing,

Fetching Files with FTP

When the Internet started out, it wasn't much more than a gigantic file warehouse. Businesses and individuals stored files on various Internet servers, where other people could come and copy (download) those files. It was like a huge swap meet for computer nerds.

FTP Short for *File Transfer Protocol*, FTP is a set of rules that govern the transfer of files between computers. True nerds use this acronym as a verb. For example, "You can ftp to the NSCA site and download the latest Mosaic."

As the Internet grew and diversified, it had to assign specific jobs to different servers. World Wide Web servers were given the task of storing hyperdocuments, newsgroups were set up to act as bulletin boards, and FTP servers became the file warehouses. What does this have to do with you? You can connect to many public-access FTP servers and copy programs, text files, graphics, and anything else that can be stored electronically.

As with most Internet sites, you can access FTP sites most easily by using a Web browser. When you connect to the site, you get a list of files and directories that appear as links. To grab a file, you click on it, tell your computer where to store it, and then give your final okay.

If the Web browser idea doesn't appeal to you, you can use a special FTP program to transfer files. These programs are usually set up something like the Windows File Manager, allowing you to copy files by dragging them from one window to another.

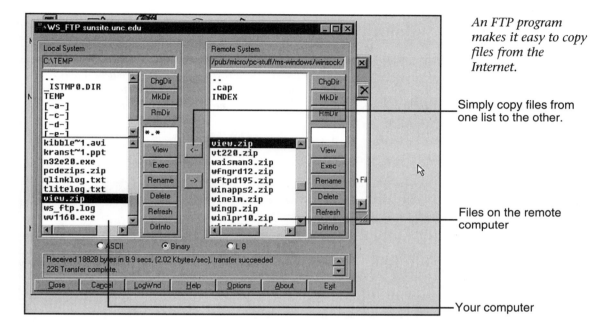

An FTP program makes it easy to copy files from the Internet.

Simply copy files from one list to the other.

Files on the remote computer

Your computer

Using Gopher Menus To Navigate

Gopher is an indexing system that enables you to access various Internet services through menus. Whenever you connect to a Gopher site, it presents you with an opening menu. When you select a menu item, the server presents you with *another* menu containing additional options and/or files. These options may send you off to another Gopher site, an FTP site, a newsgroup, or other Internet sites. You proceed through the menus until you find the file or information you want—or reach a dead end.

Telnetting (When Your Computer Just Isn't Enough)

Have you ever tried using someone else's computer? You never know what you're going to find. Maybe a menuing system, maybe some fancy graphical interface like Norton Desktop. Maybe you even get...horror of horrors...a DOS prompt! That's sort of what telnetting is like. You connect to another computer, and you enter commands just as if you were sitting at its keyboard. However, you're never sure what you're going to encounter—a texty menu system, a prompt, or a spiteful warning explaining what will happen to you if you go any further.

With most Telnet sites, you can log in as a guest. The site then displays a crude menu system that allows you to ferret out the information you're looking for.

Chatting Away

Commercial online services offer their own chat rooms, where you can rack up huge charges talking to other members all night. The Internet also has a chat feature. You use a special chat program to connect to a *chat server* (a computer that lets people use it for chatting). You then tune into a *channel*, which is sort of like a virtual coffee house, where other users are talking. As you type messages, they appear on the screens of all the other users on your channel. And, as they type messages, those messages appear on your screen. If you land on a channel with a bunch of fast typists, things can get pretty chaotic.

You can have live conversations with other users.

Your messages and other people's messages appear on your screen.

Type your message and press Enter.

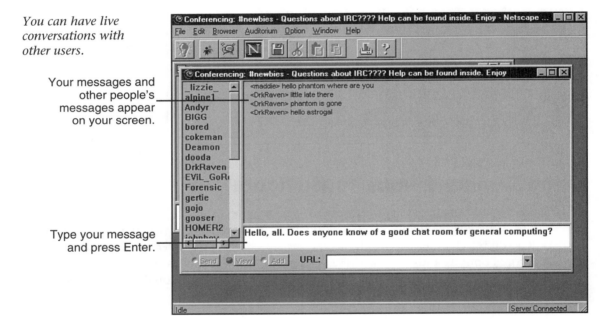

The Least You Need To Know

This chapter provides a mere smattering of what you'll find on the Internet. To experience this vast resource, get a fast modem and an Internet connection, and start playing. Here are some tips:

➤ Use a 14,400bps or faster modem.

➤ Try the World Wide Web first; you can do most of the other stuff from the Web. (You'll need a Web browser.)

➤ URLs are addresses that indicate where each item on the Internet is stored.

➤ Internet e-mail allows you to send messages to anyone who's connected to the Internet.

➤ Use newsgroups to read and post messages on an electronic bulletin board.

➤ You can ftp using your Web browser much more easily than by using an FTP program.

Part 6
Guerrilla Computing

You know the basics. You can make it with any application, rearrange your files, and even connect to an online service. You can use your computer to perform specific tasks.

But if you have to buy a new computer, do you know what to look for? Can you set the computer up when you get it home? If your computer is running out of memory and disk space, do you know what to do? When you receive an error message, do you have to call a friend or relative for help?

In this section, you'll learn how to survive in the trenches. You'll get the advanced tools you need to prepare for, prevent, and recover from common disasters. You'll also learn how to keep your computer in tip-top shape and optimize it for peak performance.

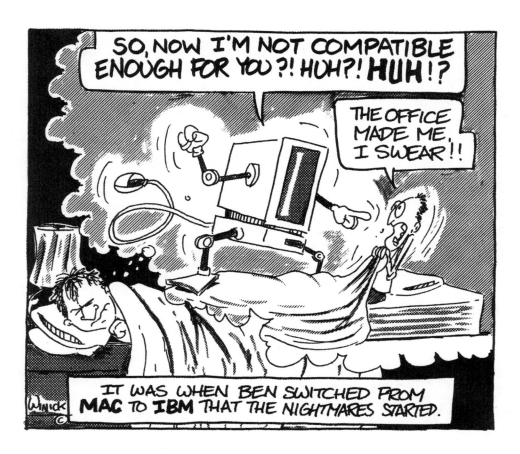

Chapter 25

Buying and Setting Up a Computer

By the End of This Chapter, You'll Be Able To:

➤ Buy a computer that won't be obsolete in a year

➤ Pick the fastest and the most affordable chip

➤ Get a hard disk drive that's big enough...and fast enough

➤ Connect all the computer parts without blowing up anything

If you already bought your dream computer, reading this chapter may be hazardous to your mental health. You may find out that the computer you have is already obsolete (I know mine is). Maybe you should have gotten 16 megabytes of RAM instead of 8. Maybe the slimline (space-saving) case wasn't the best choice, and you really should have considered buying a 64-bit graphics accelerator card (whatever that is). All these doubts and second-guesses can only make you bitter (and broke), so skip ahead to the next chapter and retain your blissful ignorance.

For the rest of you, you chronic procrastinators who have put off buying a computer, read on. These pages will show you that although you really can't afford the ideal computer, you can make the right trade-offs to get the best computer for your budget. You'll also learn how to set up your computer once you bring it home.

Finding a Brainy Computer (Chip)

One of the first things you'll encounter in any ad is the name of the computer's microprocessor (the computer's brain). This may appear as 486DX2, Pentium (or P5), or PowerPC. The chip label, which is printed on the chip and usually on the front of the system unit, tells you three things:

Chip number   The chip number (for example, 486) tells you the chip's IQ. A 286 is a dropout; 386 is a slow learner; 486 is above average; and the Pentium (586) is a genius.

Chip speed   Chip speed is measured in megahertz (pronounced "MEG-a-hurts"). The higher the number, the faster the chip works. But be careful: a 75MHz Pentium processes data faster than a 100MHz 486, because the Pentium is more advanced. Compare speeds only between chips that have the same name or number.

Chip type   The chip name may be followed by an abbreviation such as SX, DX, or DX2. The SX chip is a scaled-down version of the DX; for example, the 486SX is a 486DX without a math coprocessor. The 2 after the DX (DX2) indicates that the chip has a *clock doubler* that makes the chip process at twice the speed; for example, a DX2 66MHz chip is a 33MHz chip with a clock doubler. For portable computers, SL is commonly added to the chip type, indicating that the chip is specially designed for portable computing.

If you want some free advice, here goes. Look for a computer with a Pentium processor (a 586 chip), or better. Don't even think of buying a 386. And, unless you're buying a laptop computer, stay away from the 486, as well. If you heard something about the Pentium having a manufacturing defect, that's old news; Intel has fixed the Pentium, and it is a heck of a lot better than a 486.

Techno Talk

All Chips Are Not Created Equal

Several factors contribute to making one chip better than another: data bus structure, clock speed, and built-in cache size. The *data bus structure* determines how much information the processor can handle at one time: 16 bits (286), 32 bits (386 and 486), or 64 bits (Pentium). The *clock speed* determines how fast the chip cycles (think of it in terms of RPMs). A *built-in cache* is memory that's on the chip; this provides the processor with quick access to data, so the chip doesn't have to fetch data from RAM. 486 chips have an 8K cache, and Pentiums have a 16K cache. Some computers come with extra cache, sometimes called *internal*, which makes the chip even faster.

Thanks for the Memory (RAM)

Whenever the microprocessor is deep in thought, it's shuffling instructions and information into and out of RAM (random-access memory). When it runs out of RAM, it has to use the hard disk drive, which is much slower. Don't settle for less than 8 megabytes; if you can afford it, get 16 megabytes.

Also, make sure the computer comes with RAM *cache* or *external cache* (pronounced "cash"). This is a set of fast memory chips that stand between the normal (slower) RAM and the microprocessor. The RAM cache stores frequently used instructions and data, so the microprocessor can get the instructions and data more quickly. Most computers offer a 128K or 256K RAM cache.

The latest, greatest RAM on the market is EDO (which stands for Extended Data Out). EDO RAM is faster than the average (non-EDO RAM). You'll also hear the term *burst mode* used in conjunction with EDO. Burst mode is the EDO RAM's capability to deliver large amounts of information at a single moment. But don't worry about how it works; EDO is good, and you should look for a computer that has it.

You Don't Hear Much About the BIOS

Every computer has a built-in set of instructions called the BIOS (pronounced "BUY-ose," short for Basic Input Output System). Think of the BIOS as the little black box inside new cars that keeps everything working in sync. The three most common BIOSs are AMI (pronounced "AM-ee"), Phoenix, and Award. Of those three, AMI has the best reputation.

In addition to the BIOS manufacturer, check the BIOS date. Some computer manufacturers cut corners by using an old version of the BIOS. The BIOS date usually displays when you first turn on the computer, but it's easier to just ask the salesperson.

As you shop, you'll come across some computers that boast a *flash* BIOS. A flash BIOS allows you to update the BIOS later by using special software (instead of having to replace the BIOS chip).

A Hard Disk: How Big? How Fast?

Consider two things when you're looking at hard drives: size and speed. Size is measured in megabytes, and they range from 200 megabytes to over a gigabyte (1,000 megabytes). Most home computers now come with gigabyte hard drives; business computers come with even larger drives. If that sounds massive to you, consider the fact that Windows 95 gobbles up at least 40 megabytes, and the latest version of Quicken can take up 80 megabytes!

Speed is advertised as access time, which is expressed in milliseconds (ms)—the lower the number, the faster the drive. Good access times are between 10 and 15 ms. Stay away from anything over 17 ms.

Floppy Disk Drive Size and Capacity

A computer should have at least one floppy disk drive so you can transfer programs and data files from floppy disks to your hard disk. When considering floppy drives, look at size and capacity:

Disk size   Most new computers come with a single 3 ¹/₂" floppy disk drive. This should suffice unless you share files with people who use 5 ¹/₄" disks or you have old programs on 5 ¹/₄" disks.

Capacity   New computers come with high-capacity drives. You won't find a low-capacity drive unless you buy the computer at a garage sale. For more details about disk capacities, see Chapter 3, "Feeding Your Computer: Disks, Files, and Other Munchies."

Monitors: Get the Picture?

When you shop for a monitor, pretend you are shopping for a TV. You want a big clear picture. In addition to those obvious points, look for the following:

SuperVGA (SVGA)   Super VGA displays clear pictures with lots of colors. If you get a lower display standard (such as VGA), photos and movie clips will look blocky and fuzzy.

Size   Most computers come with a 14" or 15" monitor. The bigger 17" to 21" monitors are excellent for desktop publishing and graphics, but expect to pay dearly for the increased size.

Dot pitch   Dot pitch is the space between the dots that make up the display. In general, the closer the dots, the clearer the picture: .28mm is good, .39mm is fair, .52mm is bad.

Noninterlaced   Look for a noninterlaced monitor. Interlaced monitors have an imperceptible flash that can be hard on your eyes. Noninterlaced monitors don't flash.

Tilt/swivel base   You'll want to adjust your monitor for comfort, so be sure the base can be adjusted easily.

Flat screen   Most monitor tubes are curved, making them more susceptible to glare. Look for a flat screen.

Antiglare   Some monitors are built to prevent glare. With other monitors, you have to purchase a special antiglare screen that fits over the monitor; these can be cumbersome.

Swedish MPR II low-emissions standard   If you're worried that your monitor is going to cause a goiter to start growing on your forehead, make sure the monitor meets the Swedish MPR II low-emissions standards.

When you're looking at monitors, you may encounter the terms *video memory, local bus video,* and *graphics accelerator.* Don't let these terms scare you. A graphics accelerator card is a circuit board inside the system unit that the monitor plugs into. This card increases the speed at which data is sent to the monitor to create the display. Look for a 64-bit (not a 32-bit) accelerator card.

Video memory is a separate storage area that the computer uses to display pictures on the screen. Giving the monitor its own memory helps it display pictures faster. You should try to get a computer that offers at least 1 megabyte (preferably 2 megabytes) of video memory. Local bus just means that the monitor communicates directly with the computer, increasing the display speed.

CD-ROM: Information and Great Games

The most important consideration when shopping for a CD-ROM drive is speed. The current standard is the 4X or quadruple-speed drive (don't settle for a 2X drive). Many computers include even faster CD-ROM drives, such as the 6X. The faster the better. Keep an eye on the computer ads to see what the standard speed is when you purchase your computer.

So you won't have to keep swapping CDs into and out of the drive, consider getting a three- or five-CD changer. This is nice, especially if you have youngsters who enjoy playing all the CD computer games in a single session.

Sound FX with Sound Boards and Speakers

Many computers come with a CD-ROM drive but without a sound board. I guess the manufacturer expects you to plug a set of earphones into the CD-ROM drive and pretend you're wired to a 20-pound Walkman. If no sound board is included, have it added on; in most cases, you can add a sound board for 150 to 200 dollars. Also, make sure the sound board is 16- or 32-bit. Older, 8-bit sound cards cannot take full advantage of the sound enhancements in newer games and CDs.

303

Modems: Fast and Feature Rich

Most computers come with a modem that allows you to connect with other computers and services over the phone line. Look for a 28,800bps (28.8kbps) or faster data/fax modem. If you want to use your computer for voice mail, make sure the modem offers voice support. If you want to know more about modems, see Chapter 22, "Buying, Installing, and Using a Modem."

All-in-One: The Multimedia PC

You'll see a lot of ads for multimedia PCs. Trouble is, some of the people writing these ads think that a multimedia PC is one that can display a picture and occasionally beep. Truth is, a multimedia PC is a somewhat powerful computer that can display good-looking video in stereo. To do that, the computer needs some high-powered hardware. These are current minimum requirements for a multimedia PC (that is, current as of the writing of this book):

➤ A 75MHz or higher Pentium processor.

➤ Eight megabytes of memory.

➤ 540 megabyte hard drive.

➤ Quad-speed (4X) CD-ROM drive compatible with multisession PhotoCD standards.

➤ Wavetable sound (a step above 16-bit stereo sound).

➤ MPEG-1 video playback standard.

What's MPEG? If you've ever played a movie clip on a PC, you know how fuzzy and jerky it can appear. MPEG is a standard developed by the Moving Pictures Experts Group, to help overcome the problems with playing video clips on PCs.

Now that you know all that, watch out for ads that claim their PC as having MPEG video playback support. This support can be in the form of software (a quick, inexpensive, second-rate way to offer MPEG) or as special MPEG hardware (the only real way to display quality video). Before buying a PC that offers special MPEG video, make sure you're getting the MPEG *hardware*.

MPC1, MPC2, MPC3?

Multimedia PCs are often labeled with the MPC logo, meaning that they meet the MPC (Multimedia PC) requirements. During the writing of this book, the standard is MPC3, but before you purchase a computer, find out the current MPC standards, and make sure the computer exceeds them. These are minimum requirements; the latest, greatest CD games usually require more than the mere minimum.

The All-Important Ports

The back of every system unit has receptacles (called *ports*) for plugging in other equipment. Most system units come with the following standard ports:

Printer port   To connect a printer.

Communications port   To connect a mouse, printer, or modem.

Monitor port   To plug your monitor into the system unit.

Keyboard port   To plug the keyboard into the system unit.

Mouse port   To connect a mouse to your computer. You can connect the mouse to the mouse port or the communications port.

Game port   This really isn't a standard port, but it's nice to have if you plan on playing many computer games. You can plug a joystick (sort of like a stick-shift lever) into the port for controlling the game, rather than having to use the awkward mouse or keyboard. Most sound cards have a built-in game port.

Planning for Expansion

After you shell out two thousand bucks for a computer, the last thing you want to think about is spending more money to make it better. However, sooner or later, you'll want to add something to your computer: a bigger hard drive, more memory, maybe a scanner. When shopping for a computer, you want to make sure that you can add to it. The following sections explain what to look for.

Adding Internally with Expansion Boards

Every part of a computer plugs into a big circuit board (inside the system unit) called the *motherboard*. The motherboard contains several *expansion slots* that enable you to increase the capabilities of your system by plugging in *expansion boards* (or *cards*). For example, you can plug a soundboard into the slot so you can connect speakers and a microphone, or add an internal modem to your computer by plugging it into one of the slots. Make sure you get a computer that has at least four open expansion slots.

To further complicate matters, all expansion slots (and boards) are not created equal. There are four expansion standards you may encounter:

➤ **ISA** (Industry Standard Architecture) is for older expansion boards, and you'll want two or three of those to handle some of the expansion boards that are currently on the market.

➤ **PCI** (Peripheral Component Interconnect) is the newest popular standard, and you'll want two or three PCI slots to handle any current and future technology.

➤ **VESA** (Video Electronics Standard Association) is similar to PCI, but less popular at this time.

➤ **MCA** (Micro Channel Architecture) is IBM's standard, which never caught on. You might want to avoid MCA expansion slots, because very few manufacturers support that standard.

Again, don't feel as though you have to understand all the standards; just keep in mind that you want some ISA slots and some PCI or VESA slots.

Check This Out...

Cases Big and Small

An easy way to tell whether a system is expandable is to look at the case. Space-saving cases (usually called *slimlines*) usually have few expansion slots and unoccupied drive bays. Tower cases usually have eight drive bays and six or more expansion slots. Standard cases fall in the middle but provide sufficient expandability for most folks.

Drive Bays: For Floppy Drives or CD-ROM

Some computers come with only one floppy drive, but they contain additional *drive bays* so you can add drives later (for example, a CD-ROM drive, another floppy drive, or a tape backup unit). Look for a computer with at least four bays: one for a 3 $\frac{1}{2}$" drive, one for a CD-ROM drive, and two open drive bays (so you can add another hard drive, tape backup drive, or other type of drive later).

Adding Memory to Your System

Find out how much memory you can add to the computer. Most computers come with 8 megabytes of RAM and are expandable to 32 megabytes (or more). But knowing that you can add memory to your computer later is not enough; adding memory to some types of computers can be costly and difficult. Watch for the following traps:

➤ **Memory chip swapping required.** With some computers, you have to remove and discard the old chips to add chips that have a greater storage capacity. You should get a computer that lets you add at least 8 megabytes of memory without having to pull out the RAM chips that are already there.

➤ **Proprietary memory chips only.** Some computers require that you use only brand name chips that usually cost twice as much as a generic brand.

➤ **Memory board required.** You shouldn't have to install a memory board in order to add memory. You should be able to add memory by plugging chips (or *SIMMs*, single in-line memory modules) into the motherboard.

All Keyboards Are Not Created Equal

Keyboards look different because they have different arrangements and numbers of keys, but there's not much difference between them; they all perform the same tasks. The important thing is how the keys feel to you. Some keys click when you press them, some offer little resistance, and some just feel funny. Buy a keyboard that feels comfortable.

You might also want to look at the new, ergonomic keyboards. After breaking my wrist a while back (and not being able to rotate it to align my fingers with the keys), I was forced to buy an ergonomic keyboard. The keyboard I use is from Lexmark (no, they didn't pay me for the plug). It lets you split the keyboard in half and adjust each half independently. My wrist is back to normal, but I'm still using my new keyboard—I'll never give it up. Some ergonomic keyboards, such as Microsoft's, are not adjustable, but they do conform more closely to the natural position of your hands.

Printers: Quality, Speed, and Price

The price of a computer rarely includes the price of a printer, so you usually purchase that separately. For low-cost printing, look for a dot-matrix printer. For affordable quality, check out inkjet printers. For high-quality and speed, lasers are the best choice. When comparing printer prices, consider the price of the printer and its *consumables*. Consumables are office supplies (ink ribbons, toner cartridges, paper) that you use during printing. If you want to print in color, make sure you get a color printer.

Selecting a Printer

Printer Type	Price Range	Consumables	Output Quality	Speed
Dot-matrix	$150-$500	1/2–2 cents per page	180–360 dpi*	1–4 ppm* 80–450 cps*
Inkjet or Bubblejet	$200–$600	2–10 cents per page	300–360 dpi	2–4 ppm
Laser	$400–$3,000	3–7 cents per page	300–1000 dpi	4–10 ppm

* dpi stands for dots per inch, cps stands for characters per second, and ppm stands for pages per minute

Getting More for Your Buck with IBM-Compatibles or Clones

IBM-compatible computers (sometimes called *clones*) work exactly like IBMs, except that many compatibles are faster, cost less, and use higher quality parts than their IBM counterparts. You may have heard of some of the better known IBM-compatible computers, including Compaq, Gateway 2000, Packard Bell, and ZEOS.

Check This Out...

Bad Reps

The word **clone** is a derogatory term describing a compatible computer assembled by a local computer dealer. Clone computers have the same status as generic food—they cost less, but may not offer the same quality as the name-brand compatibles. I say *may not* because some clones are actually superior to their name-brand counterparts.

Software Included?

Some dealers include the cost of the operating system in the price they quote you; others don't. (Most systems come with DOS and Microsoft Windows, which are described in Chapters 7, 8, and 9.) If the computer does not come with an operating system, you won't be able to use it, so complain loudly and make sure the dealer installs it for you.

Many dealers also offer free applications with a computer. For example, computers often come with Microsoft Works installed. When you're comparing prices, consider this, too.

It's Not Easy Being Green

As you shop for a computer, you may encounter dealers offering "green PCs," and you may wonder why they don't look green. The "green" label marks the PC as meeting the U.S. Environmental Protection Agency's criteria for its Energy Star program. To meet these criteria, the computer must consume no more than 90 watts (30 for the system unit, 30 for the monitor, and 30 for the printer) when not in sleep mode (not in use). Some computer manufacturers go even further, making their computers out of recycled plastic and being careful about the waste materials produced during manufacturing.

Don't Buy Just for Freebies
Don't purchase a computer solely because it comes with a lot of freebies. Often, dealers will bundle a bunch of software with a computer to sucker the buyer into purchasing an obsolete computer.

Setting Up Your New Computer

When you get your computer home (or in your office), set all the boxes on the *floor*, so nothing will fall and break. Before doing anything else, read the following (long) list of cautions and tips:

➤ House the computer next to a phone jack and a grounded outlet. If you're in an old house and you're not sure if the outlet is grounded, go to the hardware store and buy an outlet tester; it has indicator lights that show if the outlet is properly grounded.

➤ Don't plug the computer into an outlet that's on the same circuit as an energy hog, such as a dryer or air conditioner. Power fluctuations can hurt your computer and destroy files.

➤ Place your computer in an environment that is clean, dry, and cool. Don't place it near a radiator, next to a hot lamp, or in your new tanning bed.

➤ Don't shove any part of the computer up against a wall, or stack books or other things on top, under, or around any part of the computer. The computer has fans and vents to keep it cool. If you block the vents, the computer might overheat. You don't want a two-thousand dollar piece of toast.

➤ Keep the computer away from magnetic fields created by fans, radios, large speakers, air conditioners, microwave ovens, and other appliances.

➤ When you unpack, pull the items out of the box; don't pull the box off the items. Otherwise, the items might fall and break.

➤ Don't cut into boxes with a knife. You might scratch something or hack through a cable.

➤ If your computer was delivered to you on a cold day, let it warm up to room temperature. Any condensation needs to dissipate before you turn on the power.

➤ Clear all drinks from the work area. You don't want to spill anything on your computer.

➤ Don't force anything. Plugs should slide easily into outlets. If you have to force something, the prongs are probably not aligned with the holes they're supposed to go in. Forcing the plug will break the prongs.

➤ Don't turn anything on till everything is connected.

To figure out where to plug things in, look for words or pictures on the back (and front) of the system unit; most receptacles are marked. If you don't see any pictures, try to match the plugs with their outlets. Look at the overall shape of the outlet and look to see if it has pins or holes. Count the pins and holes and make sure there are at least as many holes as there are pins. As a last resort, look for the documentation that came with the computer.

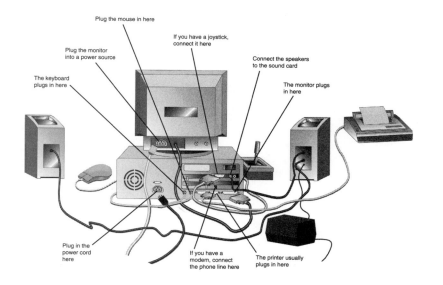

Plug the mouse in here

If you have a joystick, connect it here

Plug the monitor into a power source

Connect the speakers to the sound card

The keyboard plugs in here

The monitor plugs in here

Plug in the power cord here

If you have a modem, connect the phone line here

The printer usually plugs in here

The back of the system unit usually shows where the plugs go.

The Least You Need To Know

Okay, I admit it, this is way too much information to remember. As you're shopping for and setting up your computer, keep the following list handy:

➤ Get a Pentium processor chip 75MHz or faster.

➤ Get 16 megabytes RAM, expandable to 32 megabytes on the motherboard.

➤ You want a 1 gigabyte hard drive.

➤ Shop for an SVGA monitor, and a 64-bit graphics accelerator card with 2 megabytes of video memory.

➤ Go with a 28.8kbps data/fax modem.

➤ Look for a 4X CD-ROM drive (preferably with a three-CD changer).

➤ Get a 16-bit sound card with speakers.

➤ Make sure the system unit has four drive bays, at least two unoccupied.

➤ You want five open expansion slots: three ISA and two PCI or VESA.

Chapter 26

Upgrading: Making Your Good Computer Even Better

By the End of This Chapter, You'll Be Able To:

➤ Install a joystick on your computer

➤ Install a multimedia upgrade kit (or at least understand what's involved)

➤ Name five ways to give your computer more storage space

➤ Add a video accelerator to speed up your computer

If you have a couple thousand bucks sitting in a money market account, this chapter will help you spend it. You'll learn how to install a multimedia upgrade kit to the tune of seven hundred bucks, add memory for fifty bucks per megabyte, add a hard drive for about three hundred bucks, slap on a fax modem for a couple hundred bucks, and add a joystick for about forty bucks. I'll give you a couple pointers on how to save money, too.

Upgrade or Buy New?

Like a house, a computer can be a money pit. One month, you decide you need a new hard disk. The next month, you just gotta have a CD-ROM drive and a sound card. And you always need more memory. By the time you're done, you're a thousand bucks poorer, and you have a desk full of fancy new equipment yoked to your incredibly slow 386.

To prevent this from happening to you, make a list of all the upgrades your current computer needs to make it what you want it to be. Add up the costs for the items, and then compare the total cost to what it would cost for a brand-spankin' new computer that has everything you want. Chances are, there won't be much difference. Buy a new computer (see Chapter 25), give your old computer to a charity, and take the tax deduction. You'll be happier in the long run.

Putting Off the Upgrade for As Long As Possible

If you're having a hard time parting with your old PC, you may be able to string it out for a year or so. That way, prices for more powerful computers will drop, making them more affordable. The following list provides some suggestions of how to wring more power out of your computer without spending much money on it:

➤ If you need more disk space, more memory, or a faster computer, I show you some ways to "optimize" your computer in Chapter 27. Check this out before you spend your money.

➤ If you want sound, instead of adding a sound board, you may be able to get by with a free program for Windows that allows your dinky computer speaker to make similar sounds. You can get the program from an online service or a local user group.

➤ If you need a fax modem, first consider how often you'll use it. If you send only one or two faxes a month, you might not need a fax modem. You can send a fax through most online services. It may cost a couple bucks per fax, and it's not as convenient, but it may suit your needs.

If these cheap fixes don't quite do it, you may have no choice but to buy a bag of ram chips, a new hard disk, or some other hardware. If that's the case, read on.

Safety Precautions for All Upgrades

Before you start poking around under the hood of your system unit, you should be aware of some safety precautions. Because so many delicate electrical components reside there, you have to be careful. Follow these standard precautions:

➤ Make sure all the parts of your computer are turned off.

➤ Before you start, touch a metal part of the system unit to discharge any static electricity from your body.

➤ Unplug the system unit.

➤ New computer parts usually come in antistatic bags. Before handling a part, touch a metal part of the system unit case to discharge static electricity from your body.

➤ Keep parts in their electrostatic bags (not on top of the bags) until you are ready to use them.

➤ Hold parts by their edges and mounting brackets. Avoid touching any components or solder on the parts.

➤ Never slide parts over your work surface. This can build up a static charge in the part.

➤ Keep plastic, vinyl, furs, and Styrofoam out of your work area. And don't rub your stocking feet over a vinyl carpet either.

➤ If your new toy arrives on a cold day, let it warm to room temperature before installing it. Any condensation on the new part could damage your system.

➤ If you drop a stray screw inside the system unit, stick some tape on a pencil eraser and try to fish out the screw; don't use your fingers.

Slapping in an Expansion Board

Nine out of ten upgrades require you to "install" an expansion board (also called a *card*). An expansion board is an integrated circuit board that plugs into the main circuit board (the *motherboard*) inside your system unit. An internal modem is an expansion board. A sound card is an expansion board. In some cases, you might even have to install a card to add a floppy drive, CD-ROM drive, or hard drive to your system.

The Tricky Part: Addresses and Interrupts

In case you haven't heard, Windows 95 has ushered in the era of plug-and-play expansion boards. You simply plug the expansion board into an expansion slot on the motherboard (see "Rock the Board in Place," next), boot up with Windows 95, and follow the on-screen instructions to set up your new device.

However, many expansion boards on the market do not conform to the rules of plug-and-play. With these types of boards, you have to make sure that the new board will not use the same settings as an existing board. Typically, there are three settings you need to worry about:

➤ **IRQ** stands for *interrupt request* and is a number that enables a device to demand attention from the central processing unit. If two devices have the same IRQ, they demand attention at the same time, confusing the CPU.

➤ **DMA Channel** is a path to your computer's RAM. Most computers have eight DMA channels. If two devices have the same DMA channel, usually only one device gains access to RAM. The other device simply won't work.

➤ **I/O port address** is a designation that allows a device to take in and output information at a certain location. As with IRQs and DMAs, if two devices use the same I/O setting, problems occur.

You change these settings on the expansion board by flipping tiny switches or by sliding jumpers over or off of wire posts on the card. The documentation that comes with the card shows how to position the switches or jumpers to change the interrupt, DMA channel, and I/O port setting for the card.

The trouble is that the average person doesn't know all the settings of the existing boards. The solution? Try installing the expansion board with the factory settings (don't change anything). If the board doesn't work, start flipping switches or rearranging the jumpers till you get a configuration that does work.

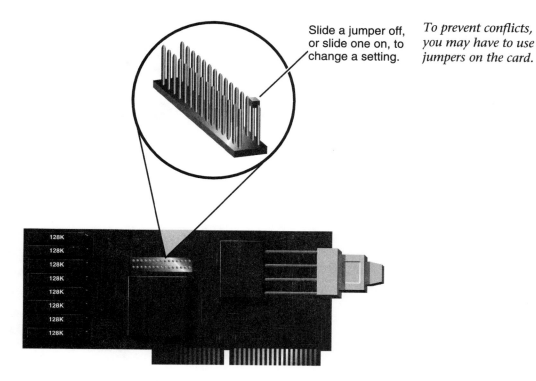

Slide a jumper off, or slide one on, to change a setting.

To prevent conflicts, you may have to use jumpers on the card.

Rock the Board in Place

To install an expansion board, first remove the system unit cover. The expansion slots are on the motherboard, near the back of the system unit (where your printer and monitor plug in). Find an expansion slot that matches the size of the board you need to plug in. If you're installing an expansion board that requires an external connection (such as an internal modem or sound card), remove the metal cover near the expansion slot, as shown in the next figure.

To install the expansion board, insert the contacts at the bottom of the board into one of the expansion slots, and then press down on the card while rocking it back and forth. Expect the fit to be snug, but don't push so hard that you crack the board. Make sure the board is seated securely in the socket, and that it is not leaning against any other boards. Secure the board in place using the screw you removed from the cover plate.

If the expansion board connects to something outside the system unit, remove the cover plate.

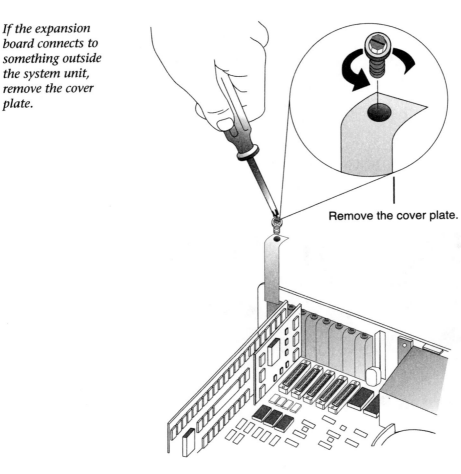

Remove the cover plate.

When you're done, don't replace the system unit cover. If the expansion board does not work, you will have to get inside the system unit again and play with the jumpers. Your computer will work fine with the cover off; just don't touch anything inside the computer when it's on.

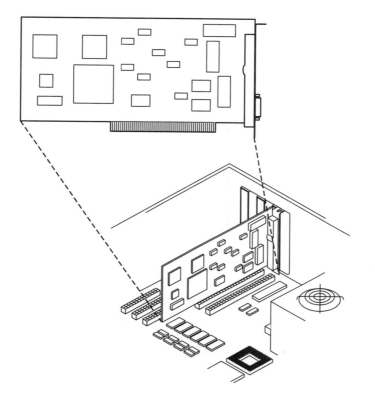

The expansion board slides into an expansion slot on the motherboard.

Run the Setup Program

Many expansion boards come with their own software (on disks) that you need to install. The software tells your computer how to work with the expansion board, and tells the expansion board how to do its job. Follow the instructions that came with your expansion board to run the setup or installation program.

Adding New Hardware in Windows 95

If you have Windows 95, after you connect a new piece of equipment to your computer, you can have the Add New Hardware Wizard search for it and set it up. The wizard takes care of all the complicated settings such as interrupts and I/O settings, to prevent the new device from interfering with the operation of any existing devices. To run the Add New Hardware Wizard, take the following steps:

1. Exit all running programs. This prevents you from losing any data in case Windows locks up during the process.

2. Click the **Start** button.

3. Move the mouse pointer over **Settings**, and then click **Control Panel**. The Control Panel window appears.

4. Double-click the **Add New Hardware** icon. The Add New Hardware Wizard appears, informing you about what the wizard will do.

5. Click the **Next** button. Wizard asks if you want it to search for new hardware on your system.

6. Make sure **Yes (Recommended)** is selected, and then click the **Next** button. If you know the type of hardware you want to install, you can select **No**, then skip ahead to the next section and select the item yourself (rather than having the wizard search for it.)

7. Click the **Next** button to have the Wizard search for new hardware. Wizard searches your computer for any new hardware that's installed. This takes a long time. Don't panic.

8. Wait until the detection process is complete (several minutes), and then click the **Finish** button. The wizard installs the new device. If the device conflicts with another device in your system, Windows displays a dialog box informing you of the conflict, and offering to help you resolve it.

9. Follow the on-screen instructions to complete the setup.

Cramming in the RAM

Just before Windows 95 hit the market, I bought a Gateway 75MHz Pentium computer with 8 megabytes of RAM. Eight megabytes! Eight megabytes was way more than I needed, but I figured I'd splurge. Six months later, when I was surfing the Internet and running my word processor with a couple other programs, my computer started to seem as sluggish as my old 386SX with 4MB RAM. Fortunately, Gateway had sent me a mouse pad with a 1-800 number to call for upgrades. I was on the phone, ordering another 8 megabytes of RAM for my "cutting edge" computer.

If you're facing the same predicament, you're probably wondering what it takes to install more memory. The following sections will help.

Shopping for the Right RAM Chips

Installing RAM isn't the hard part. The hard part is deciding which chips to buy. The easiest way to do this is to check the documentation or call the computer manufacturer. Chips differ with respect to three things:

Chip type: The *chip type* can be DIP (Dual In-line Package), SIP (Single In-line Package), or the more popular SIMM (Single In-line Memory Module). A SIMM is basically a small card that has a bunch (three or nine) DIPs plugged into it.

Capacity: Capacity is expressed in megabytes. RAM typically comes in units of 1, 2, 4, 8, or 16 megabytes. Check your computer's documentation or ask the dealer to find out the maximum capacity of the sockets into which you plug the memory. In most cases, you can't install just one SIMM; you have to install a pair of SIMMs (for example, two 4MB SIMMs) at a time. Computers typically come with four or more SIMM sockets into which you plug the new SIMMs. Some or all of the slots may be occupied by existing SIMMs.

The Great RAM Conspiracy

Manufacturers commonly trim costs by using low-capacity SIMMs in their machines. For example, they might occupy all four SIMM sockets with 2MB SIMMs instead of using two 4MB SIMMs and leaving two SIMM sockets open. This is bad for you, because if all the SIMM sockets are occupied, you have to remove the low-capacity SIMMs to make room for the higher capacity SIMMs. Some companies will buy back the low-capacity SIMMs, but you still lose out.

Speed: This is measured in nanoseconds (ns), and ranges from 50ns to 120ns. Don't mix chips of different speeds. If you're not sure what type of chips you need, ask at your local computer store or look in a catalogue. Most places have a chart that shows the type of RAM chip used in most of the popular computer brands.

Installing RAM

Once you have the additional memory, how do you install it? The answer is, "It depends." With most computers, you add memory by inserting SIMMs into the SIMM sockets. Other computers require a special memory board. The board contains the RAM chips. You insert the board into one of the expansion slots inside the system unit. To install SIMMs, take the following steps:

1. Turn off the computer, and remove the cover from the system unit.

2. Touch the system unit case to discharge any static electricity from your body. A small zap can damage the SIMM or other sensitive components.

3. Locate the SIMM sockets. Refer to your computer's documentation; these sockets can be anywhere on the mother board.

4. If you need to remove SIMMs, gently pull them from their sockets. Each SIMM socket may have two clips to hold the SIMM in place. You may have to gently pry them away from the SIMM as you lift.

5. Insert the new SIMMs into the empty sockets with a gentle rocking motion.

6. Replace the system unit cover.

Most computers automatically detect the new memory when you start the computer. Turn on the computer, and watch the monitor. It should show the total amount of memory in your computer. Other computers may require you to run a setup program. You can usually run this program by pressing a special key (such as F1) while your computer is booting, or by entering **setup** at the DOS prompt. Check your computer documentation to find out.

You can plug SIMMs directly into SIMM sockets on the motherboard.

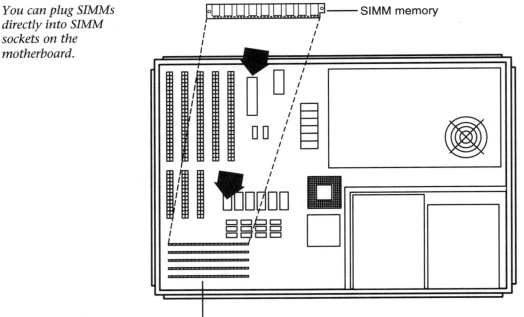

SIMM memory

RAM expansion slot

Some older computers require a special memory board. To install memory, you must plug a memory board into an expansion slot inside the system unit. For details on how to install an expansion board, see "Slapping in an Expansion Board" earlier in this chapter.

Replacing (or Adding) a Hard Drive

Before you run out and buy a new hard drive, you should ask yourself a few questions, such as if there is room in your computer for another hard drive. Look at the documentation or call the computer manufacturer, and find out the following information:

➤ Do you have an open drive bay? You can figure this out by opening the system unit and looking inside. Look for an opening around your existing floppy disk drive.

   If you don't have an open bay, you have two choices. You can purchase an external hard drive that connects to the system unit with a cable, or you can replace the current drive with one that stores more. No novice should attempt the second option; hire a qualified technician to replace the drive for you.

➤ Is the drive bay half-height or full-height? A full-height hard drive won't fit in a half-height bay, even if you use a crowbar.

➤ Do you need a hard drive controller card? If your current hard drive is connected with an IDE or SCSI (pronounced "scuzzy") cable, the cable should have another outlet into which you can plug in your new hard drive. If not, you may have to plug a controller card into an expansion slot, and then plug the drive into that board.

➤ What kind of hard drive do you need? Do you need a SCSI drive or IDE? If your current drive is an IDE drive, your new drive should be IDE, too.

➤ Does the power supply have an open outlet? Your hard drive needs electricity (from the power supply); most power supplies have several outlets. If yours doesn't have an extra outlet, you'll need an adapter that lets two devices plug into the same outlet.

➤ Does the new hard disk drive have a *cache* or *buffer*? The cache is built-in memory that stores often-used data electronically so the computer can get it quickly. The cache size should be anywhere from 64K to 256K, the more the better.

➤ Make sure the drive comes with the mounting brackets and cables you need.

The UPS guy shows up with your new hard drive, complete with cables and mounting bracket. Now what? Reread the safety precautions given earlier, and then take the following steps:

1. Pop the top off your system unit.

2. Attach the mounting bracket to the hard drive, and lay the drive inside the drive bay. Don't mount the drive to the bay just yet; you may have to jiggle things around to connect the cables.

3. If you need to install a hard drive controller board, skip back to the section called "Slapping in an Expansion Board," to find out what to do.

4. If you have an existing IDE or SCSI drive that has a data cable (a wide, flat cable, typically gray) with an open plug on it, plug it into the data outlet on the new drive. Otherwise, connect the hard drive to the hard drive controller board using the data cable that came with the drive.

5. Connect the hard drive to the power supply. (In most cases, you simply insert a plug from the power supply into the outlet on the hard drive.)

6. Now, secure the hard drive to the drive bay using the mounting screws, and replace the system unit cover.

Two IDE hard drives can use the same cable.

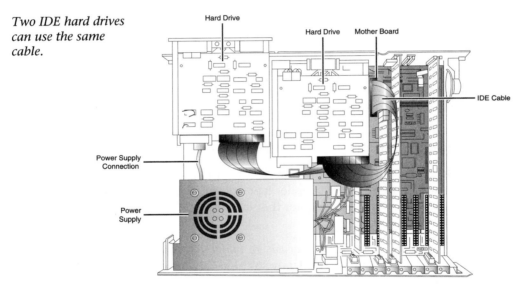

Now the hard drive is in your computer, but the computer doesn't know that. Run your computer's setup program (the procedure varies from one computer to another, so refer to your computer's documentation). You'll get a screen that lets you set up various devices. Select a drive that's marked as not installed (usually drive D or E), and enter settings for the drive as specified by the hard drive manufacturer.

You may also have to use the FDISK and FORMAT commands on the new drive. Check the documentation to be sure. When formatting, make sure you enter the FORMAT command with the letter of the new drive. If you use the letter of an existing drive, you'll destroy all the information on that drive.

Installing a CD-ROM or Floppy Drive

The procedure for installing a CD-ROM drive or another floppy disk drive is very similar to that of installing another hard drive. You must find an open drive bay and use mounting brackets to secure the drive inside the bay. You must then connect the drive to the motherboard or to a drive controller card, using a special cable, and plug the drive into the power supply.

Once you've installed a drive, you must run your computer's setup program (for a floppy drive), or install special software (for a CD-ROM drive).

> **Do You Have an Auto Detect Option?** If your setup program has an Auto Detect option for a drive, select it. You can then save the settings, exit the setup program, and restart your computer. Your computer will automatically find the new hard drive and enter the required hard drive settings for you.

> **Half-Height and Combo Drives**
>
> If you have a thin, space-saving computer, you may have only two drive bays. However, you may want to install three drives: a 3.5-inch floppy, a 5.25-inch floppy, and a CD-ROM drive. In such a case, you can purchase a dual floppy drive that includes both the 3.5-inch and 5.25-inch and fits into a single drive bay. You can then use the other drive bay for your CD-ROM drive.

Game Cards and Joysticks

Before you run out and buy a joystick and game card, spin your system unit around and look to see if you have a game port on the back. Some computers have a built-in game port. If you have a sound card, it may have a game port as well. In either case, you can buy a joystick and connect it to this port without having to purchase a game card. If you don't have a game port, you'll have to buy a game card and a joystick.

When shopping for a joystick, don't just look at the price tag. I bought a joystick for twenty bucks, but its movement was so jerky that I couldn't fly my warship for a nautical mile without crashing. Look for a joystick that uses both analog (for older games) and digital (for newer games) technology. In addition to providing greater control, digital joysticks calibrate themselves.

If your computer doesn't have a game port, first install the game card for your joystick. See "Slapping in an Expansion Board," earlier in this chapter for details. Turn off your computer. Then, simply plug your joystick into the game port.

Joining the Multimedia Madness

Calibrating a Joystick If your joystick doesn't work correctly, you may have to calibrate it. You can do this in most games that use the joystick. If you have Windows 95, double-click the **Joystick** icon in the Control Panel. In the dialog box that appears, click the **Calibrate** button and follow the on-screen instructions to calibrate your joystick.

If you had the foresight (and money) to buy a multimedia PC, complete with sound board and CD-ROM drive, you can skip this section on multimedia. For the less fortunate, before you start thinking about upgrading your computer, read "All-in-One: The Multimedia PC," in Chapter 25, to determine the latest minimum requirements for multimedia.

Once you know what you need, where do you get it? You have two options: buy a multimedia upgrade kit, or buy the components separately. The easiest option is to go with the kit. That way, you know that the CD-ROM drive and sound card will work together and that you'll get all the cables and software you'll need to get the system up and running. Most upgrade kits also include a small collection of CDs so you get immediate gratification. Creative Labs, IBM, and Sony offer upgrade kits for under $700.

To upgrade to multimedia, you basically install a CD-ROM drive and a sound card, as explained earlier in this chapter.

Lightning-Fast Video

Because Windows likes to do somersaults with graphics, your entire system works up a sweat trying to keep up. Standard video cards just aren't up to the task. To help, you can get a video accelerator or Windows accelerator card. The card should handle 1,024 by 768 resolution and 256 colors. It should have a 72Hz refresh rate and 1MB (2MB is better) video RAM (VRAM). Watch out for cards that have 70Hz or slower refresh rate; the slower refresh rate causes the image to flicker.

Yank your old video card out, plug the video accelerator board in the now open slot, and plug your monitor into the card. Most video accelerators also come with a disk that contain drivers, which tell the computer how to use the board. The process for installing these drivers varies depending on the manufacturer.

The Least You Need To Know

If this chapter merely whet your appetite for upgrade information, you can purchase another book called *The Complete Idiot's Guide to Upgrading PCs* that contains scads of information about upgrading. If, however, the detail I provided was overwhelming, here's a boiled-down version:

➤ If upgrading your current computer is going to cost almost as much as buying a new one, buy a new one.

➤ Handle expansion boards by their edges and mounting bracket. Avoid touching any of the electronic components on the board.

➤ When shopping for RAM, make sure the RAM chips you get are the type, capacity, and speed that your computer can use.

➤ When shopping for a joystick, make sure your system unit has a game port, or you must purchase a game card, as well.

➤ Multimedia upgrade kits come with a CD-ROM drive and sound card that work together. These kits may also include CDs.

Chapter 27

Optimizing Your Computer

By the End of This Chapter, You'll Be Able To:

➤ Remove programs from your hard drive

➤ Remove Windows features that you don't use

➤ Double your hard disk storage for free

➤ Give your programs more memory without installing more RAM

➤ Make your CD-ROM drive run faster in Windows 95

Your computer is like a car. You might be able to use it without ever tuning it up or changing the oil, but it probably won't last as long or run as well. In this chapter, you will learn some basic computer maintenance that will help keep your computer running trouble-free and at peak performance.

If you don't feel comfortable with some of the performance-boosting tips covered in this chapter, just skip them. The tips aren't mandatory, but they will help you squeeze the maximum performance out of your PC.

Uninstalling Programs That You Don't Use

Check This Out...

Removing DOS Programs DOS programs are easy to remove. Simply delete the program's directory and all the files in it. You can do this in File Manager, Windows Explorer, or with the DELTREE command at the DOS prompt. See Chapter 20, "Making and Deleting Directories (or Folders)," for details.

When you buy a new computer, it seems as though it has an endless supply of hard disk space. A 540 megabyte hard drive seems big until you install a few programs that take up 80 megabytes each. It's easy to stick programs on your hard drive. You install the program, use it for a few months, lose interest, and find a new program to install. Pretty soon, your disk is full.

It's tempting to just delete the folder that contains the program's files. That gets rid of the program, right? Well, not entirely, especially if the program you're trying to get rid of is a Windows program. When you install a Windows program, it commonly installs files not only to the program's folder, but also to WINDOWS, WINDOWS\ SYSTEM, and other folders. The following sections explain how to uninstall a program to remove it entirely.

Remove Windows 95 Programs

When you install a program that's designed to work under Windows 95, it typically adds its name to a list of programs you can remove (however, not all Windows 95 programs do this). If you have a Windows 95 program that is on the list of programs you can uninstall, or if you're not sure, take the following steps:

1. Click the **Start** button.

2. Rest the mouse pointer on **Settings** and then click **Control Panel**. The Control Panel window appears.

3. Double-click the **Add/Remove Programs** icon. The Add/Remove Programs Properties dialog box appears.

4. Click the **Install/Uninstall** tab, if it is not already selected. At the bottom of the screen is a list of programs you can have Windows uninstall.

5. Click the name of the program you want to remove.

6. Click the **Remove** button. A series of dialog boxes will lead you through the uninstall process, asking for your confirmation.

7. Follow the on-screen instructions to complete the process.

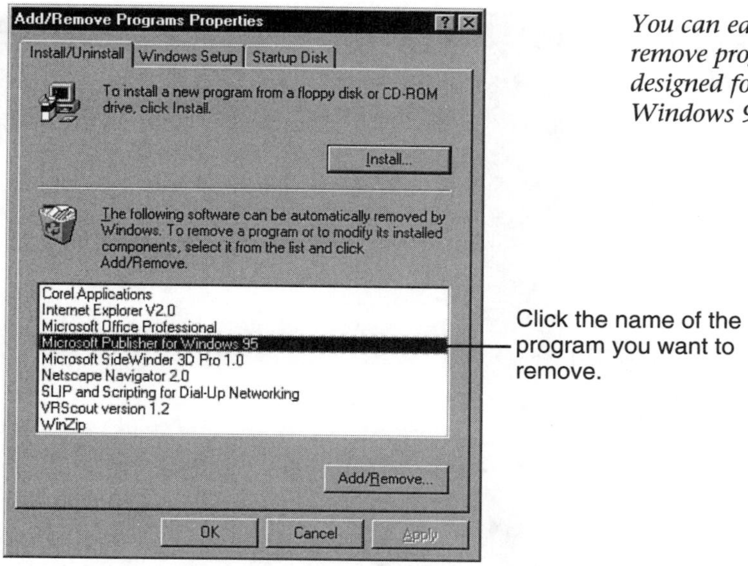

You can easily remove programs designed for Windows 95.

Click the name of the program you want to remove.

Uninstall a Program Using Its Setup Utility

If you don't have Windows 95, or if the name of the program you want to install doesn't appear in the list of programs you can remove, you may be able to use the program's own setup utility to remove the program. Take one of the following steps:

➤ In Windows 95, use My Computer or Windows Explorer to display the contents of the folder for the program you want to remove. If you see a **Setup** or **Install** icon, double-click it, and follow the on-screen instructions to remove the program.

➤ In Windows 3.1, open the program's program-group window. If you see a **Setup** or **Install** icon, double-click it, and follow the instructions to remove the program.

If you don't see a Setup or Install button, the best thing to do is to obtain a program that's designed especially to help you remove other programs from your hard drive. Uninstaller and Clean Sweep are two of the more popular programs. The other option is to remove the program manually, as explained in the following section.

331

Many programs have their own Setup utilities that let you remove the programs.

You can remove the entire program or parts of it.

Remove Programs Manually (Only If You Must)

If you have a Windows program that can't uninstall itself, you can remove it by deleting its directory (or folder). However, deleting the program's files leaves a lot of other garbage that you have to clean up. After deleting the program's directory or folder, take the following steps to remove anything the program left behind:

➤ In Windows 95, the program's name will still appear on the Start, Program menu. To remove the program, right-click on a blank area of the taskbar, and click **Properties**. Click the **Start Menu Programs** tab, click the **Remove** button, and use the dialog box that appears to remove the program from the Start menu.

➤ In Windows 3.1, go to the Program Manager, and reduce the program's group window to an icon. Press the **Delete** key, and then click **Yes** to confirm the deletion.

When you install a program, the installation utility usually edits the Windows startup files (WIN.INI and SYSTEM.INI) for you, adding commands to help the program run efficiently. You should delete any command lines that refer to the program or its directory. Take the following steps:

1. Copy **WIN.INI** and **SYSTEM.INI** from the WINDOWS directory (or folder) to another directory on your hard disk. (If you run into problems after editing these files, you can copy the originals back to the WINDOWS directory.)

2. Take one of the following steps to run System Editor:

   In Windows 95, open the **Start** menu, click **Run**, type **sysedit**, and click **OK**.

   In Windows 3.1, open Program Manager's **File** menu, click **Run**, type **sysedit**, and click **OK**.

3. Change to the **SYSTEM.INI** window, and delete any text lines that refer to the program or its directory. (You can use the Search/Find option to help you find specific text.)

   Caution: Delete only those lines that refer specifically to the program you removed. If you delete lines that other programs use, you may not be able to run those programs.

4. When you are done editing SYSTEM.INI, open the **File** menu and select **Save** to save your changes.

5. Repeat steps 3 and 4 for the WIN.INI file.

6. Open the **File** menu, and select **Exit**.

7. Exit Windows and restart it.

Remove Windows Features You Don't Use

When you (or the manufacturer) installed Windows, you probably chose to do a complete installation. This installs all the fonts, accessories, and games that come with Windows. However, if you're strapped for disk space, you might want to consider removing the parts of Windows you don't use.

In Windows, 95, you can easily remove Windows components. Double-click **My Computer**, double-click the **Control Panel** icon, double-click the **Add/Remove Programs** icon, and click the **Windows Setup** tab. A list of all the components that make up Windows appears. To remove a component entirely, click its check box to remove the check mark. To remove only some parts of a component, double-click the component's name. This displays a list of items that make up the component; click a check box to add or remove a check mark. When you're done, click **OK** and follow the on-screen instructions.

Windows 95 lets you remove some of its components.

If no check mark appears, Windows will remove the component.

Click a check box to add or remove a check mark.

Add/Remove Programs Properties

Install/Uninstall | Windows Setup | Startup Disk

To add or remove a component, click the check box. A shaded box means that only part of the component will be installed. To see what's included in a component, click Details.

Components:

☐ Accessibility Options	0.0 MB
☑ Accessories	3.5 MB
☑ Communications	1.4 MB
☑ Disk Tools	1.1 MB
☑ Microsoft Exchange	4.5 MB

Space required: 0.3 MB
Space available on disk: 114.5 MB

Description
Includes options to change keyboard, sound, display, and mouse behavior for people with mobility, hearing and visual impairments.

0 of 1 components selected | Details...

Have Disk...

OK | Cancel | Apply

Windows 3.1 also allows you to remove some of its components. Open the **Main** group window, and double-click the **Windows Setup** icon. Open the **Options** menu, and click on **Add/Remove Windows Components**. A dialog box appears, showing the names of the components that make up Windows. To remove an entire component, click its check box to remove the X. To remove parts of a component, click the **Files** button next to it, and use the dialog box that appears to deselect files you want to remove. When you're done, click **OK** and follow the on-screen instructions.

Remove Useless Files from Your Hard Disk

Your hard disk probably contains temporary and backup files that your programs create without telling you. These files can quickly clutter your hard disk drive, taking room that you need for new programs or new data files you create. The following sections explain how to quickly find and remove these files in Windows 3.1 and Windows 95.

Check This Out...

Deleting Backup Files

When you save a file you created, most programs create a backup file that contains the previous version of the file. If you mess up a file, you can open the backup file instead. Before deleting backup files, make sure that you don't want the previous versions of your files.

Deleting Temporary and Backup Files in Windows 95

To find temporary files in Windows 95, open the **Start** menu, point to **Find**, and click **Files** or **Folders**. In the Named text box, type ***.tmp**, and then click the **Find Now** button. Wait until Windows is done finding all the temporary (.TMP) files. Open the **Edit** menu, and click **Select All**. Press the **Delete** key, answer a few confirmation messages, and the files are gone. (Remember to empty the Recycle Bin to permanently remove the files.)

Repeat the same steps to find and delete backup files. However, instead of typing ***.tmp** in the Named text box, type ***.bak**. Most programs give their backup files the extension *.BAK.

Delete Temporary and Backup Files in Windows 3.1

In Windows 3.1, use File Manager to locate temporary files. Open File Manager's **File** menu, and click **Search**. In the **Search For** text box, type ***.tmp**. In the **Start From** text box, type **c:**. Make sure **Search All Subdirectories** is selected. Click **OK**. When Windows is done searching, it displays a window showing the names of all the files it found. Open the **File** menu, and click **Select Files**. In the dialog box that appears, click the **Select** button and then click **Close**. This selects all the temporary files. Now, open the **File** menu, select **Delete**, and respond to the confirmation warnings.

Repeat the steps to find and delete backup files. However, instead of typing ***.tmp** in the Search For text box, type ***.bak**.

Speeding Up Your Hard Drive

Whenever you delete a file from your hard disk, you leave a space where another file can be stored. When you save a file, your computer stores as much of the file as possible in that empty space, and the rest of the file in other empty spaces. The file is then said to be *fragmented*, because its parts are stored in different locations on the disk.

File fragmentation is a natural process that occurs as you delete files, install programs, and create new files. However, when a large percentage (ten percent or more) of your files becomes fragmented, your hard drive has to work harder to read all the file parts scattered around the disk. It's also more likely that the file will be lost or damaged.

> **Check This Out...**
>
> **Caution** If you have Windows 95, never use the DOS Defragmenter program. It can't handle the long file names that Windows 95 allows for. It might also destroy some of your files. Use only the Disk Defragmenter that comes with Windows 95.

Every month or so, you should run a defragmentation program to determine the fragmentation percent and to defragment your files, if necessary. The following sections explain how to run Disk Defragmenter (in Windows 95), and Defragmenter (which comes with DOS version 6.0 and later).

Defragmenting Files in Windows 95

Windows 95's Disk Defragmenter performs a complete defragmentation operation. That is, Defragmenter shuffles the file pieces around to place each file's parts in one place, and then moves all the files to one section of the disk, so any files you save in the future will not be fragmented. To defragment your files in this way, take the following steps:

1. Click the **Start** button to open the Start menu.

2. Move the mouse pointer over **Programs**, and then over **Accessories**.

3. Move the mouse pointer over **System Tools**, and then click **Disk Defragmenter**. A dialog box appears, asking which disk drive you want to defragment.

4. Open the **Which drive do you want to defragment?** drop-down list, and click the desired drive. You can defragment all your disks by clicking **All Hard Drives**. (There's no need to defragment floppy disks.)

You can defragment any of your disks.

Click the drive you want to defragment.

5. Click **OK**. Another dialog box appears, indicating the percent of file fragmentation on the disk, and telling you whether or not you need to defragment the disk.

6. Click the **Start** button. Defragmenter starts to defragment the files on the disk.

7. Wait until the defragmentation is complete. It's best to leave your computer alone during the process; don't run any programs or play any computer games.

You may have noticed that the dialog box that appears after you select the drive you want to defragment has an Advanced button. You can click this button to specify how you want Defragmenter to proceed:

➤ **Full defragmentation** is the default setting. With this option on, Defragmenter defragments existing files and consolidates free space to prevent future fragmentation.

➤ **Defragment files only** places all the pieces of each file together but leaves the files scattered over the disk. Because the disk's free space is also scattered around the disk, this option promotes future fragmentation.

➤ **Consolidate free space only** does not defragment the files. It does consolidate the free space, so to reduce further file fragmentation.

➤ **Check drive for errors** tells Defragmenter to check the drive for any lost or missing file pieces or directories before continuing. If Defragmenter finds a problem on a disk, it will prompt you to run ScanDisk to correct the problem before proceeding. (See "Fixing Common Disk Problems with ScanDisk," later in this chapter.)

Defragmenting Without Windows 95

If you don't have Windows 95, use the DOS Defragmenter. If you're using Windows 3.1, exit Windows before running Defragmenter. Windows might interfere with Defragmenter. Then, take the following steps to defragment your hard disk:

1. At the DOS prompt, type **defrag** and press **Enter**. Defragmenter starts and displays a dialog box, asking you to select a drive.

2. Click the letter of the drive you want to defragment, and then click **OK**. Defragmenter checks the disk and displays a dialog box suggesting the defragmentation technique you should use.

3. To use the recommended defragmentation technique, click the **Optimize** button. To change the defragmentation technique, click **Configure**, and pick the desired technique.

4. Wait until Defragmenter displays a dialog box indicating that the process is complete, and then click **OK** button. A dialog box appears, asking if you want to defragment another disk.

5. Click **Exit DEFRAG**.

Fixing Common Disk Problems with ScanDisk

If you have Windows 95 or DOS 6.2 (or later), you have a program called ScanDisk that can test a disk (hard or floppy), and repair most problems on a disk. What kind of problems? ScanDisk can find defective areas on a disk and block them out to prevent your computer from using defective storage areas. ScanDisk can also find and delete misplaced file fragments that may be causing your computer to crash.

You should run ScanDisk regularly (at least once every month) and whenever your computer seems to be acting up (crashing for no apparent reason). Also, if you have a floppy disk that your computer cannot read, ScanDisk may be able to repair the disk and recover any data from it.

To run ScanDisk in Windows 95, click the **Start** button, point to **Programs, Accessories,** and **System Tools;** then click **ScanDisk.** The ScanDisk window appears. Click the letter of the drive you want to check. To check for and repair only file and folder errors, click the **Standard** option; to check the disk for defects (in addition to file and folder errors), click **Thorough.** If you want ScanDisk to fix any errors without asking for your confirmation, make sure there is a check mark next to **Automatically fix errors.** Click the **Start** button.

ScanDisk can repair most disk problems.

Pick the disk you want to fix.

Select Thorough, if you want ScanDisk to test the surface of the disk.

Make sure this option is on if you want ScanDisk to fix problems without asking you.

If you don't have Windows 95, but you do have DOS 6.2, exit all programs (including Windows 3.1) before running ScanDisk. Otherwise, ScanDisk will only be able to check for errors, not repair them. At the DOS prompt, type **scandisk** and press **Enter.** Follow the on-screen instructions to check and repair a disk.

Fixing Disks with DOS 6.0 and Earlier

If you have a version of DOS before version 6.2, you don't have ScanDisk. However, you do have a program called CheckDisk that can repair file and directory problems. At the DOS prompt, type **chkdsk /f** and press **Enter.**

Doubling Your Disk Space with DriveSpace

If you're running out of disk space, and you don't want to go through the trouble of installing another hard drive, consider using a disk compression program. Such a program doesn't actually compress the disk; it compresses the files on the disk. Most compression programs can shrink a file's size over 50 percent, doubling your drive space. If you compress a 250 megabyte drive, you'll end up with over 500 megabytes of drive space!

Windows 95 comes with a disk compression program called DriveSpace. To run it, click the **Start** button, point to **Programs**, **Accessories**, and **System Tools**; then click **DriveSpace**. Click the letter of the drive you want to compress. Open the **Drive** menu and select **Compress**. In the Compress a Drive dialog box, click the **Start** button. Another dialog box appears, asking for your confirmation; click the **Compress Now** button. Wait until the compression operation is complete; depending on the size of your hard disk, this can take several hours.

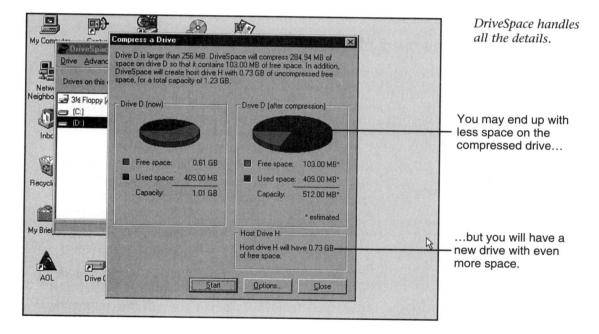

DriveSpace handles all the details.

You may end up with less space on the compressed drive...

...but you will have a new drive with even more space.

If you have DOS 6.2 or later, you can run DriveSpace from the DOS prompt. However, if you have Windows 95, DO NOT run the DOS version of DriveSpace. The DOS version cannot handle long file names; if you run it, you'll end up renaming several Windows folders and files, incapacitating Windows 95. To run DriveSpace from the DOS prompt, type **drvspace c:** (where c: is the letter of the drive you want to compress), and press **Enter**. Follow the on-screen instructions to complete the operation.

Making the Most of Your Computer's Memory

Your computer can't do anything without memory. And it can't do anything very well or very quickly if it doesn't have enough memory. There are two ways to wring more memory out of your system. One is to free up memory that your computer reserves for devices that you're not using. The other way is to use disk space as memory. The following sections explain both ways to get more memory.

Pre-DOS 6.2 Disk Compression

If you have DOS 6.0 or 6.1, you have DriveSpace, but it's called DoubleSpace. To run it, exit all your other programs, type **dblspace c:** and press **Enter**. Follow the instructions to complete the operation. Again, don't run DoubleSpace if you have Windows 95.

Make Use of Reserved Memory

All computers, even the old ones, have at least 1 megabyte of memory (RAM). 640 kilobytes of that 1 megabyte is called *conventional* memory, the main memory that your programs use. The other 384 kilobytes make up what is called *upper* memory. This memory is typically reserved for DOS itself and for other sets of instructions that your system needs to operate.

Undoing MemMaker's Changes If your system doesn't run properly after you run MemMaker, go to the DOS prompt, type **memmaker / undo** and press **Enter**. MemMaker restores your original startup files and restarts your computer.

However, this 384 kilobytes is more than what is needed, so, DOS versions 5.0 and later started using upper memory for device drivers (such as the instructions that tell your mouse and monitor how to operate). By loading these instructions into upper memory (instead of into conventional memory), DOS can make more conventional memory available to your programs.

DOS versions 6.0 and later come with a program called MemMaker that can automatically edit the commands in your startup files, so your computer will take advantage of upper memory. Simply exit any programs you're running (including Windows). Type **memmaker** at the DOS prompt, and press **Enter**. Follow the on-screen instructions (select **Express Setup** to avoid complications). At the end of the process, MemMaker shows how much conventional memory you've reclaimed for your programs.

Give Your Computer More (Virtual) Memory

Windows 3.1 and Windows 95 can use space on your hard disk as memory (*virtual memory*). Although virtual memory is slower than real memory, it can help you avoid getting **Insufficient Memory** error messages when you try to load large programs or run several programs at one time.

If you have about 20 megabytes of free space on your hard drive, first, defragment your drive using the full defragmentation option, as explained earlier in this chapter. Then, try setting up a permanent swap file. Permanent swap files work faster, because Windows doesn't have to poke around on the disk to find data.

In Windows 95, you don't have to do too much with the swap file. Windows 95 manages the swap file just fine and uses any free space on the disk as memory. When Windows needs more memory, it increases the swap file size. When it needs less memory, it decreases the size of the swap file. To make sure that Windows is in control of the swap file, open the **Control Panel**, and double-click the **System** icon. Click the **Performance** tab, and click the **Virtual Memory** button. Make sure to select **Let Windows manage my virtual memory settings**.

Make sure Windows is managing the virtual memory.

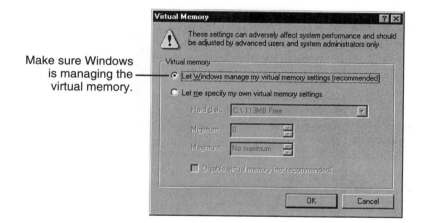

Windows 95 does a fine job of managing the virtual memory.

Speeding Up Your CD-ROM Drive and Hard Drive in Windows 95

Although your computer's hard drive and CD-ROM drive are good at storing data permanently, they are slow compared to RAM. To help increase their speed, Windows 95 lets you use a read-ahead buffer. Windows reads data off the hard drive or CD and stores it in memory before that data is actually needed. When Windows needs the data, Windows can then access it quickly from RAM.

Check This Out...

Insufficient Memory Still?!

If you run out of memory in Windows 95, you're probably low on disk space. The first thing to do when this happens is empty the Recycle Bin. If that doesn't give you the disk space you need, you'll have to remove programs and files from your disk, and/or use DriveSpace to compress your disk, as instructed earlier in this chapter.

To increase the read-ahead buffer for your hard drive or CD-ROM drive, open the **Control Panel**, double-click the **System** icon, click on the **Performance** tab, and click on the **File System** button. Click the **Hard Disk** tab, and drag the Read-ahead optimization slider to **Full**.

Click the **CD-ROM** tab. Open the **Optimize access pattern for** drop-down list, and click the speed of your CD-ROM drive. Drag the **Supplemental cache size slider** to the desired setting: increase the cache size if you frequently use the CD-ROM drive, or decrease the cache size if you rarely use it. Click **OK** when you're done.

You can use a read-ahead cache to increase the speed of your CD-ROM drive or hard drive.

File System Properties

Hard Disk | CD-ROM | Troubleshooting

Windows uses these settings for performance optimization when a CD-ROM drive is attached to your computer.

Settings

Supplemental cache size: Small [——————] Large

Optimize access pattern for: [Quad-speed or higher ▾]

Windows will use 1238 kilobytes of physical memory to perform these optimizations while data is being accessed.

[OK] [Cancel] [Apply]

Select the speed of your CD-ROM drive.

Use this slider to set the cache size.

Windows displays the cache size here.

The Least You Need To Know

As you can see, you can do a lot to keep your computer cleaned and tuned. However, if you like to do as little as necessary to keep your computer in shape, make sure you do the following regularly:

➤ Vacuum your work area monthly.

➤ Wipe your monitor with a damp cloth whenever it appears dusty.

➤ Extract fur balls from your mouse when the pointer starts to skip around the screen.

➤ Run ChkDsk or ScanDisk monthly.

➤ Run Defrag every month or two.

 WHOOPS

Chapter 28

Do-It-Yourself Fixes to Common Ailments

By the End of This Chapter, You'll Be Able To:

➤ Figure out what to do in a crisis (and what not to do)

➤ Sniff out the cause of a problem

➤ Make sense out of at least five DOS error messages

➤ Bring your mouse pointer out of hiding

➤ Get your keyboard back to normal when it flips out

Computers are fickle. You might use your computer all week without a problem. Then, on Friday, you try to run a program you've been using all week, and the following message appears on-screen:

    Bad command or filename

Or you try to print a file, and the file won't print. The printer is on, it has paper in it, and everything else seems to be okay. But no matter what you do, the printer won't print the file.

What should you do? In this chapter, you will learn how to react in a crisis and how to solve your own computer woes. Although I can't cover every problem, I will cover many common ones and give you some strategies for solving problems that aren't covered here.

Troubleshooting Tactics: Solving Your Own Problems

With a little patience, you can solve most of your own problems. You just have to know how to go about it—what to do and what not to do. The overall approach is twofold: you need to trace the problem to its cause, and not make the problem worse than it already is.

When you run into a problem that doesn't have an obvious solution, the best course of action is inaction; that is, don't do anything. If you're fidgety to do something, take a walk or watch Oprah. Then come back and try some of the following tactics.

Look for Clues

The answer to most problems is probably staring you in the face. So, the first thing you should do is look at the monitor for any messages that indicate a problem. Although on-screen messages are usually very general, they provide a starting point. If you don't see anything on screen, start asking yourself some questions.

> **Is everything plugged in and turned on?** If a part of your computer is dead—no lights, no sound, no action—it probably isn't connected or isn't turned on. Turn everything off and check the connections. Don't assume that just because something looks connected that it is; wiggle the plugs.

> **When did the problem start?** Think back to what you did before the problem arose. Did you install a new program? Did you enter a command? Did you add a new device? Recently, my sound card stopped working. I realized that the problem started after I installed a new hard drive. I had apparently knocked a tiny jumper off the sound card during the hard drive installation.

> **Is the problem limited to one program?** If you have the same problem in every program, the problem is probably caused by your computer. If the problem occurs in only one program, it is probably caused by the program.

> **When did you have the file last?** If you lost a file, it probably did *not* get sucked into a black hole. It is probably somewhere on your disk, in a separate directory. Use the **Search** menu in File Manager, or open the **Start** menu and select **Find** in Windows 95, and search for the file.

Check This Out...

Check the Obvious Many problems have quick solutions. Maybe the printer's not turned on, or a cable's loose or disconnected, or maybe you are looking for a file in the wrong directory. Sometimes you need to look away from a problem in order to see it.

It's Probably Not the Computer

Most novice computer users (and some experienced users) automatically assume that whenever a problem arises, the computer is on the blink. Although the computer itself can be the cause of some major problems, it is rarely the cause of minor, everyday problems. The problem is usually in the software: DOS, Windows, or one of your applications.

It's Probably Not a Virus

It's easy to blame a computer problem on some evil computer virus. However, 95 percent of the problems that people blame on computer viruses are actually bugs in the software, or problems with specific devices. Work on the assumption that the problem you're having is not caused by a virus.

My Computer Won't Boot

A computer is a lot like a car; the most frustrating thing that can happen is that you can't even get the engine to turn over. To solve the problem, consider these questions:

Is the computer on? Are the lights on the computer lit? If so, the computer is plugged in and is on, and make sure the power switch on the system unit is turned on.

Is the screen completely blank? Even though the screen is completely blank, the computer may have booted; you just can't see it. If you heard the computer beep and you saw the drive lights go on and off, the computer probably booted fine. Make sure the monitor is turned on and the brightness controls are turned up.

Is there a disk in drive A? If you see a message on-screen that says **Non-system disk or disk error**, you probably left a floppy disk in drive A. Remove the disk and press any key to boot from the hard disk.

Can you boot from a floppy disk? If you still can't get your computer to boot from the hard disk, try booting from a bootable floppy disk. Insert the bootable floppy disk in drive A, close the drive door, and press **Ctrl+Alt+Del**. If you can boot from a floppy, the problem is on your hard disk. You'll need some expert help to get out of this mess.

My Computer Keeps Locking Up in Windows

If you're computer keeps freezing (you can't move the mouse pointer, enter commands, or even exit your programs), press **Ctrl+Alt+Del**. A dialog box should appear, showing

345

you the names of the active programs, and allowing you to exit the program that's not responding. If you press **Ctrl+Alt+Del**, and you don't receive that dialog box, you'll have to reboot by pressing **Ctrl+Alt+Del** again or pressing the **Reset** button.

If your Windows freezes up again after you reboot, there may be an errant file fragment that's causing the problem. You can usually fix the problem by running ScanDisk. See "Fixing Common Disk Problems with ScanDisk," in Chapter 27.

If ScanDisk doesn't fix the problem, Windows might be having a problem with the mouse driver (the instructions that tell Windows how to use your mouse). Instead of using the special driver that came with your mouse, try using one of the standard drivers that comes with Windows:

➤ In Windows 95, open the **Control Panel**, and then double-click the **Mouse** icon. Click the **General** tab, and then click the **Change** button. Select one of the standard mouse types, and click **OK**.

➤ In Windows 3.1, open the Main group window, and double-click the **Windows Setup** icon. Open the **Options** menu, and select **Change System Settings**. Open the **Mouse** drop-down list, and select one of the standard (Microsoft) mouse drivers.

Mouse drivers commonly cause problems.

Select a standard mouse type.

If you're still having problems, there may be a bug in the program you're trying to run. Call the program's tech support number, and explain the problem. The company may have fixed the problem already. They can probably send you an updated program.

My Screen Is Flickering

If your screen is flickering or turning odd colors, the plug that connects the monitor to the system unit has probably come loose. Turn everything off, and then check the connection. If the plug has screws that secure it to the system unit, tighten the screws.

Magnetic fields (from speakers, phones, and other sources) can also cause your screen to freak out. You may see a band of color along one edge of the screen. Move any electrical appliances away from your monitor. In a day or so, the problem should fix itself.

I Can't Get the Program to Run

You get a new program, install it, and enter the command to run the program. The following message appears on-screen: **Bad command or file name.** What's wrong?

Are you in the drive and directory where the program's files are stored? Some programs install themselves and set up your system so you can run the program from any drive or directory. With other programs, you must change to the drive and directory that contains the program's files in order to run the program. This won't happen in Windows.

Did you type the correct command? The command must be typed exactly as specified in the documentation. If you mistype the command, the program won't run. Try retyping the command.

Did you install the program correctly? Installing some programs consists of merely copying the program's files to a directory on your hard disk. With other programs, you must run an installation program. If the program requires you to run an installation program, and you did not, the program probably won't run.

Is it a Windows program? You cannot run a Windows program from the DOS prompt. Run Windows first, and then try running the program.

I Have a Mouse, But I Can't Find the Pointer On-Screen

Once you get your mouse working, you will probably never have to mess with it again. The hard part is getting the mouse to work in the first place. If you connected a mouse to your computer and you don't see the mouse pointer on-screen, there are a few possibilities you should investigate:

Am I in a program that uses a mouse? Some old programs don't *support* a mouse, so you won't see the mouse pointer in these programs. For example, you won't see a mouse pointer at the DOS prompt. Run a program that you know uses a mouse to see if it works there.

Check This Out...

Record Your Changes It's a good idea to always write down changes you make to your system. It takes a little extra time, but it enables you to retrace your steps later.

Is the mouse pointer hidden? Mouse pointers like to hide in the corners or edges of your screen. Roll the mouse on your desktop to see if you can bring the pointer into view.

When you connected the mouse, did you install a mouse driver? Connecting a mouse to your computer is not enough. You must install a program (called a *mouse driver*) that tells the computer how to use the mouse. Follow the instructions that came with the mouse to figure out how to install the program.

When you installed the mouse program, did you specify a COM port? When you install a mouse program, the program may ask you if the mouse is connected to COM1, COM2, or COM3, the serial ports on your computer. Give the wrong answer, and your computer won't be able to find your mouse. Run the installation or setup program again and select a different COM port. Reboot after each change, and write down every change you make.

My Mouse Pointer Is Jumpy

If your mouse pointer jumps around the screen rather than moving smoothly, your mouse may have fur balls. First, exit any programs, and turn off your computer. Flip the mouse over on its back, remove the ball cover, and remove the ball. Wipe the ball with a paper towel dipped in window cleaner or rubbing alcohol. Inside the mouse are some rollers. Gently pick any dust balls out of the sides of the rollers (a toothpick works well). If you see a ring around the center of a roller, pick it off, too (try rubbing the rings off with a pencil eraser). Make sure the mouse ball is dry before you reassemble the mouse.

I Can't Get My Modem to Work

You're not the only one. Every minute of every day, someone in the world has trouble with a modem connection. Usually, the problem occurs in Windows. Some evil wizard enters the computer and messes things up. Whatever the problem, the following questions may help you resolve it:

➤ **Is the modem plugged in and turned on?** If you have an external modem, it must be plugged into a power source, to the system unit, and to a phone line, and it must be turned on.

➤ **Is the phone working?** You can check a phone jack by plugging a regular phone into the jack. Lift the phone off the hook and listen for a dial tone. If you don't hear a dial tone, the jack is dead, and your modem won't be able to dial out.

➤ **Am I dialing the wrong number?** Silly question, but it's a common cause. If you hear an angry voice coming out of the modem, you probably woke somebody up. Hopefully, he don't have Caller ID. Also, if you normally have to dial a number before dialing out (say 9), type the number, a comma, and then the phone number.

➤ **Do I have pulse or tone service?** Pick up your phone and dial a few numbers. If you hear clicks, you have pulse (or rotary) service, even if you have a phone with buttons. If you hear beeps, you have tone service. If your telecommunications program is set for tone service, and you have rotary service, it won't be able to dial out. Try resetting your telecommunications program for rotary service; it's usually as easy as checking an option box.

➤ **Does my program know where the modem is?** Most computers have two COM ports. Usually, a mouse is connected to COM1, and COM2 is left open for another device, often a modem. Your communications program or online service program allows you to specify the COM port being used by your modem. Try changing the COM port setting.

➤ **Are my communications settings correct?** If your communications program can find your modem, dial a number, and establish a connection, but can do nothing else, your communications settings are probably incorrect. If your baud setting is 9,600 bps or higher, try changing it to 2,400. If the modem works with one program but not with another, write down the communications settings from the program that works, and then use those same settings for the program that doesn't work.

➤ **Do you see On-screen garbage?** First, check the baud rate setting in your communications program. Make sure the setting matches the fastest setting that both your modem and the service provider can handle. Next, check the terminal emulation to make sure it conforms to the emulation required by the computer you're calling.

➤ **Are lines of text displayed twice?** Both your computer and the remote computer are echoing back what you type. Try turning Local Echo off, so your computer will stop echoing echoing.

➤ **Is What you type invisible?** Try turning Local Echo on.

If you have Windows 95, it can help you track down stubborn modem problems. Click the **Start** button, and click **Help**. Click the **Index** tab, and type **modems**. Under modems, double-click **troubleshooting**. This displays the modem troubleshooter, an on-screen tech support tool that asks you a series of questions to help you get your modem up and running.

Windows 95 comes with a modem troubleshooter.

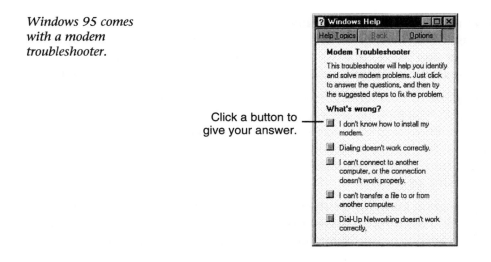

Click a button to give your answer.

The Computer Won't Read My Floppy Disk

Don't feel bad; it happens to everyone. You stick a floppy disk in the disk drive, close the drive door, change to the drive, and you get an error message saying basically that the disk is no good. Your computer can't read it or write to it or even see that it's there. What happened? That depends.

➤ **Is the disk inserted properly?** Even the most experienced computer user occasionally inserts a disk upside-down or sideways into the disk drive. Check to make sure the disk is in the right slot the right way.

➤ **Is the disk drive door closed?** If the drive has a door, it must be closed. Otherwise, you'll get an error message saying that your computer can't read or write to the disk.

➤ **Is the disk write-protected?** If the disk is write-protected, you won't be able to save a file to the disk. For a 3.5-inch disk, slide the write-protect tab so you can't see through the little hole. On a 5.25-inch disk, remove the write-protect sticker.

➤ **Is the disk full?** If you try to save a file to a disk, and you get an **Insufficient space** message, the disk has insufficient free space to hold any more data. Use a different disk.

➤ **Is the disk formatted?** If you buy new, unformatted disks, you must format the disks before you can use them.

➤ **Did you format the disk to the proper density?** If you format a high-density disk as a low-density disk, or vice versa, you will probably run into problems when you try to use the disk.

➤ **Is the disk bad?** Although it's rare, disks do go bad. Some disks even come bad from the manufacturer. If you get a **Sector not found** or **Data error** message, the disk may be bad. Then again, the drive might need a tune up. Try some other disks. If you're having problems with all disks, the problem is in the drive. If you are having trouble with only one disk, it's the disk.

Fixing Bad Disks

If a disk is bad, you may be able to salvage it using the ScanDisk, as explained in "Fixing Common Disk Problems with ScanDisk," in Chapter 27. If a drive is bad, you'll have to take it to a computer mechanic to get it fixed. Usually the problem is that the drive is not spinning at the right speed or that the arm that reads and writes data to the disk is not aligned properly on the disk.

My Keyboard Is Wacky

If whatever you type replaces existing text, you switched from Insert to Overstrike mode by mistake. In most programs, you switch modes by pressing the Ins (Insert) key. Press the key again, and you should be back in Insert mode.

Some fancy keyboards allow you to *remap* the keys. For example, you can make the F1 key on the left side of the keyboard act like the Enter key, or you can make it perform a series of keystrokes. Some advanced users like to remap keys to customize the keyboard and make it a time-saver.

However, if you accidentally press the remap key and then continue typing, you may remap your entire keyboard without knowing it. You'll know it when you press the K key and get a Z or you press the Spacebar and delete a paragraph. You can usually unmap the keyboard. If you have an AnyKey keyboard, you can return a key to normal by pressing the Remap key and then pressing the key you want to return to normal twice. If you don't have an AnyKey keyboard, consult the documentation that came with your computer.

My Keys Stick

If you have an old keyboard, or if you spilled something on the keyboard, the keys may start to stick. Take the keyboard to a computer service and have it cleaned. Or buy a new keyboard; they're cheap. If your keyboard is completely dead, or if your computer displays the message **Keyboard not found** when you boot your computer, do a quick inspection to make sure the keyboard is plugged in and the cord is in good shape.

If you spill a drink on your keyboard, don't panic. Exit any programs you're running, turn off the computer, and disconnect the keyboard. (Wipe up the spill, of course.) If you're lucky and spilled only water on the keyboard, let the keyboard dry out *thoroughly*, and then reconnect it. If you spilled something sticky, like a Pepsi, dunk the keyboard in warm water (you can use your bathtub).

My Printer Won't Print

Printers are a pain. They're a pain to set up and a pain to use. And even if you get the printer to finally work with one program, there is no guarantee that it will work with the next one. So, if you're running into printer problems, you will probably have to do more fiddling than Nero. Look for the following:

➤ **Is your printer plugged in and turned on?**

➤ **Does your printer have paper?** Is the paper tray inserted properly?

➤ **Is the printer's On Line light lit (not blinking)?** If the On Line light is off or blinking, press the **On Line** button to turn the light on.

➤ **Is the print fading?** If so, your printer may need a new toner or ink cartridge. (If you have an inkjet printer, check the print head and the area next to the print head for tape, and remove the tape. Ink cartridges usually come with two pieces of tape on them; you must remove *both* pieces.)

➤ **Is your program set up to use the correct printer?** In most programs, when you enter the **Print** command, a dialog box appears, displaying the name of the printer. Make sure the printer name is for the printer you're trying to use.

➤ **Is the correct printer port selected?** If you just set up your printer, and it is not printing at all, maybe you selected the wrong printer port.

➤ **Did you get only part of a page?** Laser printers are weird; they print an entire page at one time, storing the entire page in memory. If the page has a big complex graphic image or lots of fonts, the printer may be able to store only a portion of the page. The best fix is to get more memory for your printer. The quickest fix is to use fewer fonts on the page and try using a less complex graphic image.

➤ **Are you having problems in only one application?** If you can print from other applications, the problem is with the printer setup in the problem application.

➤ **Is it a printer problem?** To determine if the printer has a problem, type **dir > lpt1** at the DOS prompt and press **Enter**. This prints the current directory list. If it prints okay, the problem is in the Windows printer setup or the application's setup. If the directory does not print or prints incorrectly, the problem is probably with the printer.

When a document fails to print, new users commonly keep entering the Print command, hoping that if they enter it enough times, the program will start printing the document. What this does is send several copies of the same document to a print queue (a waiting line). When you finally fix the problem, you end up with a hundred copies of the same document. To prevent this from happening, do one of the following:

➤ Enter the **Print** command only once. If the document doesn't print, find the problem and fix it immediately.

➤ In Windows 95, you can check the print queue by double-clicking the **Printer** icon on the right side of the taskbar. You can then select and cancel duplicate print jobs.

➤ In Windows 3.1, Print Manager handles the print queue. To display the Print Manager, press **Ctrl+Esc**, and double-click **Print Manager**. You can use Print Manager to pause and resume printing or to cancel print jobs.

You can pause, resume, or cancel print jobs in the queue.

Windows 95 displays a list of documents it's printing.

Common DOS Messages in Plain English

As you work in DOS, you may come across some error messages and warnings and wonder what they mean. The following sections translate the DOS messages you're most likely to encounter.

All files in directory will be deleted Are you sure (Y/N)?

You probably entered the **delete *.*** command at the DOS prompt. This tells DOS to delete all the files on the current drive or directory. If you meant to do this, press **Y**. If not, press **N**.

Bad command or file name

You see this message most often when you have a typo in the command you entered. Check to make sure the command is typed correctly. If the command is typed correctly, maybe DOS cannot find the command's program file. For example, you may have to be in the DOS directory to use the DOS FORMAT command. In such a case, you must change to the directory that contains the program file before you can run the file.

File cannot be copied onto itself

You see this message if you try to copy a file into the same directory that already contains the file. To create a copy of a file in the same directory, you have to give the copy a different name.

File not found

You see this message when you try to copy, delete, rename, or perform some other operation on a file that does not exist or on a file that is in a different location from where you think it is. If you get this message, make sure you typed the file name correctly. If the file name is okay, change to the drive and directory where you think the file is stored and use the **DIR** command to view a list of files. See if the file is where you think it is.

Insufficient disk space

DOS displays this error message when you try to copy more files to a disk than the disk can hold. If you get this error message, you may need to copy the files to more than one disk.

Non-system disk or disk error Replace and press any key when ready

You may get this error message when you boot your computer. If your system files are on a hard drive, this message usually means you left a disk in drive A. Remove the disk and press any key to continue.

If you normally boot from a floppy disk, you may have forgotten to insert the DOS startup disk in drive A. Insert the DOS startup disk, close the drive door, and press any key.

Not ready reading drive A Abort, Retry, Fail?

You will usually get this message for one of these reasons:

➤ You forgot to put a disk in drive A. Insert a disk, close the drive door, and press **R** for Retry.

➤ You forgot to close the drive door. Close the drive door and press **R** for Retry.

➤ The disk in drive A is not formatted. If a brand new, never-been-formatted disk is in drive A, DOS will not be able to read the disk. Insert a formatted disk into drive A, close the drive door, and press **R**.

➤ If you changed to drive A by mistake, press **F** for Fail or **A** for Abort. This tells DOS to stop looking to drive A. A message appears telling you that drive A is no longer valid. Type **c:** and press **Enter** to return to drive C.

➤ If you have a double-density drive and put a high-density disk in the drive.

When in Doubt, Get the Heck Out

If no fix works, try rebooting your computer by pressing **Ctrl+Alt+Del**. If that doesn't work, turn everything off and leave it off for three minutes. (This lets the computer clear its head.) Turn on your monitor, then turn on your printer, and then turn on the system unit. If this doesn't fix it, call for help.

Before You Call Tech Support

Many hardware and software companies offer technical support for their products. Usually, you have to call long-distance, and you may be charged for advice. To save yourself some money, and save the tech support person some headaches, take the following steps before placing your call:

➤ Try everything in this chapter.

➤ Write down a detailed description of the problem, explaining what went wrong and what you were doing at the time.

➤ Write down the name, version number, and license (or registration) number of the program you are having trouble with.

➤ Write down any information about your computer, including the computer brand, chip type and speed, and monitor type. You can get this information by entering **msd** at the DOS prompt.

➤ Turn your printer on, change to the C:\ directory, type **print config.sys**, and press **Enter**. Type **print autoexec.bat** and press **Enter**. Keep the pages handy when you call tech support.

➤ Make sure your computer is turned on. A good tech support person can talk you through most problems, if you're sitting at the keyboard.

➤ Now you can call.

The Least You Need To Know

If you don't remember all the specifics given in this chapter, don't worry. Chances are, your specific problem isn't covered. The important things to remember are how to trace back a problem to its cause. Here are some reminders:

➤ Don't panic.

➤ Look all over the screen for any clues.

➤ Ask yourself when the problem started. Did you install a new program?

➤ Isolate the problem. Does it happen in all programs or just this one? Does it happen all the time?

➤ If you suspect a hardware problem, turn everything off and check the connections. Wiggle the plugs; a loose connection can be as bad or worse than no connection.

➤ As a last resort, turn your computer off, wait three minutes, and then turn everything back on.

Speak Like a Geek: The Complete Archive

The computer world is like a big exclusive club complete with its own language. If you want to be accepted into the Royal Order of Computer Geeks, you had better learn the lingo. The following miniglossary will help you start.

Keep in mind that you'll never achieve full geekhood by passively reading the terms and definitions. Try to say the term aloud and then use it in a sentence. When the other geeks hear you reciting computer terms to yourself, they will immediately accept you into their group.

access time   The average time it takes a device (usually a disk drive) to find a random piece of data on a disk. Access time is measured in milliseconds (the lower the number, the faster the drive). Good access times for a hard drive are between 10 ms and 15 ms. See also *transfer rate*.

application   Also known as *program*; a set of instructions that enable a computer to perform a specific task, such as word processing or data management.

ASCII file   A file containing characters that any program on any computer can use. Sometimes called a *text file* or an *ASCII text file*. (ASCII is pronounced "ASK-key.")

AUTOEXEC.BAT   A file that DOS reads whenever you boot or reboot your computer. This file contains a series of commands that DOS automatically executes.

batch file   Any file that contains a series of commands. You run the batch file just as you would run a program file (by entering its name at the DOS prompt). The most famous batch file is AUTOEXEC.BAT.

baud   A unit for measuring the speed of data transmission, which is usually used to describe the speed at which a modem transfers data, such as 2,400 baud. A more accurate measure of transmission speed is bps (bits per second).

BIOS (basic input-output system)   Pronounced "buy-ose," the start-up instructions for a computer. The BIOS tells the computer how to control traffic between the various elements that make up the computer, including disk drives, the printer, the ports, and the monitor.

bit   The basic unit of data in a computer. A computer's alphabet consists of two characters: 1 and 0. 1 stands for On, and 0 stands for Off. Bits are combined in sets of eight to form "real" characters, such as A, B, C, and D. See also *byte*.

bits per second   A unit for measuring the speed of data transmission. Remember that it takes 8 bits to make a byte (the equivalent of a single character). Modems have common bps ratings of 14,400 and 28,800.

boot   To start a computer with the operating system software (usually DOS) in place.

bps   See *bits per second*.

bulletin board system (BBS)   Not to be confused with the British Broadcasting System, a BBS is a program that enables a computer to automatically answer the phone when other computers call. The BBS allows the calling computer to copy files to it (*upload* files) and copy files from it (*download* files). Although you can purchase a BBS program to set up your own BBS, most users work with BBSs set up by computer companies and professional associations.

bus   A superhighway that carries information electronically from one part of the computer to another. There are three such highways:

➤ A *data bus* carries data back and forth between memory and the microprocessor.

➤ An *address bus* carries information about the locations (addresses) of specific information.

➤ A *control bus* carries control signals to make sure the data traffic flows smoothly, without confusion.

byte   A group of eight bits that usually represents a character or a digit. For example, the byte 01000001 represents the letter A. See also *bit*.

cache   Pronounced "cash," this is a part of memory that makes your computer run faster by holding the most recently accessed data from a disk. The next time the computer needs the data, the computer gets it from memory rather than from the disk, which would be slower. Sometimes called a *RAM cache*.

capacity   A measure of how much data a disk can store. For example, you can format a 5 1/4-inch, high-density floppy disk to store 1.2MB; 1.2MB is the disk's *capacity*.

CD-ROM (Compact-Disk Read-Only Memory)   A storage technology that uses disks similar to those you play in an audio CD player for mass storage of computer data. A single disk can store over 600MB of information. Pronounced "see-dee-rahm."

cell   The box formed by the intersection of a row (1,2,3...) and column (A,B,C...) in a spreadsheet. Each cell has an *address* (such as B12) that defines its column and row. A cell may contain text, a numeric value, or a formula.

chat   To "talk" to another person by typing at your computer. What you type appears on the other person's screen, and what the other person types appears on your screen. You can chat on the Internet or on an online service, such as Prodigy or America Online.

click   To move the mouse pointer over an object or icon and press and release the mouse button once without moving the mouse.

client   Of two computers, the computer that's being served. On the Internet or on a network, your computer is the client, and the computer you're connected to is the *server*.

Clipboard   A temporary storage area that holds text and graphics. The cut and copy commands put text or graphics on the Clipboard, replacing the Clipboard's previous contents. The Paste command inserts Clipboard data into a document.

CMOS (Complementary Metal-Oxide Semiconductor)   Pronounced "SEA-moss," CMOS is an electronic device (usually battery operated) that stores information about your computer.

COM port   Short for COMmunications port. A receptacle, usually at the back of the computer, into which you can plug a serial device such as a modem, mouse, or serial printer. If your computer has more than one COM port, the ports are numbered COM1, COM2, and so on.

command   An order that tells the computer what to do. In command-driven programs, you have to press a specific key or type the command to execute it. With menu-driven programs, you select the command from a menu.

computer   Any machine that accepts input (from a user), processes the input, and produces output in some form.

CPU (central processing unit)   See *microprocessor*.

crash   Failure of a system or program. Usually, you realize that your system has crashed when you can't move the mouse pointer or type anything. The term *crash* is also used to refer to a disk crash (or head crash). A disk crash occurs when the read/write head in the

359

disk drive falls on the disk. This would be like dropping a phonograph needle on a record. A disk crash can destroy any data stored where the read/write head falls on the disk.

cursor A horizontal line that appears below characters. A cursor acts like the tip of your pencil; anything you type appears at the cursor. See also *insertion point.*

cyberspace The universe created by the connection of thousands of computers. Computer users can use modems to enter cyberspace and converse with other users.

data The facts and figures that you enter into the computer and that are stored and used by the computer.

database A type of computer program used for storing, organizing, and retrieving information. Popular database programs include Access, Approach, and Paradox.

density A measure of the amount of data that can be stored per square inch of storage area on a disk.

desktop publishing (DTP) A program that enables you to combine text and graphics on the same page and manipulate the text and graphics on-screen. Desktop publishing programs are commonly used to create newsletters, brochures, flyers, résumés, and business cards.

dialog box An on-screen box that allows you to enter your preferences or supply additional information. You use the dialog box to carry on a "conversation" with the program.

directory A division of a disk or CD that contains a group of related files. Think of your disk as a filing cabinet and think of each directory as a drawer in the cabinet. By keeping files in separate directories, it is easier to locate and work with related files.

disk A round, flat, magnetic storage medium. A disk works like a cassette tape, storing files permanently, so you can play them back later. See *floppy disk* and *hard disk.*

disk drive A device that writes data to a magnetic disk and reads data from the disk. Think of a disk drive as being like a cassette recorder/player. Just as the cassette player can record sounds on a magnetic cassette tape and play back those sounds, a disk drive can record data on a magnetic disk and play back that data.

DOS (disk operating system) DOS, which rhymes with "boss," is an essential program that provides the necessary instructions for the computer's parts (keyboard, disk drive, central processing unit, display screen, printer, and so on) to function as a unit.

DOS prompt An on-screen prompt that indicates DOS is ready to accept a command. It looks something like C> or C:\.

download   To copy files from another computer to your computer, usually through a modem. See also *upload*.

e-mail   Short for *electronic mail*, e-mail is a system that enables people to send and receive messages from computer to computer. E-mail is usually available on networks and online information services.

EMS (Expanded Memory Specification)   See *expanded memory*.

environment   A setting in which you perform tasks on your computer. Microsoft Windows, for example, displays a graphical environment that lets you enter commands by selecting pictures rather than by typing commands. This makes it much easier to use your computer (assuming you know what the pictures stand for).

executable file   A program file that can run the program. Executable files end in .BAT, .COM, or .EXE.

expanded memory   Additional memory that a computer uses by swapping data into and out of a reserved portion of a computer's standard memory area. With expanded memory, additional memory is added to the computer in the form of memory chips or a memory board. To access this additional memory, an expanded memory manager reserves 64 of the standard 640 kilobytes as a swap area. The 64 kilobytes represent 4 *pages*, each page consisting of 16 kilobytes. Pages of data are swapped into and out of this 64 kilobyte region from expanded memory at a high speed. Old DOS programs commonly used expanded memory, but Windows and its programs prefer extended memory. See also *extended memory*.

expansion slot   An opening on the motherboard (inside the system unit) that allows you to add devices to the system unit. Expansion slots allow you to add an internal modem, sound card, video accelerator, or other enhancements.

extended memory   Any memory above the standard 640 kilobytes that performs the same way as the standard memory. Extended memory is directly available to the processor in your computer, unlike expanded memory, where data must be swapped into and out of the standard memory. Most additional memory in new computers is extended. See also *expanded memory*.

extension   The portion of a file's name that comes after the period. Every file name consists of two parts: the base name (before the period) and an extension (after the period). The file name can be up to eight characters in DOS and Windows 3.x (up to 255 characters in Windows 95). The extension (which is optional) can be up to three characters.

field   A blank in a database record, into which you can enter a piece of information (for example, a telephone number, ZIP code, or a person's last name).

file   A collection of information stored as a single unit on a floppy or hard disk. A file always has a file name to identify it.

file allocation table (FAT)   A map on a disk that tells the operating system where the files on the disk are stored. It's sort of like a classroom seating chart for files.

File Transfer Protocol (FTP)   A set of rules that govern the exchange of files between two computers on the Internet. To copy a file from the Internet, you need a special program that can handle FTP file transfers.

fixed disk drive   A disk drive that has a nonremovable disk, as opposed to floppy drives, where you can insert and remove the disks.

floppy disk   A wafer encased in plastic that stores magnetic data (the facts and figures you enter and save). Floppy disks are the disks you insert in your computer's floppy disk drive (located on the front of the computer).

folder   Windows 95's name for a directory, a division of a hard disk or CD that stores a group of related files. See also *directory*.

font   Any set of characters of the same *typeface* (design) and *type size* (measured in points). For example, Times Roman 12-point is a font: Times Roman is the typeface, and 12-point is the size. (There are 72 points in an inch.)

format (disk)   To prepare a disk for storing data. Formatting creates a map on the disk that tells the operating system how the disk is structured. The operating system uses this map to keep track of where files are stored.

format (document)   To establish the physical layout of a document, including page size, margins, running heads, line spacing, text alignment, graphics placement, and so on.

FTP   See *File Transfer Protocol*.

function keys   The 10 or 12 F keys on the left side of the keyboard, or 12 F keys at the top of the keyboard (on some keyboards there are both). F keys are numbered F1, F2, F3, and so on, and you can use them to enter specified commands in a program.

geek   1. An overly obsessive computer user, who will sacrifice food, sleep, sex, and other pleasantries of life to spend more time at the keyboard. 2. A carnival performer whose act usually includes biting off the head of a live snake or chicken.

gigabyte   A thousand megabytes. See also *megabyte*.

Gopher   An area of the Internet that allows you to navigate the Internet by using menus. You use a menu to tell the Gopher what you want. The Gopher will then "go for" the item you requested.

graphical user interface (GUI, pronounced "GOO-ey")   A type of program interface that uses graphical elements, such as icons, to represent commands, files, and (in some cases) other programs. The most famous GUI is Microsoft Windows.

hard disk   A disk drive that comes complete with a nonremovable disk.

Hayes-compatible   Used to describe a modem that uses the Hayes command set for communicating with other modems over the phone lines. Hayes-compatible modems usually are preferred over other modems because most modems and telecommunications software is designed to be Hayes-compatible.

HTML   Short for *HyperText Markup Language*, the code used to create documents for the World Wide Web. These codes tell the Web browser how to display the text (titles, headings, lists, and so on), insert anchors that link this document to other documents, and control character formatting (by making it bold or italic).

icon   A graphic image on-screen that represents another object, such as a file on a disk.

initialize   To reset a computer or program to some starting values. When used to describe floppy or hard disks, the term means the same as *format*.

insertion point   A blinking vertical line used in most Windows word processors to indicate the place where any characters you type will be inserted. An insertion point is the equivalent of a *cursor*.

integrated program   A program that combines the features of several programs, such as a word processor, spreadsheet, database, and communications program. The names of integrated programs usually end with the word *Works*.

interactive   A user-controlled program, document, or game. Interactive programs commonly display on-screen *prompts* asking the user for input so they can determine how to carry out a particular task. These programs are popular in education, allowing children to follow their natural curiosity to solve problems and gather information.

interface   A link between two objects, such as a computer and a modem. The link between a computer and a person is called a *user interface*, and refers to the way a person communicates with the computer.

Internet   A group of computers all over the world that are connected to each other. Using your computer and a modem, you can connect to these other computers and tap their resources. You can view pictures, listen to sounds, watch video clips, play games, chat with other people, and even shop.

keyboard   The main input device for most computers. You use the keyboard to type and to enter commands.

kilobyte (K)   A unit for measuring the amount of data. A kilobyte is equivalent to 1,024 bytes (each byte is a character).

load   To read data or program instructions from a disk and place them in the computer's memory, where the computer can use the data or instructions. You usually load a program before you use it or load a file before you edit it.

macro   A recorded set of instructions for a frequently used or complex task. In most programs, you create a macro by telling the program to record your actions. You then name the macro or assign it to a keystroke combination. You can replay the macro at any time by selecting its name or by pressing the keystroke combination you assigned to it.

megabyte   A standard unit used to measure the storage capacity of a disk and the amount of computer memory. A megabyte is 1,048,576 bytes (1000 kilobytes). This is roughly equivalent to 500 pages of double-spaced text. Megabyte is commonly abbreviated as M, MB, or Mbyte.

memory   An electronic storage area inside the computer, used to temporarily store data or program instructions when the computer is using them. The computer's memory is erased when the power to the computer is turned off. Also referred to as RAM.

menu   A list of commands or instructions displayed on-screen. Menus organize commands and make a program easier to use.

microprocessor   Sometimes called the central processing unit (CPU) or processor, this chip is the computer's brain; it does all the calculations for the computer.

modem   An acronym for MOdulator/DEModulator. A modem is a piece of hardware that enables a computer to send and receive data through an ordinary telephone line.

monitor   A television-like screen on which the computer displays information.

mouse   A hand-held device that you move across the desktop to move an arrow, called a mouse pointer, across the screen. Used instead of the keyboard to select and move items (such as text or graphics), execute commands, and perform other tasks.

MS-DOS (Microsoft Disk Operating System)   See *DOS (Disk Operating System)*.

multitasking   The process of performing two computer tasks at the same time. For example, you might be printing a document from your word processor while checking your e-mail in Prodigy. One of the primary advantages of Windows is that it allows you to multitask.

newsgroup   An Internet bulletin board for users who share common interests. There are thousands of newsgroups ranging from body art to pets. Newsgroups let you post messages and read messages from other users.

online Connected, turned on, and ready to accept information. Used most often in reference to a printer or modem.

pane A portion of a window. Most programs display panes, so you can view two different parts of a document at the same time.

parallel port A connector used to plug a device, usually a printer, into the computer. Transferring data through a parallel port is much faster than transferring data through a serial port, but parallel cables can carry data reliably only 15 or 20 feet.

partition A section of a disk drive that's assigned a letter. A hard disk drive can be divided (or *partitioned*) into one or more drives, which DOS refers to as drive C, drive D, drive E, and so on. (Don't be fooled; it's still one disk drive.) The actual hard disk drive is called the *physical* drive; each partition is called a *logical* drive.

path The route that the computer travels from the root directory to any subdirectories when locating a file.

peripheral A device that's attached to the computer but is not essential for the basic operation of the computer. The system unit is the central part of the computer. Any devices attached to the system unit are considered *peripheral*, including a printer, modem, or joystick. Some manufacturers consider the monitor and keyboard to be peripheral, too.

pixel A dot of light that appears on the computer screen. A collection of pixels forms characters and images on the screen. Think of a pixel as a single peg in a Lite Brite toy.

ports The receptacles at the back of the computer. They get their name from the ports where ships pick up and deliver cargo. In this case, the ports allow information to enter and leave the system unit.

post To tack up a message in a bulletin board or newsgroup for all to see.

POST (Power-On Self Test) A series of internal checks the computer performs on itself whenever it is first turned on. If the test reveals that any component is not working properly, the computer displays an error message on-screen giving a general indication of which component is causing problems.

PPP Short for Point-to-Point Protocol, which probably means as little to me as it does to you. What's important is that when you choose an Internet service provider, you get the right connection: SLIP or PPP. See also *SLIP*.

program A group of instructions that tell the computer what to do. Typical programs are word processors, spreadsheets, databases, and games.

prompt A computer's way of asking for more information. The computer basically looks at you and says, "Tell me something." In other words, the computer is *prompting* you or *prodding* you for information or for a command.

protocol   A group of communications settings that control the transfer of data between two computers.

pull-down menu   A menu that appears at the top of the screen, listing various options. The menu is not visible until you select it from the menu bar. The menu then drops down, covering a small part of the screen.

random-access memory (RAM)   Where your computer stores data and programs temporarily. RAM is measured in kilobytes and megabytes. In general, the more RAM a computer has, the more powerful the programs it can run. Also called *memory*.

record   Used by databases to denote a unit of related information contained in one or more fields, such as an individual's name, address, and phone number.

ROM BIOS   See *BIOS (basic input-output system)*.

scanner   A device that converts images, such as photographs or printed text, into an electronic format that a computer can use. Many stores use a special type of scanner to read bar code labels into the cash register.

scroll   To move text up and down or right and left on a computer screen.

server   Of two computers, the computer that's serving the other computer. On the Internet or on a network, your computer is the *client*, and the computer you're connected to is the *server*.

service provider   The company that you pay in order to connect to their computer and get on the Internet.

shareware   Computer programs you can use for free, and then pay for if you decide to continue using them. Many programmers start marketing their programs as shareware, relying on the honesty and goodwill of computer users for their income. That's why most of these programmers have day jobs.

shell   A program that enables you to enter commands to the operating system by choosing them from a menu. Shell programs make it easier to use the operating system.

SLIP (Serial Line Internet Protocol)   A type of Internet connection that allows you to connect directly to the Internet without having to run programs off your Internet service provider's computer. See also *PPP*.

software   Any instructions that tell your computer (the hardware) what to do. There are two types of software: operating system software and application software. *Operating system software* (such as DOS) gets your computer up and running. *Application software* enables you to do something useful, such as type a letter or chase lemmings.

spreadsheet   A program used for keeping schedules and calculating numeric results. Common spreadsheets include Lotus 1-2-3, Microsoft Excel, and Quattro Pro.

status bar   The area at the bottom of a program window that shows you what's going on as you work. A status bar may show the page and line number where the insertion point is positioned, and indicate whether you are typing in overstrike or insert mode.

style   A collection of specifications for formatting text. A style may include information for the font, size, style, margins, and spacing. Applying a style to text automatically formats the text according to the style's specifications.

switch   A value you can add to a command to control the manner in which the command is carried out. For example, in DOS, you can use the /V switch with the COPY command to have DOS verify that the copied files are exact duplicates of the originals.

TCP/IP (Transmission Control Protocol/Internet Protocol)   A set of rules that govern the transfer of data over the Internet. In order to do anything on the Internet, you need a TCP/IP program. This program connects your computer to your service provider's computer, which is part of the Internet. You can then run other programs that let you do fun stuff, like browse the World Wide Web.

telnet   The process of connecting to a server and using it to run programs, just as if you were sitting at its keyboard (or sitting at the keyboard of a terminal that's connected to the server). Think of it as using the computerized card catalog at the local library.

trackball   A device, often used with laptop computers, which works like an upside-down mouse. It requires less desk space for use because instead of moving a mouse around the desk to move the pointer on-screen, you pivot the trackball in its socket to move the pointer. Some arcade video games use devices similar to trackballs.

transfer rate   A measure of how much information a device (usually a disk drive) can transfer from the disk to your computer's memory in a second. A good transfer rate is in the range of 500 to 600 kilobytes per second. The higher the number, the faster the drive. See also *access time*.

uninterruptible power supply (UPS)   A battery-powered device that protects against power spikes and power outages. If the power goes out, the UPS continues supplying power to the computer so you can continue working or safely turn off your computer without losing data.

upload   To send data to another computer, usually through a modem and a telephone line or through a network connection.

URL (Uniform Resource Locator)   An address for an Internet site. The Web uses URLs to specify the addresses of the various servers on the Internet and the documents on each server. For example, the URL for the Whitehouse server is **http://www.whitehouse.gov**. The **http** stands for HyperText Transfer Protocol, which indicates a Web document. **www** stands for World Wide Web. **whitehouse** stands for White House. And **gov** stands for government.

virtual memory   Disk storage that is treated as RAM (memory). Both Windows 3.1 and Windows 95 can use disk space as virtual memory.

virus   A program that attaches itself to other files on a floppy or hard disk, duplicates itself without the user's knowledge, and may cause the computer to do strange and sometimes destructive things. The virus can attack the computer by erasing files from the hard disk or by formatting the disk.

Web browser   A program that lets you navigate the World Wide Web (the most popular feature of the Internet). The World Wide Web consists of documents (pages) that may contain text, graphics, sound clips, video clips, and other items. A Web browser pulls the pages into your computer (through modem or network connection) and displays them on your screen. See also *World Wide Web*.

wild card   Any character that takes the place of another character or a group of characters. Think of a wild-card character as a wild card in a game of poker. If the Joker is wild, you can use it in place of any card in the entire deck of cards. In DOS, you can use two wild card characters: a question mark (?) and an asterisk (*). The question mark stands in for a single character. The asterisk stands in for a group of characters.

windows   A way of displaying information in different parts of the screen. Often used as a nickname for Microsoft Windows.

word processor   A program that lets you enter, edit, format, and print text.

word wrap   A feature that automatically moves a word to the next line if the word won't fit at the end of the current line.

World Wide Web   A part of the Internet that consists of multimedia documents that are interconnected by links. To move from one document to another, you click on a link, which may appear as highlighted text or as a small picture or icon. The Web contains text, sound and video clips, pictures, catalogues, and much, much more. See also *Web browser*.

write-protect   To prevent a computer from adding or modifying data stored on a disk.

368

How To Use the CD at the Back of This book

What You Need To Run the CD

To use the Microsoft Home CD-Sampler your computer must meet the following minimum requirements:

➤ 386DX/33 or better central processing unit (486 recommended)

➤ 4MB memory

➤ 2.5MB available hard disk space

➤ CD-ROM drive

➤ VGA or better monitor (capable of displaying 256 colors)

➤ Microsoft mouse or compatible pointing device

➤ Sound card and speakers

➤ One of the following two configurations:

Microsoft Windows 95

MS-DOS version 5.0 or later with Windows 3.1 or Windows for Workgroups

And that's not all. The previous list of hardware gets you up and running with the CD Sampler, but your computer needs a few extras to run Fury3:

➤ 486DX/66 or better central processing unit

➤ 8MB memory

➤ 15MB free hard disk space

➤ Double-speed CD-ROM drive

➤ Joystick or other flight control recommended (although you can use your keyboard or mouse)

And if you plan on using Internet Explorer, you'll also need a 14,400bps modem or faster, and an Internet account. See Part 5 for details.

Running Microsoft's CD Sampler

If you have Windows 95, you can run CD Sampler simply by inserting the CD in your CD-ROM drive. Windows 95 automatically starts CD Sampler, and displays a window that lets you start using it. First, pick the language you want to use: English, German, Spanish, or French. After listening to the introduction, click on the **Products** button, and then click on the type of product (in the Categories list) you wish to look at. You can then click on tabs and buttons to view demos, see a list of features for a given application, and even install and use demonstration versions of some of the programs.

CD Sampler Lets You Preview Over 70 Microsoft Products

If you have Windows 3.1 or Windows for Workgroups (3.11), take the following steps to run CD Sampler:

1. Insert the CD into your CD-ROM drive.

2. Open Program Manager's File menu and select Run.

3. In the Command line text box, type **d:\cdsample** (where "d" is the letter of your CD-ROM drive), and click on OK.

Internet Explorer is a Web browser. If you don't know what a Web browser or the World Wide Web is, check out Chapter 24, "Doing the Internet Shuffle." You'll also need to refer to Chapter 24 to learn how to set up your Internet connection. Without a connection, you can't use Internet Explorer.

Index

H

I

X-Z

Check out Que® Books on the World Wide Web
http://www.mcp.com/que

As the biggest software release in computer history, Windows 95 continues to redefine the computer industry. Click here for the latest info on our Windows 95 books

Make computing quick and easy with these products designed exclusively for new and casual users

Examine the latest releases in word processing, spreadsheets, operating systems, and suites

Find out about new additions to our site, new bestsellers and hot topics

Desktop Applications & Operating Systems

que®

new users

what's new?

Que's Publishing Areas

Windows 95

Internet And New Technologies

The Internet, The World Wide Web, CompuServe®, America Online®, Prodigy®—it's a world of ever-changing information. Don't get left behind!

Calendar of Events

DEVELOPER AND EXPERT USERS

ZD ZIFF-DAVIS PRESS

Que's Top 10 Titles

Macintosh & Desktop Publishing

In-depth information on high-end topics: find the best reference books for databases, programming, networking, and client/server technologies

A recent addition to Que, Ziff-Davis Press publishes the highly-successful *How It Works* and *How to Use* series of books, as well as *PC Learning Labs Teaches* and *PC Magazine* series of book/disk packages

Stay on the cutting edge of Macintosh® technologies and visual communications

Find out which titles are making headlines

With 6 separate publishing groups, Que develops products for many specific market segments and areas of computer technology. Explore our Web Site and you'll find information on best-selling titles, newly published titles, upcoming products, authors, and much more.

- Stay informed on the latest industry trends and products available
- Visit our online bookstore for the latest information and editions
- Download software from Que's library of the best shareware and freeware

que®

Complete and Return this Card
for a *FREE* Computer Book Catalog

Thank you for purchasing this book! You have purchased a superior computer book written expressly for your needs. To continue to provide the kind of up-to-date, pertinent coverage you've come to expect from us, we need to hear from you. Please take a minute to complete and return this self-addressed, postage-paid form. In return, we'll send you a free catalog of all our computer books on topics ranging from word processing to programming and the internet.

Mr. ☐   Mrs. ☐   Ms. ☐   Dr. ☐

Name (first) ☐☐☐☐☐☐☐☐☐☐☐☐ (M.I.) ☐ (last) ☐☐☐☐☐☐☐☐☐☐☐☐☐☐☐☐☐

Address ☐☐☐☐☐☐☐☐☐☐☐☐☐☐☐☐☐☐☐☐☐☐☐☐☐☐☐☐☐☐☐☐

City ☐☐☐☐☐☐☐☐☐☐☐☐☐☐☐☐☐☐ State ☐☐ Zip ☐☐☐☐☐ ☐☐☐☐

Phone ☐☐☐ ☐☐☐ ☐☐☐☐ Fax ☐☐☐ ☐☐☐ ☐☐☐☐

Company Name ☐☐☐☐☐☐☐☐☐☐☐☐☐☐☐☐☐☐☐☐☐☐☐☐☐☐☐☐☐

E-mail address ☐☐☐☐☐☐☐☐☐☐☐☐☐☐☐☐☐☐☐☐☐☐☐☐☐☐☐☐☐

1. Please check at least (3) influencing factors for purchasing this book.

Front or back cover information on book .... ☐
Special approach to the content .... ☐
Completeness of content .... ☐
Author's reputation .... ☐
Publisher's reputation .... ☐
Book cover design or layout .... ☐
Index or table of contents of book .... ☐
Price of book .... ☐
Special effects, graphics, illustrations .... ☐
Other (Please specify): _____ ☐

2. How did you first learn about this book?

Saw in Macmillan Computer Publishing catalog .... ☐
Recommended by store personnel .... ☐
Saw the book on bookshelf at store .... ☐
Recommended by a friend .... ☐
Received advertisement in the mail .... ☐
Saw an advertisement in: _____ ☐
Read book review in: _____ ☐
Other (Please specify): _____ ☐

3. How many computer books have you purchased in the last six months?

This book only .... ☐   3 to 5 books .... ☐
2 books .... ☐   More than 5 .... ☐

4. Where did you purchase this book?

Bookstore .... ☐
Computer Store .... ☐
Consumer Electronics Store .... ☐
Department Store .... ☐
Office Club .... ☐
Warehouse Club .... ☐
Mail Order .... ☐
Direct from Publisher .... ☐
Internet site .... ☐
Other (Please specify): _____ ☐

5. How long have you been using a computer?

☐ Less than 6 months   ☐ 6 months to a year
☐ 1 to 3 years   ☐ More than 3 years

6. What is your level of experience with personal computers and with the subject of this book?

	With PCs	With subject of book
New	☐	☐
Casual	☐	☐
Accomplished	☐	☐
Expert	☐	☐

Source Code ISBN: 0-7897-0787-x

7. Which of the following best describes your job title?

Administrative Assistant .... ☐
Coordinator .... ☐
Manager/Supervisor .... ☐
Director .... ☐
Vice President .... ☐
President/CEO/COO .... ☐
Lawyer/Doctor/Medical Professional .... ☐
Teacher/Educator/Trainer .... ☐
Engineer/Technician .... ☐
Consultant .... ☐
Not employed/Student/Retired .... ☐
Other (Please specify): _____ ☐

8. Which of the following best describes the area of the company your job title falls under?

Accounting .... ☐
Engineering .... ☐
Manufacturing .... ☐
Operations .... ☐
Marketing .... ☐
Sales .... ☐
Other (Please specify): _____ ☐

9. What is your age?

Under 20 .... ☐
21-29 .... ☐
30-39 .... ☐
40-49 .... ☐
50-59 .... ☐
60-over .... ☐

10. Are you:

Male .... ☐
Female .... ☐

11. Which computer publications do you read regularly? (Please list)

_____
_____
_____
_____
_____
_____
_____
_____
_____
_____

Comments: _____

Fold here and scotch-tape to mail.

Licensing Agreement

By opening this package, you are agreeing to be bound by the following: